MAKING WAVES
AND RIDING THE CURRENTS

MAKING WAVES AND RIDING THE CURRENTS

Activism and the Practice of Wisdom

CHARLES HALPERN

BERRETT-KOEHLER PUBLISHERS, INC.
San Francisco
a BK Currents book

Berrett-Koehler Publishers, Inc.
235 Montgomery Street, Suite 650
San Francisco, CA 94104-2916
Tel: (415) 288-0260   Fax: (415) 362-2512   www.bkconnection.com

Ordering Information

Quantity sales. Special discounts are available on quantity purchases by corporations, associations, and others. For details, contact the "Special Sales Department" at the Berrett-Koehler address above.

Individual sales. Berrett-Koehler publications are available through most bookstores. They can also be ordered directly from Berrett-Koehler: Tel: (800) 929-2929; Fax: (802) 864-7626; www.bkconnection.com

Orders for college textbook/course adoption use. Please contact Berrett-Koehler: Tel: (800) 929-2929; Fax: (802) 864-7626.

Orders by U.S. trade bookstores and wholesalers. Please contact Ingram Publisher Services, Tel: (800) 509-4887; Fax (800) 838-1149; E-mail: customer.service@ingrampublisherservices.com; or visit www.ingrampublisherservices.com/Ordering for details about electronic ordering.

Berrett-Koehler and the BK logo are registered trademarks of Berrett-Koehler Publishers, Inc.

Printed in the United States of America

Berrett-Koehler books are printed on long-lasting acid-free paper. When it is available, we choose paper that has been manufactured by environmentally responsible processes. These may include using trees grown in sustainable forests, incorporating recycled paper, minimizing chlorine in bleaching, or recycling the energy produced at the paper mill.

Library of Congress Cataloging-in-Publication Data

Halpern, Charles, 1939-

    Making waves and riding the currents : activism and the practice of wisdom / Charles Halpern.
      p. cm.
    ISBN-13: 978-1-57675-442-9 (hardcover : alk. paper)
      1. Halpern, Charles, 1939 2. Political activists—United States—Biography. 3. Social reformers—United States—Biography. 4. Lawyers—United States—Biography. 5. Wisdom—Social aspects United States. 6. Social change—United States. 7. Public interest—United States. 8. Center for Law and Social Policy. 9. City University of New York. School of Law at Queens College. 10. Nathan Cummings Foundation. I. Title.
    CT275.H2584A3 2007
    973.92092—dc22

                                              2007034438

First Edition

12 11 10 09 08 07   10 9 8 7 6 5 4 3 2 1

INTERIOR DESIGN: Gopa & Ted2, Inc.   CANOE ICON: Jon Friedman
COPY EDITOR: Sandra Beris   INDEXER: Kay Banning
PRODUCTION: Linda Jupiter, Jupiter Productions   PROOFREADER: Henrietta Bensussen

FOR SUSAN

CONTENTS

Foreword by His Holiness the Dalai Lama. xi

Foreword by Robert B. Reich xiii

Prologue 1

1: Awakening. 9

2: Breaking Out. 25

3: Social Entrepreneur. 53

4: Creativity in the Courtroom. 81

5: Community and Consciousness. 107

6: Facing a Tough Reality. 143

7: Beginning Meditation 175

8: Convergence. 209

9: The Northwest Passage 239

Epilogue: Practicing Wisdom 257

Acknowledgments. 261

Notes. 267

Bibliography and Resources 273

Index 275

About the Author. 289

AUTHOR'S STATEMENT

THE EVENTS in this book are primarily drawn from memory. For public events—the creation of a new organization or filing a lawsuit—I have consulted available official documents. For my own reflections and private interactions, I have relied on memory, buttressed by personal notes and check-ins with friends. Needless to say, all quoted conversations are reconstructed from memory, not from transcriptions.

FOREWORD
BY HIS HOLINESS
THE DALAI LAMA

I MET CHARLES HALPERN when, as president of the Nathan Cummings Foundation, he supported a rich and productive dialogue between prominent Tibetans here in Dharamsala and representatives of the world Jewish community. Such imaginative initiatives are typical of a life dedicated to positive social change.

In this new book, *Making Waves and Riding the Currents*, he shows the importance of fostering basic human values like compassion in our relations with others and of working to generate inner peace. If we are able to do this, we will make our lives and our work meaningful, and ultimately contribute to the welfare of all living beings.

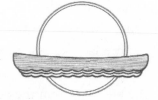

FOREWORD
BY ROBERT B. REICH

I F YOU'RE LIKE most people, you're working harder than ever before. That's mainly because the economy has become so competitive that all customers, clients, and investors have many other options. Unless you work hard to attract and keep them, they'll leave for better deals elsewhere. Even if you're a professional or working in the nonprofit sector, your organization is likely to be feeling more competitive heat. Lawyers, journalists, and doctors used to be in business to serve the public; nowadays, their organizations are in business to make money, and the competition is intense. Philanthropies, universities, museums, and concert halls used to be dedicated to the poor, to learning, or to artistry. Now they're in competitive races for resources and attendees. As a consumer or investor, all this new competition is giving you more for your money. But as a person trying to make a living while finding meaning in one's work and life, it's wreaking havoc.

If you're also trying to be an agent of change—a public official, organization leader, or social entrepreneur seeking a fairer or healthier society—your job is doubly difficult. Market forces are allied against you. When jobs are so insecure and wages so unstable, the public is less willing to take chances on ideas that may sound good in theory but could rock the boat even more. When the private sector offers huge monetary rewards to financial entrepreneurs who merely rearrange the pieces of the pie, talented young people are more likely to seek law degrees or M.B.A.'s that lead to prestigious law firms and financial powerhouses than to accept jobs that help redistribute the pie away from the very rich. When the economy allows investors to reap fortunes from hedge funds and private-equity partnerships, there's less money for or interest in changing the economic order.

So how is one to proceed? In the following pages, Charles Halpern offers a way forward. As you will see, Halpern's life has been dedicated to positive social change—to comforting the afflicted and afflicting the comfortable. As a founder of the Center for Law and Social Policy, the first public interest law firm in the nation; as dean of City University of New York Law School, among the first public interest law schools; and then as president of the Nathan Cummings Foundation, itself dedicated to making the world a better and more humane place, Halpern has collected his share of stars and scars. But what is likely to make this book particularly useful to you—whether you are seeking a more just society or are merely seeking to navigate the difficult currents of a career—is Halpern's lifetime journey toward finding a place within himself that has allowed him to bear these pressures while simultaneously maintaining his humanity.

As one who has known Charlie Halpern for many years and watched with admiration all that he has accomplished, and the struggles—both professional and personal—in which he has engaged, I can attest to the truth of this story. As one who has had his own share of stars and scars, I can attest to its importance. There is no way for a human being to endure the challenges of social leadership, let alone manage the tumult of a job and a family in this age of supercapitalism, as I have called it, without having the means of discovering and holding on to a part of yourself that remains invulnerable. The more we are able to discover and hold on to this core, the easier our life journey will be. Halpern terms this the *practice of wisdom*.

Halpern's personal journey illuminates and integrates two overarching social movements that have occupied what is commonly referred to as "the Left" over the last forty years. One has been focused on the potential for a more just society and world. This movement began with the goal of achieving civil rights for African Americans and was extended to ending the Vietnam War, giving women equal rights, expanding opportunities for the poor or others who have been socially excluded, honoring human rights at home and abroad, and achieving a cleaner and safer environment.

The other overarching movement, by contrast, has looked inward. It has focused on the potential within every person for a full and meaningful life. This second movement began with the goal of expanding the capacity of individuals to be in touch with their feelings and to utilize their intuitions, and was extended to gaining a deeper knowledge of the relationship between the mind and the body, exploring the power of alternative medicines, meditating, and finding other means to spiritual well-being.

These two overarching movements—one exterior and one interior, if you will—have evolved separately. Agents of social change rarely come into contact with agents of personal change, except perhaps when former activists "burn out" and seek solace in discovering their inner lives. Religious movements on the political Right have more fully integrated the exterior and the interior, although from a more authoritarian perspective. But many activists on the Left have long rejected or denied the importance of religion or spirituality, just as many people on the Left who have sought spiritual meaning are deeply cynical about social and political change. Yet, as Halpern helps us understand, fundamental societal change cannot occur without personal change on a large scale, and the agents of societal change cannot muster the resources they need without calling upon their inner strengths. Nor, for that matter, can personal change occur on a large scale unless society is reformed to make enough room for it. Just as decent citizens form decent societies, decent societies form decent citizens. The lives and the great influences of Mahatma Gandhi, Nelson Mandela, Martin Luther King, Jr., and the Dalai Lama exemplify this basic interdependence.

By finding the means of weaving the two movements together in his own life, Halpern invites you to do the same in yours. And in so doing, he offers a means of discovering the balance, clarity, compassion, and effectiveness you may need—and that our society and our world desperately need in these tumultuous times.

ROBERT B. REICH
Professor of Public Policy, University of California,
at Berkeley; former U.S. Secretary of Labor

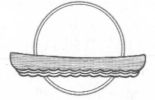

PROLOGUE

THIS BOOK is about working for a more just, compassionate, and sustainable world while cultivating the wisdom that supports and deepens this work. Over the course of my career as a social entrepreneur and activist, I have launched public interest law firms, designed and led a new public interest law school, and served as founding president of a major foundation. I had a growing intuition that something was missing, and I sought ways of developing inner resources that complemented my cognitive and adversarial skills. These explorations led me to the conviction that the practice of wisdom is essential both to my own effectiveness and well-being and to our collective capacity to address the challenges of the twenty-first century successfully.

A critical juncture in my inner explorations occurred in 1990. On a beautiful autumn day, I began a pilgrimage to Dharamsala for a meeting with the Dalai Lama. I spent an afternoon in the crowded streets of New Delhi, gasping for breath in the fetid air and bargaining for gifts in the teeming bazaars. I took a night train to Patankot, wedged into a bunk bed between gun-toting guards and maroon-clad monks. The taxi to Dharamsala detoured around religious demonstrations, where the smoke of burning tires hung in the air. Then I found myself in the foothills of the Himalayas, sitting in the tranquility of the Dalai Lama's parlor with a group of monks and rabbis, listening to wide-ranging exchanges between the Dalai Lama and some of the great living masters of Kabala and Jewish mysticism. As president of the Nathan Cummings Foundation, I had helped to convene this unlikely meeting, a dialogue unprecedented in the long history of the two religions.

While the substance of the discussions was interesting, from comparative mysticism to the challenge of retaining traditions in diaspora, I was transfixed by the qualities of the Dalai Lama himself: his presence, clarity, and kindness. He had an enormous and inclusive curiosity, an incisive and penetrating intelligence, and a resounding laugh. I was as impressed by the way he listened—with complete presence and unwavering attention—as by the words he spoke.

His compassion for the suffering of the Tibetan people was profound. Although he was a vigorous, courageous champion of the Tibetan cause and a staunch opponent of Chinese domination of Tibet, he spoke of the Chinese with equanimity and without hatred. His daily, intimate exposure to the suffering of his people had not undermined his inclusive humanity or his joy in living.

I felt I could learn something here that might help me pull together the sporadic efforts to cultivate wisdom that I had pursued in parallel with my work as an activist and social entrepreneur. As I listened to the Dalai Lama speak, I thought, "So this is what it looks like when inner work and committed work in the world come together."

I realized that my inner work had prepared me to engage with the Dalai Lama fully and receptively, to set aside my lawyerly skepticism and ingrained irony, and to open to the Dalai Lama in his total being—to the fullness of who he was, to his humility and compassion. My perception of the Dalai Lama's wisdom led me to reflect that wisdom is not just an abstract possibility, and that anyone can commit to developing wisdom.

The word *wisdom* rarely appears in legal, political, and scholarly discourse.[1] Different from being smart, well-educated, and discriminating, wisdom entails a way of being—grounded, reflective, insightful, and compassionate. Each of us can do that, I thought— we can work toward wisdom, cultivating these qualities, living our lives in a way that makes us wiser, not with the expectation of attaining the Dalai Lama's level of wisdom, but with the belief that cultivating wisdom can move us toward greater balance and clarity, broader compassion, and improved effectiveness in our work in the world.

This book is for anyone who wants to explore that possibility. Each person who wants to pursue this path will have to make decisions about how he or she wants to balance competing objectives: taking risks and finding security, personal life and career, idealism and compromise, service to the larger community and concern for self. I have weighed these choices in many circumstances, in large career shifts and in the small everyday decisions that shape a life. I hope that sharing my experience will inspire readers, make these choices less lonely and daunting, and encourage them to do the inner work needed to be able to make those choices more wisely.

As I walked from the Dalai Lama's residence to the Kashmir Cottage, the guest house where I was staying, on a path that followed the contour of the hill between the snowcapped mountains and the plains of northern India, I reflected on the long meandering path that had brought me to this remote place and prepared me to be a responsive participant in this unlikely conversation.

After I left the practice of law in a prestigious Washington firm, I moved into the creation of public interest law firms and a new law school, then resurfaced as the president of a new foundation. In each of these positions I had the opportunity to work for social justice and challenge conventional thinking. As I launched these new ventures, I began to explore edges of personal growth and relationship that had been invisible to me when I was working in a highly structured, hierarchical law firm. At the time, those explorations seemed to be peripheral to the "real work" that I was doing as a public interest lawyer and institutional innovator, remote from my world of lawyer's logic. Some of them were physical, drawing me out of the city and into primitive places. In others, I built up my inner resources through workshops grounded in psychoanalytic theory and in the human potential movement. Most important, I began to practice meditation regularly, sitting each morning in silence, finding a place of quiet within me that I could come back to during the course of a conflict-filled day. Later, as I undertook meditation retreats with wise teachers, I began to realize that my meditation practice was opening the possibility of the cultivation of wisdom.

As I looked back, I realized that some of my early experiences had already put me on the wisdom path, though I didn't know it at the time. As a teenager I had found pockets of serenity in the summer by going to a remote camp on an island in central Ontario. I was intrigued by the elegance and simplicity of the canoe—its shape, its cedar ribs and flooring, the taut canvas of its skin. In those Canadian summers I developed an abiding love of the interlocking lakes, streams, and marshes of the northern wilderness. It was on this island, too, away from home and my life of right angles and logical analysis, that I met Susan, who later became my wife, and fell in love with her grace, cheerful optimism, and infectious laugh.

I saw that this was where I first experienced moments of deep inner peace and an intuitive intimation that all life on earth is interconnected and interdependent. Those shadowy beginnings of perception in my teen years were the seeds that germinated years later, pushing through the hard-packed soil of intellectual sophistication, ambitious striving, and professional success.

My extracurricular explorations began to affect the ways in which I did my work, becoming a critical component of my effectiveness rather than a diversion or respite. These explorations were laying the foundations for my practice of wisdom. I found that in the midst of turmoil I was able to respond to strong pressure with less anger and reactivity. I was able to see things more clearly. I was able to empathize with a broader range of people and identify the things we shared. This book is about my progressive efforts to reintegrate the part of myself that had awakened in the lakes of northern Ontario with the activist and social entrepreneur.

Each of us can return to points in our lives when we had an awakening—an insight that suggested that the world was larger than what we had thought it was. Often these are not the sort of incidents that show up on our résumés, and we sometimes don't talk about them with the people we work with. By sharing such incidents in my life, I want to encourage each of us to lift up such events, to reflect on how they enrich our lives and how they can be more fully integrated into our work for a more peaceful and just world.

Since moving to California at the start of the new millennium, I have increased my efforts to integrate the practice of wisdom with my activist engagement in the world. Although there are many paths to the practice of wisdom, this book maps the guideposts that have been most relevant to me, giving me resources to confront the inevitable crises that have arisen in my personal life and in the public sphere.

Practicing wisdom involves *aligning work with values*, what the Buddhists speak of as "right livelihood." It often involves taking risks and being willing to act independently, outside the limits of conventional thinking—particularly in this time of self-absorbed individualism.

Practicing wisdom demands a commitment to *keeping life in balance*. That means living fully in order to develop a wide range of human capacities, emotional as well as cognitive, the heart, the spirit, and the body as well as the mind.

Practicing wisdom requires *time for reflection and introspection*. Meditation and other contemplative practices are tested methods to cultivate an inner silence and presence in which wisdom can evolve.

As wisdom practice develops, *clarity of vision* emerges. We hold our ideas more lightly and see reality more clearly, less circumscribed by our inherited screens and filters, biases and preferences. We become more comfortable living with paradox, holding dissonant views.

Wisdom practice makes *the interconnection of all people* more apparent. We recognize that all people have in common the desire to be happy and secure, an insight that promotes kindness and compassion.

Another dimension of wisdom practice is *the recognition of impermanence and the constancy of change*. Finally, wisdom practice helps us accept *the limits of our understanding* and the importance of *humility*, acknowledging the mystery that surrounds us.

I hope that the practice of wisdom will lead to the creation of a new activism, one that is more grounded in compassion and community and less grounded in anger and divisiveness. Each person who brings the practice of wisdom to her work can be more effective and balanced, and together we can build organizations and strategies that are more sustainable and less polarizing.

Wisdom practice is particularly valuable as we confront the radical discontinuities of the twenty-first century—terrorism, global climate disruption, the risk of pandemics, nuclear proliferation. Most of these threats can be anticipated but none can be controlled. Many people fall into fear and contraction, denial and hedonism, hopelessness and despair.

This book suggests that the practice of wisdom, though it doesn't offer answers or assurance, can infuse our activism with the staying power to remain centered in the face of powerful forces pulling us away from the point of balance and compassion. An activism grounded in wisdom can provide the capacity to deal with the global crises that we increasingly face with clarity, courage, and hope. It can infuse our politics, our individual choices, and the way we live our lives.

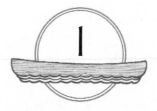

AWAKENING

I STEPPED INTO the main entrance of the federal district court-house, a sterile modern building facing the manicured lawn of the Mall, between the Capitol and the White House in the heart of official Washington. I greeted the guard by name as I walked through the green marble lobby. "How ya doin' Mr. Hapner? Nice to see you back," he said.

"I've got a big case in district court this morning," I said, as breezily as I could manage, as if I had trials and arguments in the courthouse every day. Just two years earlier, in 1965, I had been a law clerk in this same building, my first job out of law school, doing research and drafting opinions and memoranda for an appellate judge. Today I was returning, dressed in my gray pin-striped suit, carrying my new monogrammed calf-skin briefcase. I was lead counsel in a case I cared about deeply, asking the court to take unprecedented steps to protect the rights of mental patients confined in public mental hospitals against their will. I was no longer carrying the bags for a senior partner in a case for a bank or drug company. This was my first big step into professional autonomy.

I had spent months preparing, learning about mental hospitals and the diagnosis and treatment of mentally ill people, interviewing experts, and lining up witnesses. If we could establish that my client was receiving inadequate treatment, the decision would have major implications for the hundreds of thousands of patients confined in mental hospitals throughout the country. Success would mean that courts would, for the first time, look behind the sealed doors of the hospital and evaluate the activities, the tedium and neglect that characterized the patients' lives—their long days watching soap operas, their sunlight filtered through thick windows and mesh security screens, surrounded by patients on thorazine rocking back and forth and chewing their tongues. Courts would have to determine whether the hospital was providing adequate treatment for the inmates' mental condition to justify their incarceration for an indefinite term.

As I entered the courtroom I felt a mix of excitement, anticipation, and terror. This was a highly visible case and Jim Ridgeway was covering it for *The New Republic*.[1] He greeted me at the courtroom door with a big, gap-toothed smile. "Is your client like McMurphy? Is Nurse Ratched beating him down? Does this case involve an effort to hit back at the whole repressive system that is clamping down in this country?"

"I am just focusing on this hearing, this morning," I answered. "It is about one guy who has been held without treatment for over four years. The Constitution doesn't permit that."

Of course, I had read *One Flew Over the Cuckoo's Nest*, the Ken Kesey novel that had been published just a few years earlier, along with R. D. Laing and Thomas Szasz, and I knew the sociological and cultural implications of this challenge to psychiatric authority.[2] But this was a law case in a courtroom, and I had never conducted a hearing before. I was too tense for a casual conversation about sociology or literature.

By the time I arranged my papers at the counsel table and sat down, my client was brought into the courtroom by two marshals.

Charles Rouse looked confident and hopeful despite his ride from St. Elizabeths Hospital in handcuffs, alone in a bus with security screens on the windows. He was a man in his mid-twenties, dressed in an ill-fitting gray suit and a narrow black tie, his skin pallid from his years locked away from the sunshine, with the demeanor of an ambitious used car salesman. His black hair was slicked back, and he wore dark-rimmed glasses that enlarged and framed his darting eyes. There was a little swagger in his walk, as if he were pleased to be the focus of attention. We shook hands.

"How are you feeling?" I asked him.

"Nervous," he said.

"Me too," I said.

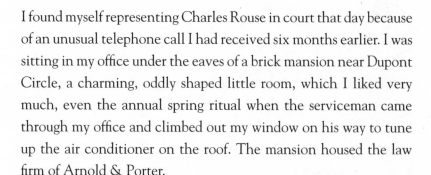

I found myself representing Charles Rouse in court that day because of an unusual telephone call I had received six months earlier. I was sitting in my office under the eaves of a brick mansion near Dupont Circle, a charming, oddly shaped little room, which I liked very much, even the annual spring ritual when the serviceman came through my office and climbed out my window on his way to tune up the air conditioner on the roof. The mansion housed the law firm of Arnold & Porter.

The firm had been founded in the fifties by three veterans of the New Deal. It was known for its smart, innovative lawyers—effective advocates for major corporations, as well as, paradoxically, flinty independents willing to take on unpopular clients, like accused subversives in the McCarthy years. It was a pleasingly eccentric place to begin my career, but the initial blush of novelty had faded. I was becoming impatient with work on issues that I didn't care about—license agreements for marketing laundry soap and joint ventures for shopping malls—drafting legal memoranda

in long days in the library, and client conferences where my job as
a junior associate was to take notes and try to look interested.

On that afternoon I was drafting testimony for a trade association
executive for a congressional hearing on bank interest rates when I
received a call from David Bazelon, the chief judge of the Federal
Court of Appeals, where I had served as a law clerk. I was familiar
with Judge Bazelon's reputation at Law School, a restless and creative judge who used his judicial authority to work for social change.
To do this, he was willing to reach out to promote novel legal theories. He was particularly identified with probing exploration of the
insanity defense.[3] Because I hadn't worked directly under him, I had
been spared the often tense exchanges he had with his own clerks,
with whom he could be demanding and ill-tempered.

"Can you come down to see me at the courthouse?" he asked,
with no preliminary small talk.

"When?"

"Now."

I looked over the testimony that I had been drafting. "Sure," I
said. When the chief judge asks, I thought, it was a good idea to say
yes. I knew that he often reached out to his former clerks to assist
him in drafting speeches and developing new legal theories. But
since I had not been one of his clerks, I was flattered that he was
calling on me. And there was a good chance that he wanted to talk
about something more interesting than the maximum interest rates
that can be charged on an unsecured loan.

The chief judge's suite of offices looked over the Mall, at the west
façade of the Capitol, which was glowing pink in the setting sun.
It looked to me like the kind of picture postcard view that tourists
send home. To my left the dome of the Capitol hovered. At the
other end of Pennsylvania Avenue stood the White House. The
Mall was surrounded by sprawling government buildings housing
cabinet departments, each with endless corridors leading to beige

cubicles, spreading out in huge rectangles from classical entrance colonnades. The bureaucratic decisions flowing from those offices came to this court for review.

When Judge Bazelon's secretary showed me into his office, the judge remained seated, the overhead lights making a halo of his silvery hair. He hardly looked up as he gestured me to a chair, across a large expanse of desktop covered with drafts of half-completed opinions and marked-up lawyers' briefs. On the wall behind his head he had hung a dramatic etching of himself—younger, ruggedly handsome, and darkly introspective. What kind of person decorates his office with such a picture of himself? I wondered. I knew that he gave inscribed etchings to his law clerks at the end of their year's clerkship, and many of these portraits decorated the offices of partners in the city's most prestigious firms.

Judge Bazelon wasted no time. "Look, I have just handed down an opinion that has huge implications for the way courts deal with insanity." He tossed the printed advance sheet, a little pamphlet, across the desk toward me. "The case will go back to the district court for a hearing and I want to make sure that it is handled right. Read the opinion and go back to the firm and tell them that I want you to handle the case in the district court. I'll bet that they will let you do it."

"What do you want me to do in the district court? Will there be an evidentiary hearing?"

"How do I know? I want you to figure it out. Our court has held that involuntary mental patients must be given adequate treatment. This poor schmuck Rouse has been in the hospital for four years after committing a misdemeanor. He's just a kid. It looks like they aren't giving him any treatment at all. He could spend the rest of his life there. And," he added, with a laugh, "if all else fails, you can try a writ of *rachmunes*."

"*Rachmunes*? What's that?"

"Don't you know *any* Yiddish?" he said with mock surprise. "*Rachmunes* is basic human feeling, compassion, sharing someone else's sorrow. This is the generation gap." True, my parents protected me from the Yiddish language as part of the project of making me thoroughly American, and I sometimes feared that the substance of *rachmunes* itself was lost in their desire to equip me to compete effectively in the American struggle to excel.

"Look, just read my opinion, talk to the big shots, and get back to me."

I left the courthouse thinking that the case Judge Bazelon had just handed me sounded like a big opportunity, and my supervisors at the firm agreed to let me handle it. At Yale Law School I had been inspired by the Justice Department's work under Robert Kennedy. He had created a separate division to promote civil rights for racial minorities, mirroring and supporting the work of effective civil rights advocates like Thurgood Marshall, who had used federal litigation patiently and systematically for decades to attack racial segregation.[4] As I drove home that night, I imagined myself acting in the tradition of Kennedy and Marshall, bringing the law's protection to the helpless, neglected people confined in mental hospitals.

I had been intrigued by the issue of insanity and the criminal law ever since taking a law and psychiatry seminar at Yale that was taught jointly by two professors—one a lawyer, the other a psychoanalyst. Anna Freud co-taught the course as well, as a visiting professor. Her presence in the small, paneled seminar room lent it a special quality and everyone deferred to her comments. She wore long simple dresses and spoke softly, with an English accent, and with surprising diffidence.

We discussed moral responsibility, free will, and the limits of criminal penalties for mentally impaired people, analyzing legal, philosophical, and psychological issues. The psychoanalyst urged us to look more deeply at our own motivations lying behind our arguments. The mix of legal doctrine and psychological insight whetted my appetite to know more.

"Isn't it risky to give the psychiatrists too much authority?" Miss Freud asked in her soft voice. "It sounds like the psychiatrist is a magician who can determine with certainty whether a particular mental state causes a particular act. I am not sure that anyone can do that." That opinion about the psychiatric profession struck me as excessively modest, especially coming from Freud's daughter. At that time it seemed to me that psychiatrists had a fascinating and powerful tool for seeing into the human heart, penetrating the screen of words and rationalizations in which we wrap our actions. I was interested in exploring those mysterious depths, although it remained an academic inquiry for me.

The call to Judge Bazelon's office changed that. Far from an academic exercise, the task I was about to begin could transform the way the government treated mentally ill people. The core of the inquiry in law school was about the responsibility of insane people for their criminal conduct, never following the defendant into the mental hospital and asking what happened to him there, and how long he could be incarcerated. The *Rouse* case was an opportunity to begin a legal process of looking behind the walls of mental hospitals and reforming the hospitals' practices. I was flattered that Judge Bazelon had called on me to handle this case, and I liked the fact that I was going to be in charge, with final responsibility for making the decisions.

Several weeks later, I went to meet Charles Rouse on "S" Ward at St. Elizabeths Hospital, the mental hospital run by the federal government for the District of Columbia. This was the hospital where Ezra Pound had been warehoused after World War II, rather than being tried for treason, and where John Hinkley has been held since he shot Ronald Reagan.

St. Elizabeths is on a large, campus-like tract of land spotted with century-old trees in rolling meadows, in a distant part of the District of Columbia, on the far side of the Anacostia River. The building for the criminally insane, the John Howard Pavilion, stands in a remote corner of the grounds. To get to Rouse's ward, I passed through four locked doors and a key-operated elevator. Most of the people on his ward had been found not guilty by reason of insanity, and some of them behaved in bizarre ways, staring, muttering, growling, gnawing their tongues. Later I learned that much of their behavior was induced by the drugs they were given, and the effects of their prolonged hospitalization and enforced idleness. The only activities available in the dayroom were TV and ping-pong. The nursing aides sat in a fortified bunker in the middle of the ward, encased in shatterproof glass and surrounded by files describing and categorizing the people on the ward and by the pills they could use to alter their behavior.

Rouse was a few years younger than I was. He looked like the kind of kid you'd find hanging around a garage in a small town after school, with a pack of cigarettes rolled up in his T-shirt sleeve and a Coke in his hand, trying to look tougher than he was. I saw nothing bizarre or inappropriate about his behavior.

"I just want to get out of here," he said, as soon as we started talking. "Nobody is getting adequate treatment. They should just close this place down, take the locks off the doors and the security screens off the windows, and turn the hospital into a junior college."

At the outset, in Judge Bazelon's office, I was excited by the *Rouse* case, as an important, precedent-setting piece of test litigation. If I succeeded in proving that Rouse had not received adequate treatment and was entitled to be released, a new era of judicial scrutiny would begin, and mental hospitals could no longer be used as human warehouses.

After our meeting at the hospital, the nature of my commitment to the case changed. It was no longer a matter of abstract legal principles. Charles Rouse was a person, and I felt his youth had been taken from him. Indeed, if he had been convicted of the crime, the maximum sentence would have been one year. Instead, he was trapped in a Kafkaesque world of locked wards and thorazine, in which he tried his best to guess at the combination of changes in attitudes and behaviors he could make to get himself released. As I passed outside into the brilliant sunlight, I realized I wanted desperately to help him recover his freedom. I was beginning to get a sense that the commitment to lawyerly abstractions, even noble ones like due process and equal protection, was much stronger if it was coupled with human connection and empathy.

I began preparing for trial, reviewing Rouse's records and interviewing the psychiatrist in charge of his unit. According to the records, it appeared that there was no systematic plan for treating Rouse and that he was receiving virtually no treatment. The psychiatrist claimed that his ward was a "therapeutic milieu" and that confinement in such a place was in itself adequate treatment. It seemed to me that the milieu at St. Elizabeths was just about as therapeutic as the milieu in *One Flew Over the Cuckoo's Nest*.

I also had the advantage of sociologist Erving Goffman's brilliant analysis, based on the year he had spent working at St. Elizabeths as an orderly, researching his classic book, *Asylums*.[5] He found that doctors, custodians, and patients made their way through a complex maze of relationships, isolated from the outside world, and that the therapeutic encounter, the theoretical justification for the whole venture, often was barely discernible. His clear-eyed look at the hospital, free of the wishful thinking of mental health professionals, revealed how limited the therapeutic potential of the place was.

I went to discuss the case with Goffman, who was then a visiting professor at Harvard. We met on a dismal, rainy night in the little apartment he was subletting near Harvard Square. I thanked him for seeing me and explained the case to him.

"Aren't you being sociologically disingenuous?" he asked. "Of course they're not providing adequate treatment in St. Elizabeths Hospital. Everyone knows that. But it's something that society tolerates in order to get some troublesome people off the street and out of sight."

"Disingenuous or not," I said, "there's no legal justification for holding Rouse without treating him. This case is a way of making people face up to this hypocrisy. Besides, Charles Rouse is getting screwed, and I want to get him out of there."

We had a pleasant conversation, during which Goffman was dismissive of the idea that real therapy was taking place at St. Elizabeths. But as we talked I decided that Goffman was probably too introspective and shy to be an effective witness. In any case, he did not want to take time from his current projects to travel to Washington and familiarize himself with the case—and subject himself to the unpleasant experience of cross-examination.

I located two eminent psychiatrists with long experience as superintendents of mental hospitals who would familiarize themselves with Rouse, his records, and the circumstances of his confinement. They had enough prestige in the field to testify convincingly whether St. Elizabeths really was offering adequate treatment for Rouse. Both of them knew a great deal about the strengths and weaknesses of public mental hospitals, and they were willing—without compensation—to stick their necks out, to be critical of their own profession, in order to serve what they saw as a larger good.

On the day of the hearing, I came to the courthouse with the feeling that I was as well prepared as I could be. I had developed a tight legal argument, learned a great deal about public mental hospitals, and identified two outstanding experts to testify about the inadequacy of Rouse's treatment.

When I met him in the courtroom, Rouse turned to me and asked, "What do you know about this judge?"

"I'm not counting on him to be too sympathetic," I said.

"All rise," the bailiff said, cutting our conversation short. The Federal District Court for the District of Columbia is now in session, Judge Alexander Holtzoff presiding." I knew that Judge Holtzoff, a crusty old conservative—small, bald, and waspish—had no use for innovative theories and no use for activist judges like Bazelon. This hearing was a skirmish in a long-running battle.

Indeed, Judge Hotzoff treated me like Bazelon's surrogate throughout the hearing. My arguments were disregarded, my objections overruled, my expert witnesses treated disrespectfully. It was a long and painful courtroom debut.

The judge's head was barely visible above the bench, and the expression on his face suggested that he smelled something disagreeable. As I spoke he tapped his pencil on the bench in front of him impatiently. I tried to keep my focus, to speak confidently and persuasively. I tried to put the case in context. "In this novel case, we will show that my client has been held for three and a half years without treatment, after he had been found not guilty by reason of insanity for an offense that carried a maximum sentence of one year. Our expert testimony will show that the hospital's claim to have given him 'milieu treatment' is a sham. He has been denied his right to have adequate treatment during his incarceration, and he is entitled to be released."

"How long will your presentation of the case take, Counsel?" Judge Holtzoff broke in.

"Probably two days, Judge Holtzoff."

"Counsel, you'd better think of ways to cut your testimony short. We are a busy court here. While you and the chief judge may claim that this case is unique and deserving of special attention, all litigants think that their cases are uniquely important. We have a busy calendar."

Realizing that this could become a debacle, I began imagining a confrontation in Bazelon's chambers. "You what?" he would snarl, his face twisted in anger. "You didn't present your witnesses' testimony? There's no record for us to consider? You certainly made a mess of this! Perhaps Fortas chose the wrong associate. Perhaps you chose the wrong profession."

I looked over at my client, who was slumped down in his chair, visibly deflated, imagining a return to his endless days in the mental hospital. "Relax," I whispered. "The fight isn't over. There will be more than one round."

One of my psychiatric experts, Israel Zwerling, was able to help me recover my equanimity and confidence during the first break in the trial. "This is outrageous," I said to him, my voice rising, as we huddled in the corridor outside the courtroom. "We have a difficult legal issue to deal with, and this poor bastard Rouse's freedom is at stake. This judge is playing crazy games because he has issues with Bazelon and his authority in the courtroom." I was furious as I saw my crusade for improved treatment for the mentally ill going up in smoke before it even began.

"Just hang in there," Zwerling said. "Hold onto your temper. There are strange rules that govern the courtroom, as you know better than I do. You can win this case without persuading Holtzoff. And who knows? We might be able to bring him around."

However, judging from his comments, grimaces, and yawns, Judge Holtzoff was having none of it. As the witnesses testified, he interrupted them with skeptical questions, impatient requests for briefer testimony, and sarcastic asides. "Don't you have any problems in your mental hospitals in Colorado? How do you have time to come here and tell us how to run ours?"

Rouse was taking it all in. During a break in the trial, he leaned over to me and whispered, "Holtzoff is up there trying to bash Bazelon. Bazelon is trying to enhance his reputation as an innovator. You're launching your career as a reformist lawyer. The prosecutor is trying to get ahead by showing how tough he is on the criminal element. Everybody is trying to manipulate, one way or another. Why am I the only one who's locked up and labeled a manipulator and a sociopath? What's going on here? Why me?"

I was taken aback by his insight, which sharply drew me out of my lawyer's role, forcing me to see the situation through Rouse's eyes. The courtroom looked different from his perspective, and I felt another rush of sympathy for him—having to sit passively while his life in confinement for the past three years was dissected and his future determined, as if he were not a full participant in his own life. Each of us was acting out his own drama in the courtroom, and Rouse's life and liberty were at stake. "I don't have an easy answer," I said. "Life isn't fair. You got caught up in the whirlpool where criminal process and mental health systems flow together. I'm trying to get you out of it. That's the best I can do."

Since Judge Holtzoff did not disguise his hostility to Rouse and to the principle of a right to treatment, I was not surprised when he ruled against Rouse from the bench at the end of the day, sending him back to an open-ended period of confinement. Of course, I was not about to let the matter rest there with Holtzoff's prejudgment and hostility. I owed it to Rouse to appeal, and I thought that we would have a good chance of success.

Rouse was crestfallen and angry about this outcome. As the marshals led him out of the courtroom, his head bowed, he said to me in a loud stage whisper, "What good is a fucking right to treatment if the judge isn't going to pay attention to expert witnesses, if he is just going to support the hospital no matter what the experts say?" He did not respond to my assurances about a likely reversal in the court of appeals.

On appeal, I focused the bulk of my argument on challenging Holtzoff's conclusion that Rouse was receiving adequate treatment. I also raised an issue that I had discovered in the course of a conversation with Rouse during the hearing: his original commitment had been illegal, I argued, because he had not consented to the plea of insanity that his lawyer had entered on his behalf. The court of appeals accepted this argument and ordered Rouse released because of his unlawful commitment. The opinion made no finding on the adequacy of Rouse's treatment.[6]

I was pleased for Rouse's sake, but disappointed by the court's failure to address the inadequacy of his treatment. Rouse was happy to be free. "I hope you can help some of the other poor bastards in that place to get out," he said to me as we parted. "Me, I'm going out for a beer."

As Rouse reentered his interrupted life, I returned to mine feeling that I had some unfinished business. I had looked deep into the system that confined thousands of mentally ill people against their will in custodial institutions that were little more than prisons with a psychiatrist as warden. No one was challenging these mental hospitals and holding their practices up to Constitutional scrutiny.

Thurgood Marshall and the NAACP Legal Defense and Education
Fund were expanding and enforcing the rights of African Americans. Who was giving comparable attention to the rights of the
mentally ill?

Despite the battering I had taken in Judge Holtzoff's courtroom,
I found the entire experience energizing and exhilarating. I had
learned an enormous amount, reading widely in psychiatric texts
and consulting with some of the senior mental health profession-
als in the country. I had enjoyed acquiring the language of another
discipline and translating their concepts into the language of non-
specialists. I had stood up to intense pressure and come out all right.
It was my first success in court and I realized, with some surprise,
that my legal training had really prepared me to handle a trial com-
petently.

When I went back to Yale for my fifth Law School reunion, I
enjoyed the conversations initiated by my professors who had
taught my law and psychiatry course. "Where do you think the right
to treatment is heading?" they asked. "Is it likely to be adopted by
other courts?" Although I felt a little guilty about it, I also liked the
publicity, particularly Ridgeway's articles in *The New Republic*. I
began an internal dialogue about the seductions of fame and
celebrity, modest as mine was—about the ways that self-aggrandize-
ment can interfere with service to a client or a cause. From that
point forward I could never assume that my motivations were
untainted.

I saw in this case the possibility of using the courts as a vehicle
for reforming oppressive mental institutions. The courts could end
the entrenched practice of using mental hospitals as a dumping
ground of last resort for difficult and disruptive people. I wanted to
stir things up, to make waves. I saw the possibility of establishing
the rights of the mentally ill through creative and persistent legal
effort, creating a new body of law where none existed, bringing the

protection of the Constitution into mental institutions. I wanted to try using the class-action technique to challenge the inadequacy of treatment in whole systems, not simply the injustice of one person's incarceration. If mentally ill people in institutions had a right to adequate treatment, I wanted to pursue the idea that mentally retarded people should have a similar right. I wanted to be the person who built on the right to treatment principle.

The *Rouse* case suggested that I had some useful skills and important perceptions. I was pleased with my own entrepreneurial ability—raising a modest amount of foundation money to bring in experts, consulting psychiatrists to help shape the case, and working with journalists to bring the story to a broader public. I had a fresh insight into how I could do creative and useful work in the world, to work for social justice and paint on larger canvases.

When I graduated from Yale Law School, I had an abstract interest in contributing to solutions of the world's problems and reducing poverty and injustice. But I did not have the degree of focus and clarity that would have permitted me to escape from the powerful current flowing through the Law School, which carried most of the graduates into corporate law practice. My level of commitment to service wasn't enough to get me to effectively challenge the conventional advice about career path and success. The *Rouse* case helped me to wake up, to create a vision of a life of meaning in the law, and to begin a process of reorienting my life.

BREAKING OUT

SHORTLY AFTER the *Rouse* case was decided, Paul Porter, one of the senior partners in the firm, stopped me in the hall. "Congratulations," he said, draping a long arm over my shoulder. "I read about your victory in your effort to bring law and order to the dank back wards of Bedlam. I hope this means that you'll be able to bill some hours next month."

Porter's remark brought to a head the dilemma I had been worrying about for some time. The *Rouse* case had given me a taste of running my own show, dealing with big issues that I really cared about. Now I was back in my old slot as a junior associate in a big firm whose business was representing large corporations. After the public policy challenges and emotional highs and lows of the *Rouse* case, I was immersed once again in the routine business of the firm: the junior person advising a bank in New York City that wanted to open a branch on Long Island, working for Coca-Cola before the Federal Trade Commission to avoid a requirement that it list its caffeine content on the bottle.

What was I doing in this place, doing this kind of work?

My path to Arnold & Porter began long before law school. By the time I was in eighth grade, I was already thinking about legal principles and the important role played by the courts. My father was a judge, and the dinner table conversation in my home often focused on that day's cases in his courtroom. If he had an interesting case before him, such as the case about the unequal treatment of female bartenders, then called barmaids, he would lay out the facts for my brother Jim and me and solicit our opinions on how it ought to be decided. He was good-humored about it, relishing funny stories and probing and critiquing our efforts to put together just decisions.

One case that was famous around our dinner table involved the death of a ruptured pig. The farmer had filed suit against his garage mechanic, who had failed to fix his truck on time, making it impossible for the farmer to get his ruptured pig to the veterinarian and thus causing the pig's premature death. It was an unusually valuable pig and much loved by the farmer, and he was tenaciously pursuing his legal rights against the mechanic. Jim and I were invited to think about the mechanic's liability and to formulate a just rule that would take care of this situation and others like it. We concluded that it was the farmer's tough luck, that the mechanic had no way of knowing that the late delivery of the farmer's truck would cause a prize pig to die, and that the mechanic's supplier may have been slow in getting him the necessary parts. From that time forward in our house, whenever I made a claim that I had lost some treasured possession, I was met with the rule in the ruptured pig case—it was just my own tough luck, and I was going to have to learn to live with the consequences of my action and my sense of grievance.

My father was a rationalist. He believed that law fostered order and justice. And to the extent that disorder and injustice persisted, that was a challenge and opportunity for rational analysis and reform through law. I wonder whether his commitment to rationality was in part a way of distancing himself from the irrational

horrors that had overtaken the Jews of Europe in his lifetime, overwhelming the German legal system. Although the rationalist training he gave me was invigorating and useful throughout my life, it
was also unbalanced; my emotional skills were not honed with the
same vigor, and the legal analysis did not leave a great deal of room
for compassion.

Before deciding to join Arnold & Porter, I had interviews at a number of corporate firms in New York and Washington, including such
pillars of the Wall Street establishment as Sullivan & Cromwell,
recommended to me by a brilliant young professor, Ronald
Dworkin, who had recently left that firm to teach at Yale Law
School. "Excellent training," he said.[1] As I walked along Wall
Street for an interview, surrounded by lawyers and investment
bankers striding purposefully to their offices in dark topcoats and
regimental Brooks Brothers striped ties, I began to have doubts. It
wasn't that I didn't look like one of them—I did—but I felt that I
shouldn't, that I was wearing a disguise. I stopped and bought a pret-
zel from a street vendor, and slathered it with mustard. I was still
wiping mustard off my fingers as I stepped into the oak-paneled elevator to ascend to the firm's office for my interview. I didn't know
much about myself at the time, but I knew enough to know that
this place wasn't right for me.

Sullivan & Cromwell and a few other firms offered me jobs—and
some firms did not. I was most interested in Arnold & Porter
because of its reputation for outstanding legal work, for unconven-
tionality, and for taking on politically controversial clients.

One of the firm's eccentricities was that it delegated to Victor
Kramer the responsibility for recruiting new lawyers. Kramer was a
small, irascible antitrust lawyer who prided himself on absolute

candor. When I went for an interview, he paced around the office with manic energy, frequently consulting his fat, gold pocket watch, puffing nervously on his pipe and peppering me with questions, sometimes from behind me when his pacing carried him to the far end of the office. "Why do you want to practice law? Why do you want to join this firm? Do you think that this kind of practice will satisfy your impulse to do good? Have you thought about going to the government first and coming here when you've gotten public service out of your system? Do you realize that if you spend five years here you may not be able to afford to leave?"

He never made any offers until he had established that the offer would be accepted. It was an extremely awkward process and Victor's personal quirks did not make it easier. When I succeeded in persuading him that I thought that the firm would be a good place for me to begin practice, he made an offer. At that time the firm was called Arnold, Fortas & Porter, but a few months later it lost its middle name, when Abe Fortas was appointed to the Supreme Court. I was the thirtieth lawyer in the firm, an intimate and informal office with few visible indications of hierarchy. Still, I had to struggle to get comfortable calling senior partners by their first names.

The named partners were New Deal alumni who had been creative designers of government institutions and programs to promote the public welfare. Paul Porter, the first chairman of the Federal Communications Commission when it was established in the mid-thirties, was a tall, elegant Kentuckian with oiled-back hair and immaculately tailored suits. A two-martini lunch was, for him, the kind of lunch you have if you have important business to do in the afternoon. Otherwise, you didn't stop with two. His great skill was not legal analysis, but wooing clients. One of his younger partners said of him, "He is like necessity; he knows no law." But that did not stop Paul from being a critically important partner in this firm.

Abe Fortas was a powerful legal mind, an intimate counselor to Lyndon Johnson, and the center of the firm. He had the reputation of being the shrewdest tactician in the Washington bar. His career in government during the New Deal era gave him an intimate knowledge of its workings. A superb draftsman, who had turned the legal brief into an art form, he was famous for his brutality to associates and partners who made mistakes or failed to live up to his high standards of performance. Some quite senior partners in the firm still bore the scars of their encounters with him. Unfortunately, their experience had not made them kinder to their juniors.

Fortas enjoyed the wealth that law practice had brought him. He and his wife, Caroline Agger, the head of the firm's tax department, lived in a mansion in upper Georgetown. Famous for her misanthropic toughness, she dressed in subtle pastels and smoked thick cigars. "Our swimming pool has two deep ends," she said, "so that people aren't tempted to drop by with their small children for a swim on a hot summer day." Fortas was a serious amateur violinist who played chamber music with Isaac Stern when Stern was in town for concerts.

The third named partner, Thurman Arnold, had grown up in Wyoming and once served as mayor of Laramie. He later became a professor at Yale Law School and wrote *The Folklore of Capitalism*, an irreverent and influential book that won him the attention of President Roosevelt, who appointed him head of the antitrust division of the Justice Department and later a court of appeals judge in Washington.[2] By the time I met him, he was a profane, messy old man, full of salty frontier humor and utter disdain for conventional thinking and habits. He had made peace with capitalism in a way that seemed to have deepened his cynicism.

Neither Porter nor Arnold could see a balloon without sticking a pin in it, usually with wit and enthusiasm. They presided over cocktails in the firm's garden room every day at six o'clock, telling stories about Washington during the New Deal and the ways in which people had been making fools of themselves for decades. They were wonderful storytellers, their tales always drawing from a good-natured belief that people are absurd and greedy and that anybody who does not look out for his own interests is a fool. I once asked Judge Arnold why he had resigned from the court of appeals, where he had a lifetime appointment, to start a law practice. "Simple," he said, shaking with laughter and sprinkling his vest with cigar ashes. "I'd rather talk to a bunch of damn fools than listen to them."

Shortly after I joined the firm, Fortas was persuaded by Lyndon Johnson to take a seat on the Supreme Court. By all accounts, he had wanted to stay in private practice, at which he was exceedingly successful, and also to take advantage of his intimate ties to the occupant of the White House. Nonetheless, Johnson's legendary persuasive powers moved Fortas to the Supreme Court. I was still at the firm a few years later, when he resigned from the Court in disgrace because of an inappropriate financial relationship with a former client, a convicted felon with business before the Supreme Court. I wondered if his ethical failure had something to do with the peculiar schizophrenic career he lived as a lawyer—a New Deal liberal and a brilliant legal innovator in his youth who later offered his unique gifts to corporations selling cigarettes.[3]

I postponed my starting date at the firm to spend a month in Louisiana with the Lawyers Constitutional Defense Committee doing volunteer legal work in support of the civil rights movement. The previous summer was the Mississippi Freedom Summer, when many northerners went south to work in the civil rights movement and three heroic civil rights workers were murdered in rural Mississippi. Though I had not been actively involved in the civil rights movement before, I felt that I wanted to be part of it. The risk in going to Louisiana did not seem to be inordinate, and I thought that going as a lawyer might afford me a measure of protection.

In Shreveport, in the tough northern section of the state, I shared a small rental house with two other northern lawyers in the black part of town. We ate our meals in black restaurants, where we were the only white customers. I had never lived in a black world and eaten collard greens before, nor had I ever seen such deep poverty. In virtually every town we came to, I could tell where the black neighborhood began because the streetlights and the street paving ended, giving way to darkness and dusty unpaved roads.

At the time I was there, the Free Southern Theater—an integrated company of actors and improvisers doing political theater to nurture the growing civil rights consciousness among the local black population—was touring Monroe and Jonesboro and the smaller towns in the northern tier of the state. The company was harassed everywhere they went, and much of my time was spent getting them out of rank and dangerous county jails before guards or inmates could beat them up. At a confrontation in Jonesboro, one of the lawyers with me, a soft-spoken man on leave from the Coast Guard judge advocate's office, was arrested for talking too aggressively to a sheriff's deputy. We talked him out after a few hours in jail. The jail was overshadowed by the huge paper mill operated in the town by the Crown-Zellerbach Corporation, with a strictly segregated workforce, reserving the high-paying jobs for white workers.

One night I attended a meeting in a rural black church near Monroe, addressed by the charismatic James Farmer, then president of CORE, the Congress of Racial Equality. The audience was made up of local people—shopkeepers, students, and sharecroppers, who were risking their livelihoods and possibly their lives by being there—a few civil rights organizers, and two white lawyers. After hearing Farmer's resonant voice describe a new world in which blacks would be able to vote and to go to integrated schools, we all sang "We Shall Overcome." It was a powerful moment for me. I believed in the possibility of Farmer's vision, and I thought we could overcome, and that I was part of the "we" who would make it happen. We walked out the double doors at the back of the sanctuary, shaking hands with the pastor who had offered his church for this meeting, into the moonless night, under a dense canopy of stars. We got into our car, drove slowly past the squad cars pulled off the road by the church driveway with their lights off. All the way back to Shreveport, I kept an eye on the rearview mirror.

I was deeply impressed by the civil rights workers and the local people I met—by their courage, commitment, and optimism. The other lawyers and I believed that the license plates on our rental car were registered with the police and that we had been placed in the category of carpetbaggers, Communists, and outside agitators. If I saw a police car pull in behind us on the highway, I knew that an enemy was following me. For the first time, I was on the wrong side of the law.

Sometimes, brief experiences can assume a large psychological significance. My few weeks in northern Louisiana were a small episode in a long career in law, and I was on the periphery of the civil rights movement that was remaking the country. Yet those few weeks had a disproportionately large impact on the way I thought about myself and the future direction my life should take.

I joined the firm in the fall of 1965, after my life-changing experience in Louisiana. I had a different perspective on the firm and on the compromises I was prepared to make. I had glimpsed another kind of law practice. I didn't want to let go of the intensity, the exploration of new experiences, and the sense of meaningful engagement I had felt during my time in Louisiana. I wanted to see if these feelings could exist in the urbane, self-satisfied, and legalistic world of Dupont Circle. The firm was still a small group of lawyers and a pleasant place to work. From my early days there, I was considered a person with an overactive social conscience, a type often drawn to the firm because of its well-known history.

Some of these young lawyers left after a few years; some made peace with themselves and their work. There were a number of partners who thought that this level of tension was a positive thing, giving the firm its distinctive character, and helping some of the corporate lawyers to feel good about themselves in their profession. There was room for an associate who would push the boundaries, who would be recognized in the bar as a leader in pro bono work. Perhaps I could find a niche here.

Most of the lawyers in the firm were liberal Democrats who spent their days representing large corporations, managing with apparent ease the built-in dissonance between their politics and their careers. It was clear that I was going to have to make some compromises in my life, and this firm might be able to accommodate my needs. I valued the professional prestige and its national leadership in pro bono work. Here was a group of lawyers who apparently had values like mine, and they seemed to enjoy their very lucrative work.

In general, I was assigned to cases that were intellectually interesting and relatively neutral from a moral perspective. I was one of the utility infielders who would be sent into the library to research a novel point of law that arose when one of our corporate clients was trying to buy a competitor. I developed a nodding familiarity with antitrust, banking, food and drug, real estate, and litigation. I was never assigned to work on the ethically toxic matters involving Philip Morris and the Tobacco Institute.

Like many lawyers, I did this work that I basically didn't believe in, taking satisfaction in the skillful and responsible way that I executed my assignments. I was thoroughly familiar with the theory: lawyers work in an adversarial process. Judges reach just results if contesting parties represented by skilled advocates present their arguments as forcefully and effectively as they can. The legal system is set up for zealous advocates who need not think too much about the value or merit of any particular position they take. But this justification never fully satisfied me.

My colleagues thought of me as tough-minded, aggressive, and lawyerly. When they came to dinner and met my children, they found something quite different. Susan and I had moved into a small brick house just north of the District of Columbia, with a dogwood tree in the front yard. We had married young and promptly began to have babies—two by the time I came to Arnold & Porter, a third by the year I left. Although neither of us had ever taken care of a baby for even one hour before we brought our first baby home, Susan was a competent, grounded, and loving mother.

I had established the habit of spending time in intense interaction with the children. When we came into the house, adult conversations were interrupted by our children bouncing up and down, shouting, "Daddy! Daddy!" Dropping legal issues immediately, I got down on the floor, entering into their play, with dolls, with building blocks, and simply with imagination. I had the ability to leave the intensity of law work behind instantly and enter into the mind and games of small children.

The double life I led saved me from some of the excesses of the law world. Being a father to small children gave me the experience of unconditional love and a deeper sense of connection to other beings than I had ever felt before. It also gave me exposure to the frustration that comes from dealing with irrational beings who are unresponsive to reason.

I did not think about cultivating wisdom at this time. The word wisdom was hardly in my vocabulary. But as I look back, I can see that I was beginning to practice wisdom, instinctively and without a plan, as I found that my family life was calling me into a life of balance, building the resources of the heart as well as the head. It helped blunt my lawyers' tendency to self-importance and to see the world as fitting neatly into logical frameworks. The time I spent with my children taught me a lesson in the limited effectiveness of logic and rules. I had certainly not planned on having my first child when I was twenty-one years old, but this proved in many ways to be a fortunate accident.

We began as an Eisenhower-era marriage, with a sharp division of responsibility and traditional gender roles—Susan's life focused in the home, mine outside. We had limited emotional resources to help us negotiate our differences and make peace after angry confrontations. Still, we improvised together and taught ourselves how to be adults, parents, and a married couple. Susan brought greater psychological sophistication into the marriage as she completed a master's degree in social work and became a psychotherapist. She helped me to constrain my lawyer's mindset, which would sometimes leech into domestic conversation, bringing rules of evidence and relevance invented for the courtroom into the bedroom.

At law school they had promised to teach us to "think like a lawyer." I had no idea what that phrase meant since I only knew one way to think: like a lawyer, the way that my father thought—logical, unemotional, doubtful of intuition and passion. My experience as a young husband and father was a milestone in my learning to think like a *nonlawyer*. My immersion in the joys and responsibilities of parenthood accelerated my enjoyment of the fullness of life. Susan and I developed together the skills we needed to build our marriage and our family. I don't believe that it was just good luck that we found each other so young, though I sometimes thought so at the time. I believe that we each responded to an inner knowing—deeply reliable but inaccessible to the rational mind— that this was the person we were to spend our lives with.

While I was finding my way in the firm and thinking about the possibility of my making a career there, I was assigned to an antitrust case, representing Allis-Chalmers, a large farm equipment manufacturer in Milwaukee, that has since been devoured by John Deere, an even larger manufacturer. It was a bread-and-butter case for the firm, a prosecution by the government involving a novel legal theory. I welcomed the assignment as a way of getting to see the inside of a major corporation.[4]

Allis-Chalmers had considered going into the lawn-mowing business by designing and building its own line of riding garden tractors, the hefty minitractors that people ride while mowing their suburban lawns. Instead, rather than developing a new product line, the company decided to acquire a successful manufacturer, Simplicity Manufacturing, in a neighboring Wisconsin town. The Justice Department claimed that this decision was anticompetitive, in violation of the antitrust laws, because it removed Allis-Chalmers as a potential competitor with its own product line and reduced the choices available to the consumer. This legal theory was novel and potentially significant in a wide range of industries, but it turned on a simple factual question: Do riding garden tractors compete in the same market as ordinary power lawn mowers, which can be bought in any hardware store? If all power lawn mowers competed in a single market, the market was huge, and any anticompetitive effect of A-C's purchase of Simplicity would be trivial. If, however, riding garden tractors were their own market, then the acquisition would be a significant anticompetitive development in a small market. Our job was to establish that the relevant market was all power lawn-mowing equipment—the $55 walk-behind power mower and the riding garden tractor that sold for several thousand dollars.

I spent weeks traveling around midwestern towns in the dead of winter, talking about lawn mowing to riding garden tractor dealers, lawn mower dealers, and manufacturers. I felt like Willy Loman on the road. Most of the people I spoke with were hostile to government interference in business, so they were naturally sympathetic to our client. I picked a half-dozen potential witnesses who saw the world our way and discarded the rest.

This case taught me how to travel well on an expense account. For the first—and only—time in my life, I flew first class. As we were sitting in the first-class cabin, enjoying a martini on a flight to Milwaukee, one of the partners I was working with told me, "They are lucky to have us working for them, coming to Milwaukee for a client conference when there is a foot of snow on the ground. They have no complaint if we travel first class. We'll get to know the best restaurants in town. I'm just sorry that we have to eat so much sauerbraten in Milwaukee. Too bad the place wasn't settled by the French."

About this time, the firm established a hiring committee, a symbol of creeping bureaucratization as efficiency-minded managers asserted their influence. It was also a polite way to retire the quirky Vic Kramer from the hiring process. Thinking it would be good for the firm's image to have a young, public-spirited associate on the committee, they chose me. At that point I had never hired anyone for anything, and I started at a rarified point of elite sensibility. My initiation was a discussion on the committee about whether the firm should look beyond the Harvard, Yale, and Columbia law schools to recruit new lawyers. The consensus: Why bother? An exception might be made for someone who was first in the class at another law school. Such a person might have had good reasons for not going to Harvard—such as the need to stay near home to care for a sick mother—and might have excelled if he or she had gone there. In addition, if a partner had business in San Francisco, he might swing by Stanford or Boalt Hall in Berkeley and talk to their best students.

I thought of asking, "Does it trouble anyone on this committee but me that if Paul Porter or Judge Arnold were graduating from law school today, neither one could even get an interview?" But I thought better of it.

During the committee's meetings I also became familiar with the distinctive humor that I came to identify as "lawyer humor." For example, when we were talking about a partner who had recently left the firm after a psychological crisis, the chairman said, "His departure did not leave a vacancy." With regard to another partner who had left Arnold & Porter to join another prominent firm, the chairman remarked, "When he moved over to the other firm, the average IQ of both firms went up." The jokes were ironic, witty, and cruel. They reminded the people who heard them about the kind of treatment they might expect from their partners when they were not in the room. Although I found them funny and I was good at the form, these jokes left me with an uneasy feeling that I was buying my way into the club at the expense of others and of my own humanity.

I didn't have the words to express it at the time, but I felt a growing disharmony between the person I was becoming and the norms of the firm—not just the clients that they represented, but the way the other lawyers lived, the things that they found funny, their competitiveness, their sense of entitlement. I felt that I could go in that direction, and I didn't want to.

Susan and I were in New York, staying at the East Side suite that Arnold & Porter maintained for traveling lawyers. It was available for recreational weekends, one of the firm's ancillary benefits. We called our old friend Fred Reinglas, whom we had met long ago at summer camp in Ontario. He was a small, intense man, the child of actors in Yiddish theater who had survived the Holocaust in Eastern Europe with their young son by traveling east, performing and hiding, always staying one jump ahead of the German army. At the war's end they moved to Toronto.

Fred's career in theater had carried him to New York. He spent several years in the mid-sixties as stage manager for the musical *Hair*—first in the New York production, and then casting touring companies and installing them in theaters around the country.[5] He was deeply engaged in the drugs and rock 'n' roll culture that the play embodied, and he had developed a flamboyant persona that suited his role. Once, he came to dinner in our home in suburban Chevy Chase dressed in dark glasses and a floor-length robe of carpetlike material with long filaments of green and orange wool. Amused by our respectable suburban lifestyle, he took particular pleasure in shocking us and initiating us into ways of life that we could barely imagine.

Fred invited us to an outdoor performance of *Hair* that would take place in Central Park. He assured us that it would be worth attending. It was easy to find the amphitheater because of the heavy haze of marijuana smoke hanging over it and the sweet smell drifting on the wind. We followed our noses to the performance.

Although there were many policemen in attendance, the concert-goers were comfortably passing joints around the audience. At first we simply passed the joints by, but after a bit we found ourselves taking a puff as each one reached us. The music seemed to improve as the afternoon wore on, and a feeling of beautiful friendship suffused the crowd. We had never smoked marijuana or had an experience like this before, and we found ourselves slipping into the ease and good humor of the moment.

The loud throbbing music was penetrating and irresistible, totally absorbing us in the rhythm and dance, in the brilliant sunshine and the joyous feeling in Central Park. We allowed ourselves to go with it and be taken over, letting go of our plans and commitments. We found ourselves on our feet, dancing alone, with each other, and with smiling strangers, moving languidly through the crowd, patiently rubbing past the pliant bodies responding to the music.

We left the concert with broad smiles and a freshness of vision that made the busy city vivid and exciting. The dense traffic seemed to be a sophisticated and complex ballet, the reds and greens of stoplights glowing like rubies and emeralds as we sat in the backseat of a taxi on the way to LaGuardia Airport.

It was a far cry from our Chevy Chase home, our two beige station wagons, and the law firm where I worked. We reflected on the self-imposed limits of our lives, acknowledging the subtle but powerful ways that my life as a corporate lawyer was narrowing our vision and isolating us from the cultural currents that were blowing through the country.

The Allis-Chalmers case wound on to a successful conclusion. We were able to marshal a convincing case in federal court in Milwau-

kee, in a long and boring trial, in which my primary responsibility
was to keep track of the voluminous exhibits and depositions. We
had hired, for a handsome fee, the former dean of the University of
Wisconsin Business School, who shared our view of the economics
of the lawn-mowing business. His testimony was persuasive to the
judge, and he ruled in our favor.

At the celebration dinner, held in a private dining room at the
Milwaukee Athletic Club, well-lubricated with alcohol, I found
myself feeling empty. Amidst all the gaiety, I confessed to myself
that I really hadn't cared at all whether we won this case or not.

About this time the firm had just finished computerizing the
time-record system, so it was easy to find out how many hours I had
spent working on our recent victory. I found that I had logged more
than two thousand hours, a full year's work, representing Allis-
Chalmers in something that made little difference to anyone.

My real satisfaction and most imaginative work during my years at
Arnold & Porter were associated with the pro bono matters that I
took on, whether formally approved by the firm or around the edges
of my work week. As the opposition to the Vietnam War grew in
intensity, I was looking for a way to support the antiwar movement
and the young people who were going to jail and risking their
futures by resisting the draft and opposing the war. Some friends
and I began to discuss ways to strengthen the legal support for people facing the draft and considering draft resistance.

Under the draft law at that time, each local draft board was free
to make its own decisions based on its interpretation of the regulations put out by the Selective Service System. This meant that
there could be wide variations, for example, in interpreting a
phrase like *conscientious objector*. Some draft boards would only

grant that status to members of peace churches like the Quakers or Mennonites, whereas other draft boards gave it to people with good-faith moral objections to war, not based on the theology of any church. Some would only recognize an objection to fighting in all wars; others would acknowledge a draftee's objection to a particular war. The district courts, which reviewed draft board decisions, usually deferred to the boards, and often the opinions of the courts were not published. Prior decisions of draft boards and many courts were unavailable to counselors who were advising potential draftees.

We launched the *Selective Service Law Reporter* to build a network of draft lawyers who would report to us on their cases. The *SSLR* gathered draft decisions, indexed them, and organized them in practical categories to make them easily accessible to lawyers and draft counselors. We added commentary that was both scholarly and practical. Twice a month, *SSLR* sent out an installment to be added to the subscriber's loose-leaf binder. Over time, lawyers were able to make increasingly sophisticated arguments to draft boards and courts, and a body of precedent emerged to replace the arbitrary decisions of draft boards. The Supreme Court decided important cases, establishing principles that were binding on courts and draft boards throughout the country. People confronting the draft could make informed choices about their risks and choices. Within a few months, we had better information about draft decisions than the Selective Service System itself. We knew we were successful when the Selective Service System ordered ten subscriptions to the *SSLR*.

Prior to the *SSLR*, the Selective Service System had existed outside the law. The arbitrary decisions of local draft boards had a radical impact on the lives of potential draftees—who went to Vietnam, who went to jail, who got deferments or exemptions. I got a firsthand look at the power of the *SSLR* when a friend of mine

called me about his draft-age brother who had dropped out of college and become part of the music scene in San Francisco. He was
prepared to go to jail rather than go to Vietnam. He actually seemed
to welcome the idea. I checked out the SSLR and advised him of
the process by which he could enroll as a part-time student and
obtain a student deferment, encouraging him to reflect on how
much more effectively he could oppose the war if he stayed out of
jail. After much soul searching, he decided to follow the less dramatic path. Thousands of draft resisters received this kind of advice
from lawyers who had consulted the SSLR.

Although this was a major pro bono project, it was not identified
with the firm. I was flying below the radar, and no one in the firm
ever raised an objection.

I was not so fortunate in regard to the Marc Raskin affair, which
developed from my work with the Institute for Policy Studies, the
progressive think tank established in the early sixties by Raskin and
Dick Barnet, with Arnold & Porter doing the legal work.[6] As I had
searched among the firm's clients looking for matters that I wanted
to work on, I thought the Institute sounded unusually interesting.

I became corporate secretary of the Institute, the person who
keeps minutes at board of trustees meetings and attends to corporate filings. It wasn't the most interesting aspect of the Institute's
work, but it gave me an opportunity to sit in on board meetings and
learn how a nonprofit organization operates. At the same time, I
was introduced to the foundation world and the possibility of creating new kinds of institutions with foundation support, learning
how to build a board of trustees and work with it.

A side benefit of my association with the Institute was the window it offered on movements growing in society. The Institute was

a magnet drawing these forces into dialogue: the civil rights movement, coping with the tensions inside the movement as "black
power" was coming to replace integrationism; the feminist movement, calling for equal treatment of women in the workplace; a
deeper rethinking of relationships within the family; the inter-
weaving of the personal with the political; and, of course, the rejection of the brutal war in Vietnam.

These forces were barely visible at Arnold & Porter. Although I
read about them in analytic articles in the *Washington Post*, the seminars at the Institute brought them alive, flowing with energy and
passion. And the energy flowed over into wonderful parties that
were held at the Institute and at Raskin's home. The conversation
was always challenging, and I met new people who introduced me
to a larger world—civil rights organizers from northern Mississippi,
diplomats from Algeria, dissident intellectuals like Paul Goodman
and Ivan Illich. At one Raskin party after a Pentagon demonstration against the war, Norman Mailer held court in one room and
Robert Lowell in another, each surrounded by a circle of beautiful
young protesters. Mailer chronicled the party in *The Armies of the
Night*.[7]

I learned at these parties that it was OK to dance. I had grown
up thinking that dancing was something that intellectuals didn't
do. But at these parties, after hours of heady conversation, some-
body would turn down the lights and turn up the music. Raskin and
other people whose minds I respected were getting deeply into the
music and dancing into the morning hours, tense debate and harsh
judgment dissolving in the intensity of Dionysian rhythm and
dance, minds and bodies becoming synchronized, opening new
sources of pleasure. The music of Dylan, the Beatles, and the
Rolling Stones was a critical part of the changes that were taking
place, and the free-form dance increased the joy of it. Susan and I
started dancing stiffly and ended up sweating, with a different sense

of our bodies' rhythms, and we experienced the joy of singing "I can't get no satisfaction," with friends and strangers, along with Mick Jagger. Our emergence as enthusiastic but tentative dancers was a small thing, but in retrospect I see that this lightening up, this grounding in our bodies, was a significant milestone in our moving toward wholeness. I began to see dancing as a metaphor for a certain way of moving through life—gracefully, with pleasure in the moment. Being a parent could be a dance. Practicing law could be a dance.[8]

The Institute became a hub of the antiwar movement, at first intellectually, later as a center for mobilizing action. At one antiwar demonstration, Marc Raskin, although he was well beyond draft age, burned his draft card in a show of solidarity with the young men facing the draft. Some months after this act, in 1968, he was indicted for conspiring with Benjamin Spock, the respected author of books on child rearing; William Sloan Coffin, the chaplain of Yale University; and others to obstruct the draft. The prosecution was a centerpiece in Lyndon Johnson's strategy to throttle the growing opposition to the Vietnam War.

The day the indictments were handed down I flew with Marc to a preliminary meeting of the accused conspirators and their lawyers. Marc had never met or corresponded with several of them. None of his activity with any of his codefendants went beyond parallel efforts to work for an end to the war, activity that was clearly protected by the First Amendment.

We met the accused conspirators and their lawyers on a snowy evening at Leonard Boudin's house in Greenwich Village. Leonard, a senior member of the left bar, had been retained to represent Dr. Spock. The defendants agreed that they would fight the charges, both legally and politically. "This trial will give us the forum that we need to indict the illegal war effort and demand the government be held to account. The courtroom will be the center of our defense, but it will overflow into the universities, the media, and the streets," Reverend Coffin said.

I attended the meeting as an informal legal adviser to Marc, assuming that Arnold & Porter would represent him—a longstanding client—through what promised to be an important and exciting trial, and that I would be spending the next several months on the defense team. But I underestimated the firm's loyalty to Lyndon Johnson and its unwillingness to displease him. Although Judge Arnold had formerly been a trustee of the Institute, he was a fierce defender of the Vietnam War and opposed our representing Raskin in what he characterized as a political trial. There was an intense debate within the firm, with me playing a leading role, and many of the younger partners supporting a commitment to the Raskin defense.

After one meeting, as we were leaving the conference room, Judge Arnold took me by the elbow. "I have an important lesson for you, Halpern," he said with a laugh that shook loose a shower of cigar ashes. "You can't piss in the soup—we all have to drink it." The firm would not risk offending the Johnson administration.

Raskin had become a good friend, and I hated the idea that I would not be able to stand by him. I read about the trial, a catalytic antiwar event, in the newspapers. Raskin was acquitted by the jury. Some of his codefendants were convicted, but all convictions were overturned on appeal.[9]

An interesting idea for a pro bono case grew out of my civil rights work in northern Louisiana. The most frightening town in that area was Jonesboro, a center of racist resistance and CORE organizing. The main employer in the town was a paper mill that had been bought by Crown-Zellerbach, a San Francisco–based corporation with a reputation for good works and community responsibility. But it had done nothing to desegregate the plant or integrate the workforce. Blacks were kept in menial and low-paying jobs, and the physical facilities were rigidly segregated. The Civil Rights Act of 1964 made these practices illegal, but the corporation did not want to disrupt its operations and unsettle the local customs by complying with the law.

It occurred to me that stockholders ought to have the right to demand that the corporation in which they owned stock comply with the law. I did some basic research on the legal theory and found that there was a good argument that a stockholder could maintain such an action. When I discussed my theory with Phil Stern, an author, activist, and philanthropist who had deep roots in New Orleans, he was ready to file suit.

I was called into Judge Arnold's office to meet with the firm's management committee. Judge Arnold, in a seersucker suit, cigar ashes streaking his shirtfront and vest, greeted me with questions: "I don't suppose that Crown-Zellerbach is doing anything different from other companies down there, do you? What does Phil Stern want to mess with it for?" After some desultory discussion, the committee turned the case down, and once again I was left frustrated, confronting the limitations on practice in a firm that is devoted to corporate representation.

My experience with the Crown-Zellerbach and Raskin cases reminded me of what I had been told at my job interview: "We are in business to make money; we are not a charitable institution." I had never been confused about the point, but these incidents reminded me of how large the number of off-limits matters was likely to be. And I didn't think that a little pro bono work on cases that were inoffensive to the firm's clients and senior partners was going to be sufficient to reconcile me to a career as a corporate lawyer.

On the day after Martin Luther King was shot, in 1968, I sat with my radio at the breakfast table, mourning the loss of yet another great leader and listening to news reports of the riots, looting, and violence that were spreading around the country and through the District of Columbia. As I drove down Sixteenth Street to my office, the city was under military occupation, with soldiers in battle gear behind sandbag bunkers at major intersections north of the White House. Sirens wailed and low-flying airplanes buzzed overhead. Clouds of smoke billowed over the Fourteenth Street corridor, which was in flames.

A group of young lawyers at the firm got together early in the morning to go down to the District of Columbia courts to provide legal representation for people who had been picked up during the disorders. With our briefcases we were prepared to thread our way through the armed and divided city to see if we could be of service.

Just as we were leaving the firm, Paul Porter pulled into the U-shaped driveway in his long black Cadillac limousine, with his driver, a smiling African American named Henry Ford, behind the wheel. Paul asked where we were going, and when we told him, he insisted that Henry drive us to the courthouse. So we drove across the city in the Cadillac limousine, with gunshots in the air and the smoke from fires from the downtown area casting a pall over the city. Paul loved the humor of it, and we imagined him retelling the story over martinis at his favorite restaurant, the Palm, a hangout of Washington insiders. We self-consciously got out of the limousine before we reached the courthouse, walking the last few blocks. This odd incident captured for me some of the incongruities of the life I was leading. About this time, the term *limousine liberals* was developing currency, used to disparage the hypocrisy of people who espoused liberal views while riding around in limousines. Its literal application made me squirm.

One warm spring night not long after the limousine incident, I sat with Susan on the screened porch behind our little house in suburban Chevy Chase, watching the moon rise over the schoolyard behind our fence and the blossom-laden apple tree that stood in the corner of our yard. "I don't want to find myself, after another twenty-five years of law practice, registering another hollow victory, spending my efforts on behalf of a client I don't give a damn about. I loved handling the *Rouse* case with the excitement and the sense of public service that went with it."

That night, as we sat, we sifted through the arguments for and against staying at Arnold & Porter. The firm was attractive in many ways. The people there were pleasant, the financial security was reassuring. It was still a small firm, fewer than fifty lawyers, and it was easy for a junior associate to engage senior partners. There was an appealing level of chaos, which gave me the flexibility to follow my own interests. And they genuinely supported pro bono work, up to a limit. "If he were alive, my father would advise me to stay and try to work things out. 'These are first-rate lawyers, and they value your work,' he would say."

"He's been dead for a while," Susan replied. "Who knows how his views would have evolved in this cataclysmic decade? You know he didn't care about money." She reminded me that his partner used to complain that he didn't charge his clients enough, and that he would be so grateful to a client who brought him an interesting legal problem that he felt that the client was doing *him* a favor. "Your father's indifference to making money was something I liked about him," she added.

I worried about what a lifetime of work in a firm like this would turn me into. I looked around at the senior partners and I did not see anyone I wanted to be like. They lived with the insecurity of having to prove themselves continually in this highly competitive environment, both by turning out a great deal of highly polished work and by attracting corporate clients.

I had no skill at schmoozing with general counsels and chief executives in the clubhouse after a round of golf. I couldn't imagine bringing new corporate business into the firm. Ultimately, that's what the firm was all about. Lawyers who lacked that skill, no matter how brilliant, stalled partway up the ladder. The meritocracy that seemed to flourish in the law schools and in the first round of law firm hiring was replaced by a different meritocracy, one that was explicitly attuned to attracting corporate clients.

Susan and I discussed a series of articles in the *New Yorker* written by Charles Reich, my old Constitutional law professor. He criticized the traditional liberal response to social problems—passing new legislation, creating a new bureaucracy to enforce the law, increasing the size and power of the federal government. He had been moving toward a different, deeper agenda for change, which he spelled out in the *New Yorker* articles and later in his book *The Greening of America*.[10] His analysis resonated deeply with me.

Reich contended that a new consciousness was emerging among young people that was going to transform our institutions, creating a new kind of revolution, one based in love, an expression of the authentic self, and an inclusive sense of community. The new consciousness was joyous, communitarian, ecological, compassionate, and spiritually rooted. His analysis seemed like a revelation, holding out a possibility of wholeness. It suggested that the intellect, the body, the emotions, and the spirit might converge.

I reflected on the orderly world I grew up in. Buffalo was a city that had been laid out in a strict geometrical grid by Pierre

L'Enfant, the Enlightenment architect, who also designed the capital. Our house was large and solid, built of dark brick at the end of the nineteenth century. It crouched like a sphinx, facing a street vaulted by enormous elm trees. My family would sit after dinner on our front porch, a few steps up from the sidewalk, rehearsing our day's activities, reading the *Buffalo Evening News*, and conversing with passersby.

"I don't want to live a life that is too predictable and orderly," I told Susan. "The lawyers in the firm have settled into lives of respectability and security—private schools, big houses, season tickets for Redskins games. Something new is emerging, and I don't want to read about it in the newspaper."

SOCIAL ENTREPRENEUR

IN 1968, I invited a group of friends to discuss the problems with our law work and the failings of the justice system. In evening meetings at my home, we were driven both by our dissatisfactions and a sense of possibility, a feeling that we could be doing better with our lives. This wasn't what we had become lawyers for. We wanted to work on problems that were socially significant, and we were prepared to make waves. We liked the idea of working as a community of friends, with people we cared about. We were in a position to take risks, since our work in prestigious legal institutions provided us a substantial safety net. We were inspired by other people who were taking bigger risks—in the resistance to the war and in the civil rights movement.

In unstructured and wide-ranging conversations, we talked about the social turmoil and the people who were challenging the sluggishness of institutions and the performance of leaders. Student takeovers closed down university campuses; urban ghettoes were in flames. The 1968 Democratic Convention became a landmark of urban disorder and police violence against young people. The assassinations of the Kennedy brothers and Martin Luther King made the search for new forms to reinvigorate democratic processes urgent. The Weathermen and the Black Panthers engaged in violence in a misguided effort to end racism and oppression. People were making big bets with their lives. They were burning draft cards and they were burning their bridges—moving to Canada to avoid going to fight in a war they condemned, going to jail, or dropping out into the worlds of spiritual quest, drugs, or rock music. People who had been on career and achievement tracks their whole lives were suddenly being derailed.

We explored the ways that a group of activist lawyers could contribute to the movement for social justice. We discussed the corporate domination of governmental decisions through the effective advocacy of Washington lawyers. We discussed the Arnold & Porter representation of Phillip Morris, how successfully the firm defeated effective regulation of the tobacco industry and muzzled government efforts to get the truth out about smoking and health.

From cataloguing our frustrations with law practice and chafing against the inadequate performance of courts and lawyers in difficult times, we moved slowly on to thinking that maybe we could do something about this. We started with the seminal work of Thurgood Marshall and the NAACP Legal Defense Fund, using federal litigation through three decades to expose the evil of racial segregation, and step by step, dismantling the structures of segregated institutions.

I had been encouraged by my experience with the *Selective Service Law Reporter*. "And look at Ralph Nader's work," I said. "He's been incredibly successful in his one-man crusade for new legislation on automobile safety, with nothing but his courage, hard work, and imagination." In 1968, the country was in the middle of an enormous release of energy for the creation of new institutions and the radical challenge of old ones. Change was in the air, making conversations like ours possible. The time was ripe.

As we sat in my living room on beanbag chairs, around a fire on a wintry evening, the outline of a project gradually emerged. I suggested that we put together a foundation proposal. I had had a little experience with foundations, so I knew that they were in the strange business of giving money away, and a few of them were interested in social change. We would set up a nonprofit organization to handle cases representing unrepresented interests in Washington, dealing with big policy issues—the environment, consumer rights, corporate responsibility, the rights of mental patients. "We can be an Arnold & Porter for the other side, as sophisticated and skillful as they are. It will be a significant experiment, and if we are successful, we could shift the dynamics of courts and law practice," I said.

My suggestion set off a long, sometimes contentious discussion. We were all good lawyers, so we led with our criticisms and caveats, putting out objections and then trying to work through them and around them. We were going to be challenging basic corporate interests, which was going to make foundations uncomfortable. In addition, foundations were notoriously fickle; they might support us for three years and then go on to whatever next caught their fancy. One participant, who was already committed to a more radical course of action, argued that our proposal was going to strengthen lawyers too much, and not strengthen the movement.

"This is an experiment," I said. "If we run this thing for three years, that's great. Who knows where it's going to lead? This is a chance for us to make a contribution to the public interest, to work together on big issues, to get out of the rigid hierarchies that we're trapped in, and do something creative and exciting."

We took environmental law as an example. The environmental movement was growing. Yet, although there was inchoate interest in environmental law, nobody was practicing in the field regularly and systematically—building a body of case law, developing experience, working with grassroots groups, getting to know the government decision makers, proposing new laws, training the next generation of activist lawyers.

We also discussed including an educational component, offering internships, and tying in some law schools. We agreed that this strategy would let us tap into the rebellious energy that was rocking university campuses, give us more person-power to increase the number of cases we could handle, and take advantage of the institutional prestige of the law schools so we would look more connected and grounded. If the people at the Ford Foundation asked why they should fund a group of thirty-year-olds to take on this project, we could respond that we were supported by these law schools that were entrusting their students to us. We could begin to build a public interest bar, and we could give those students a head start on a different way of thinking about their law career, one in better alignment with their values.

I thought about my own legal education and the impact that this kind of Washington internship would have had on my career. My classmates at Yale were an ambitious and talented group, with more than our share of valedictorians and returning Rhodes scholars.

Despite the Law School's reputation for being relatively humane and relaxed, in my first semester my civil procedure teacher, James William Moore, undertook to make sure that we did not fall into sentimental patterns of thought. A short, round man from Montana who smoked fat cigars and wore large silver belt buckles, he prided himself on his tough, frontier manner. During our first meeting he drawled, "In this class I want to you to get up on your hind legs and make sounds like lawyers." One unfortunate student said that he felt sympathy for a plaintiff who had waited too long to file a lawsuit and lost his right of action. Moore banged on the desk and barked, "I don't care how you feel about the case, just tell me what the judge's ruling and reasoning was. Your feelings are irrelevant."

The fate of the litigants—what actually happened to the particular person who filed the case—was of no interest. The court's ruling was the only significant thing—the legal principles relied on the substance and the logic of the judge's decision.

We were learning the language and the tough demeanor of lawyer discourse. Our vocabulary became skewed. Being tough-minded, hard-nosed, and thick-skinned were virtues; there was little talk of altruism or kindness. During a contract negotiation, for example, our job as lawyers was to imagine all the negative outcomes that might possibly happen and draft contract language that would protect our clients' interests in the event of fraud or chicanery by the other contracting parties. The law presented a Darwinian world, and the possibility that people would act out of selfless or generous motives was considered highly unlikely. I found it alarmingly easy to slip into this mindset—suspicious, lawyerly, aggressive.

Although this was the talk in the classroom, the conversation in the corridors was often about the burgeoning civil rights movement and the courage of the movement activists. We talked about the heroic roles played by lawyers for the NAACP and CORE. We talked about the new poverty law offices that were offering free legal services to poor people. I admired those members of the faculty who were actively involved in the civil rights movement and the defense of civil liberties—Charles Black, Louis Pollak, Tom Emerson.

The Law School was a paradox. While it supported a culture of activism and engagement, the reality was that it was training extremely smart lawyers to assume their places in corporate law firms. We quickly got used to seeing law firm recruiters on campus. I could always tell which of our classmates had interviews, because they would be wearing conservative suits—and the few women would be in business dresses or suits—on those days. It was flattering to have senior corporate lawyers courting us and dangling substantial salaries. Richard Nixon, between his terms as vice president and president, visited the Law School to recruit students for his Wall Street firm. With such solicitous attention and no obvious alternatives, it is not surprising that most of the students, who had never held more than a summer job, ended up in corporate firms.

After a long evening of discussion, I agreed to take the first crack at drafting a memorandum that would describe the organization we were setting up. I put together a half-dozen pages, proposing that we establish a nonprofit, tax-exempt organization with connections to leading law schools, supported by foundations, and directed by a board of trustees made up of activists and leaders of the bar.

We were talking about something genuinely new. Some elements of our program existed in other places—the NAACP Legal Defense Fund, the ACLU, the Legal Services program. But this combination of skills, goals, funding, and organizational structure had no precedent. A few months after we began, journalists began to refer to us as a public interest law firm, and the name persisted, eventually stretching to encompass a public interest law movement.

We agreed that we wanted to have environmental law in the mix, because there was so much stirring on the environmental front. Rachel Carson's *Silent Spring* had been published in 1964, with its radical indictment of what modern technology was doing to the planet.[1] The book received much attention, but it had not generated a shift in policy or practice. We thought we could do something to translate Carson's critique and the growing environmental awareness into court cases and to make it impossible for government bureaucrats to ignore her findings.

I circulated the draft to the others in the group, and in our next meeting we worked it over and moved toward a viable foundation proposal.

Then came a big step: we had to determine who among us was actually prepared to commit to the project, to attach our résumés to the proposal. I canvassed the people who had moved in and out of our group. It quickly became clear that most of them had enjoyed the conversations and wished the new venture well but didn't want to make a commitment. It was too risky, something else had turned up, or they had never planned to make the venture a full-time job.

I was surprised and disappointed. I probably would have dropped the whole thing if I had been the only survivor. But Bruce Terris, a veteran of the Solicitor General's Office, where he had argued many cases before the Supreme Court, was looking for something new, and he stepped forward. With his shy laugh, he said, "Well, I guess it's just you and me. I say we give it a try."

Bruce and I felt that four lawyers made a critical mass—to maintain a credible educational program and to permit some collective sharing of diverse experience and talents. We needed to bring two more lawyers into the project, one of them with environmental expertise. Our search led us to Jim Moorman, toiling in an obscure corner of the Lands Division of the Justice Department, the closest he could come, at that time, to being an environmental lawyer since there were no environmental law firms or law-oriented advocacy groups.

Moorman got excited, even evangelical, when he talked about protecting wetlands and safeguarding public lands from exploiters. We described the job and discussed salary in a hypothetical way. "You mean that you would pay me to do the work that I dream of? You are talking about the best law job in the country. Where do I sign up?" he asked.

Geoffrey Cowan, a graduate of Yale Law School who had been an activist in the civil rights movement and an innovating force in Democratic reform politics, filled the fourth spot. He had experience on Capitol Hill and an impressive Rolodex. He was full of enthusiasm, positive energy, and creative ideas for developing a practice in communications law.

The two agreed to join us in developing the new institution, and we added their résumés to ours in the appendix at the back of our proposal. Yet none of us made a firm commitment. It was always contingent—if we could bring everything together, then we would do it. I was certainly not prepared to leave my day job until we had made some substantial progress. Still, we were prepared to risk a large and public failure, because the payoff in public benefit could be tremendous.

Many tasks lay ahead of us, and they were mutually interdependent and had to be accomplished simultaneously, a problem common to many start-ups. All of the pieces had to be brought together at the same time: We couldn't recruit trustees if the project wasn't going to happen. We couldn't get commitments from law schools unless there was a real entity with educational credibility and money in hand. And we couldn't raise money without trustees, staff, and law school endorsement.

We pursued all these elements and components at the same time, trying to put together enough interest and contingent commitments to provide momentum. But we were in our twenties and early thirties, relatively young as age is measured in the law world, where forty-year-old partners often carry briefcases for their seniors when they go into combat. None of us were proven wizards in the courtroom or in organizing new institutions.

We did, however, have a number of assets that we were able to draw on. Our enthusiasm and persuasive powers were good starting points. We believed in this unformed organization enough that we

were prepared to leave the security of traditional jobs. Still, we recognized that we didn't have the gravitas, by ourselves, to persuade
a foundation to put real money into such a novel and untried enterprise. I was convinced that after four years of law practice, at age
twenty-nine, I was ready to launch a unique enterprise that was
using law in new ways, but I knew that others might not see it that
way.

Our first step was to think of a name for the venture, and stop referring to it as "our new project." We could name it after ourselves,
like a law firm—but we wanted to create something new. We were
not just a law firm. We were doing a different kind of law, creating
a new community, with students, secretaries, and lawyers working
together for the larger good. One afternoon, we sat in a bar on Connecticut Avenue and tossed around possible names. In the background the new video game, Pong, was emitting electronic beeps
and blips that mimicked a ping-pong match.

"How about naming it with some evocative words that have no
particular content?" I suggested. "Like a music group—the Jefferson Airplane, the Rolling Stones, the Grateful Dead. Or corporations that called themselves Citgo or Motorola. Why be limited to
words in the dictionary, by ordinary meanings and syntax? GreeningLawClub, Advocus, Public-Interested, Publius Central, Populegal, Newlaw, Voxpopuli. We're building for a new era, aren't
we?"

"Too far from the mainstream, too alienating to people whose
support we need," Bruce said. "It has to sound serious and weighty.
Better to err on the side of pomposity than frivolity. Better to
choose a forgettable name than one that would offend the dean of
the Yale Law School."

Institute, Center, Forum, Fund, Council, League. Public Affairs, Social Justice, Equality and Freedom, Law and a New Consciousness, Law in the Public Interest. Finally, we agreed on the Center for Law and Social Policy. A center sounded like it would house a number of functions, and maintain a variety of connections. Law and social policy—we were going to retain our identity as lawyers, and do lawyers' work, but always paying attention to social policy— what the legal issues would mean for people whose lives would be affected. And CLASP was a pleasing acronym, one that implied connection, holding things together, at a time when things were falling apart.

CLASP needed a board of trustees to lend the operation weight and reassure the foundations and law schools that we really were an institution to be trusted and taken seriously, not just a group of radical young lawyers frustrated by limited career opportunities, with a vague desire to do good. We would be dealing with serious institutions with eminent boards of trustees accustomed to dealing with institutions that were similar to them. They would want assurance that a grantee, especially one that was receiving a big, multiyear grant, was going to be around for a while, would do the things it said it would do, and would not use such poor judgment that it would get itself and its funders into trouble. Furthermore, when we started filing lawsuits that would infuriate corporations and politicians, we would need some trustees with credibility to stand up for us.

We had never assembled a board of trustees, so we had to feel our way. It is not easy to persuade busy people to join the board of an organization that does not exist. Part of the job was to make CLASP seem substantial, to appear to be something that important people would want to support. Our connections certainly helped, and we had good people to vouch for us. This was something that we deeply believed in, so our enthusiasm for the project carried people along. Drawing on our advocacy skills, we could make a credible argument that we were likely to succeed in pulling it together, and we got better at it with experience.

We decided to focus our effort on identifying the board chair. If we had the right chair, the rest of the board would fall into place. We quickly agreed that our ideal candidate was Arthur Goldberg, who had been general counsel to the AFL-CIO, President Kennedy's secretary of labor, a Supreme Court justice, and ambassador to the United Nations. Bruce knew him from his days in the Solicitor General's Office, when he was arguing before the Supreme Court and Justice Goldberg was a member of the Court. Goldberg was accustomed to working with younger people and supporting their judgments. He had worked with staff and signed letters written by someone else without grumbling over commas. We were reasonably confident that he would support the kinds of cases we were planning on bringing. But he had no particular reason to agree to serve as chairman when we approached him. In fact, he had little to gain, having just resigned from his position as ambassador to the United Nations and entered private law practice. His association with us was not likely to attract fee-paying clients.

We were excited when he agreed to see us. "This is big," I said to Bruce. "You argued before the Supreme Court all the time, but I've never even been in the same room with one of the justices."

Justice Goldberg met with us in the United Nations ambassador's luxurious suite at the Pierre Hotel in New York, with its crystal chandelier and gilded Louis XIV furniture covered in silk brocade. When we entered the suite, I knew that I was approaching a Presence. Dressed in an elegant double-breasted blue suit, his leonine head of white hair carefully combed and glowing, he was obviously at ease in these grand surroundings.

When we described the project, he listened carefully and asked probing questions, rather like a Supreme Court justice interrogating lawyers from the bench. He was unsure about the law schools' willingness to take the gamble. And he had a labor lawyer's doubts about the foundations. "They're awfully close to the corporate elites," he said. After almost an hour of conversation, he paused. We sat, anxiously awaiting his verdict. Then he said, "If there is a board to chair, I will be happy to chair it. Let me know what I can do to help make it happen."

Bruce and I left the Pierre grinning. We stopped in front of the hotel for a moment of celebration at this remarkable turn of events. "Justice Goldberg's name certainly brightens up our letterhead," I said. I felt undiluted joy as we stood on the East Side sidewalk. There had been something quixotic about our effort up to this point, and I had held the possibility that I would yet have to give up this dream and continue my career in private practice. But now it seemed that our plan was within reach.

I was in my office at Arnold & Porter, giving desultory attention to the firm's business, and trying to juggle the start-up tasks of our new venture, when I received an unsolicited call from Derek Bok, dean of the Harvard Law School and later the president of Harvard. He had never called me before; in fact, no law school dean had ever called me. "Mr. Halpern," he said. "I hear that you are planning to open a new kind of legal center that will have an educational component."

"Well, we are trying, Dean Bok," I said, attempting to sound assured but modest. "Justice Goldberg has agreed to serve as our board chair."

"Give Arthur my best."

"I'll be happy to."

"I understand that you want to be the Arnold & Porter for non-profit advocacy groups. And you want to teach law students to do that kind of law. It would be a good thing if you can pull it off. It would increase the ability of courts to do justice, and channel griev-ances off the streets and into the judicial system. Some student rad-icals don't believe the courts can do anything right. I would like to invite you to describe your project to some of our more receptive faculty members."

We had not even considered approaching Harvard with our idea. We thought it was hopeless. Bok assured me that it was not. "A long shot, perhaps, but not hopeless," he said. At that point, like many law school deans, he seemed to be concerned with the radical rebel-lion erupting on the campus, and he wanted to make it clear that he was sympathetic to innovative educational ventures and to the use of law as a tool for social change.

Bok offered to convene a dinner meeting at Harvard's Faculty Club, where Bruce and I would present the proposal to some sen-ior faculty members. I had been an undergraduate at Harvard, and I knew the Faculty Club—a modest yellow clapboard building on the edge of the campus. I had seen my professors shuffling in and out for lunch. I never thought that I would be invited in—not only invited in, but asked to make a presentation to the dukes and barons of the Harvard Law School! I brought some of the awed feelings of an uncertain freshman into the Faculty Club with me.

When I arrived at Harvard in 1957 to begin my undergraduate stud-ies, I found the place intimidating. The first night, my roommate Barney Frank and I went to dinner at the Freshman Union, and took our seats at a long, polished table beneath large chandeliers.

Barney launched into a conversation about his favorite subject, politics. As we talked, I was both impressed and appalled by the depth of his knowledge. I knew that Congress had two houses, but I had no idea what the structure of committees in the two houses was. He explained, patiently and a little ostentatiously, the significance of the seniority system and what the power of the southern senators meant for public policy. He seemed to understand these institutions as well as if he had been a congressman for a decade. "I know the names of all the senators and three-quarters of the representatives," he told me. He was willing to prove it, but I asked him not to bother. He had a well-defined, defensible political point of view, which he has continued to hone as a congressman from Massachusetts. I was embarrassed that I had none.

The basic Harvard system rested on large lecture courses with hundreds of people in the classroom and graduate assistants who made the only direct contact with the individual student. I chose a major—American History and Literature—which was familiar and broad enough to encompass both politics and culture. Arthur Schlesinger's American Intellectual History course was a core element in the major. Three days a week, dressed in his tweed sport coat and bow tie, he would enter the long narrow classroom seating three hundred students. He would clip a microphone to the front of his shirt, unzip his leather folder, and begin to read through his prepared lecture in a self-assured voice, its authority only slightly undercut by an Elmer Fudd lisp. His brilliant presentation of the intellectual history of the country was reassuring and consonant with the worldview I had learned at home. Progressive values were moving ahead, with occasional temporary setbacks. Fringe ideas would come forward for a moment but then recede in the face of centrist common sense. At the end of fifty minutes, precisely, he would finish with the Transcendentalists, the Harlem Renaissance, or the transitory influence of Gurdjieff, zip up his leather folder, and leave.

The day arrived for our meeting with the Harvard faculty. Sipping sherry in a room full of musty Victorian furniture and worn Oriental carpets, Bruce and I found the cocktail conversation unsettling. The *Harvard Crimson* had that day run an "exposé" of the existence of the Choate Club, a secret society at the Law School whose members included faculty and students, all male, of course. Membership in the club was by invitation. It met for an elaborate formal dinner once a month—brandy and cigars, eminent guests, and heady discussion. The *Crimson* story also reported the outrage of the Law School students who had been excluded and kept in the dark about this club.

My immediate reaction was to sympathize with those who had been excluded; I had no doubt that I would have been a nonmember. If I had discovered that my roommate had made up a monthly lie to explain his tuxedoed exit and his whiskeyed return to our student room, and that he was, in fact, sharing evenings with the exalted professors who held such power over our future lives, I would have been furious.

Most of our dinner companions were members of the club. They presented the story to demonstrate how utterly paranoid law students had become, so much so that they were upset about the innocent Choate Club, a venerable Law School institution. "It's not as if we invite only the brightest students to join," said one professor, who was a member. "We just look for the most interesting."

After listening to the discussions, I glanced over at Bruce, who had been a Harvard law student and a nonmember. We exchanged a look that confirmed my feeling that this dinner was not likely to produce our first law school affiliation. If these guys couldn't see any problem with this gathering between the "most interesting" law students and their professors, they were unlikely to be drawn to our novel venture that was committed to making waves—disrupting comfortable ways of doing business in order to demand attention for people who had been excluded.

I had a sudden disquieting insight—we were, despite our high-minded objectives and egalitarian rhetoric, drinking sherry at the Harvard Faculty Club, relying on our tenuous but real connections to the old-boy network. We were using all of our elite connections to pull together this new antiestablishment institution. If we weren't part of the network—albeit adjunct, probationary members—we could not have gotten this far. I began to acknowledge the paradoxes that framed our activities. We could push the edges, but we could not put ourselves outside the consensus of professional legitimacy. I was not about to jeopardize the goodwill in the room in order to tell them what I thought of the Choate Club. If I was going to bring this public interest law firm to life, I would have to live with carefully calibrated compromises and forego many opportunities to "speak truth to power." As I look back on that evening, I see that the recognition of this tension and my decision to live with it, without resolution, was a step in my growing awareness of what it meant to cultivate wisdom. It meant taking in the situation with clarity of vision, and remaining flexible enough to live with contradiction and adapt to emerging needs.

After the sherry hour, we had a conversation about our new project over lukewarm chicken and peas. We explained our plans: an opportunity for two or three of their students to spend a semester in Washington, litigating important cases, with close supervision. There was a good deal of sympathy and interest, but no hint of willingness to take so radical a step—to release a Harvard student for a full semester to a program outside the Law School. "Have you thought about undertaking the program in Cambridge for fewer credits?" Al Sacks, the associate dean, asked. "Try it here as an experiment. Maybe after you have had a couple of years of experience under your belt, we could take a look at a program in Washington."

Even though they felt that a semester in Washington for a few students was too radical a step for Harvard, these elders of the Law School seemed genuinely encouraging and supportive, and Bok gave us permission to list his name in our proposal as someone we had consulted, who supported the plan. After a glass of brandy and some secondary cigar smoke, Bruce and I bid them a cordial farewell.

As we left the club, Abe Chayes, a senior faculty member who had been chief legal adviser to the State Department during the Cuban missile crisis, joined us and said, "I'm glad that this meeting wasn't open to students. We would be in a hell of a lot of trouble."

We laughed about the idea of moving our venture to Cambridge, where it could be more closely watched by the Harvard faculty. "The whole point of it is that it has to be in Washington, D.C.," he said. "Starting the program in Cambridge would be like establishing an oceanographic institute in Omaha." Then we ran into Barney Frank, whom I was meeting for a drink. Barney was then a member of the state legislature and a second-year law student. When Abe saw Barney coming over to greet us, he said, "Oh, God, how are you going to describe this meeting to Barney? Are we going to look like a bunch of Neanderthals!"

In retelling the story to Barney, I played it for laughs—the secret club, the air thick with self-satisfaction, the proposal that we operate our program in Cambridge.

"What did you expect?" he asked. "When I applied to Law School, they told me that they didn't permit part-time students. I was already in the legislature at the time, and I thought I was too young to retire. They were actually going to reject my application. I threatened to sue, and they finally backed down. It's my business how I spend my time outside classes, so long as I keep up my grades."

He continued, "I have had a few problems. I've dozed off in class a couple times, and for an instant, wasn't sure where I was. But I've learned to pause and look around. If I'm surrounded by people with zits, I know I'm in Law School; if I see liver spots, it's the legislature. The Law School continues to run on nineteenth-century ideas. I think they aren't ready for CLASP."

"Still, they invited us to come here," I said, "and gave us a respectful hearing. I never imagined that Harvard Law School would take our project that seriously."

We were looking for foundation support to permit us to begin, enough money to open our doors and give it a try. Foundations, which have existed in this country since the early twentieth century, are pools of money established by rich people to be distributed to groups that are certified by the Internal Revenue Service to be fit subjects of philanthropy—educational, charitable, or scientific.

Since we had decided to rely on foundations to float our new venture, I tried to educate myself about the foundation world. Based on my limited experience, I knew that the great majority of foundations were small, locally focused, and supportive of establishment institutions. They gave a lot of money to the colleges attended by the donor and his family and to local museums and hospitals, and they avoided the controversial questions that we were interested in—corporate responsibility, the rights of poor people, and environmental protection. Since their philanthropy was an accurate reflection of the comfortable social status of the donors and trustees, they were not likely sponsors of our new venture.

Most of the larger, national foundations were equally unpromising. They had a tendency to support research and scholarship, and they made big grants to big, stable institutions. They were unlikely to be interested in funding advocacy, sharpening social contention, or disrupting the status quo.

That left us with a small number of foundations that had a progressive social change agenda and a willingness to deal with politically charged issues, even if there was some potential for embarrassment of the foundation's trustees at the country club. I had had firsthand experience with the support of such foundations for controversial new undertakings, so I knew that there was hope. The New World Foundation and the Stern Family Fund supported the Institute for Policy Studies, the *Selective Service Law Reporter*, and civil rights organizations. We found them receptive to our proposal, but they had small pots of money.

Among the big foundations, Ford was outstanding in its concern for social change and willingness to support innovation. It had made some early grants to provide legal services for poor people and for legal education reform. It was a critical foundation for our purposes; it had compatible interests and a large grants budget. I had hoped that they would greet us with enthusiasm and present us with a large check. Instead, we received a one-paragraph rejection letter from a Ford bureaucrat, notifying us that we were "not in an area of the Foundation's program interests." He would not even meet with us.

This was a demoralizing blow. It brought me to a point where I was almost ready to abandon the whole undertaking. I didn't see where the money would come from if Ford wouldn't give us anything. And the momentum of our project felt fragile. Maybe the Harvard faculty was right that we were trying to move too fast.

But I believed deeply in the program, and I didn't want to give it up because one foundation bureaucrat didn't get it. I was meeting interesting people, learning more about the world, and having fun. The Johnson-Humphrey administration, weighted down by the Vietnam War, had been turned out of office, and Richard Nixon was taking over, making our work seem more important than ever.

So we pressed ahead, looking for other foundations and vowing to come back the next year—not just with a proposal, but with concrete accomplishments: a board of trustees, an education program in place, and some important courtroom victories.

As we had hoped, Justice Goldberg helped us in recruiting other board members. Because they would receive an invitation from Justice Goldberg, not from us, we let ourselves aim high. Former members of the Kennedy and Johnson cabinets, Attorney General Ramsey Clark and Secretary of the Interior Stuart Udall, joined the board. The letter from Justice Goldberg opened the door, and we effectively presented the case for the Center. Udall was particularly drawn to our plans to launch an environmental program. "I've seen it from the inside," he said. "If we are going to protect the nation's resources, someone has got to start butting heads with the corporations that are poisoning the water and clear-cutting the forests."

At first, I was surprised that I could get such people on the telephone and even more amazed at how readily they agreed to serve on the board. I soon realized, though, that the recent change in administration meant there were a significant number of formerly powerful people around who no longer commanded large bureaucracies and who found that their phones didn't ring as often as they would have liked.

It was an example of what I began to think of as "the ex-great-man syndrome." People who serve in the president's cabinet often have trouble returning to the ordinary world—no chauffeured limousine, no corps of assistants and secretaries, no fawning reporters. This was a sobering and important lesson, and it made me rethink my life objectives. Becoming a cabinet member seemed much less desirable when I saw that it led inevitably to becoming an ex-cabinet member.

One reason we found it easy to recruit lawyers to join our board was that we were doing something that many lawyers felt was needed. The reputation of the legal profession was tarnished, and the imbalance in representation led to results skewed toward corporate interests. Public interest law firms might be a way to restore some balance, to show the disaffected that the system really was concerned with fairness and balanced advocacy. It was a response to the "never-trust-anyone-over-thirty" radicals who wanted to burn the courthouses down and start over. The system had its own self-correcting mechanisms. CLASP was evidence that it was possible to work within the system.

After Ramsey Clark joined the board, he suggested we invite retired Chief Justice Earl Warren. Chief Justice Warren no longer heard cases, so there would be no conflict-of-interest problem. Clark addressed a "Dear Chief" letter to him at his office at the Supreme Court, explaining the proposal to him and inviting him to join the board. We received no answer for several weeks, and we were about to resend the letter when we received a response turning down "our kind invitation," from the new chief justice—Warren Burger. It seems that our invitation had been delivered to the wrong office by the Supreme Court mailroom, and Chief Justice Burger had not read the address carefully. "It could have been worse," Clark said with his dry Texas drawl. "He might have accepted." (We sent another letter to Chief Justice Warren, who praised the concept but said that he lacked the time.)

Of course, the eminent board substantially enhanced our credibility, but it also subtly affected our behavior. We did not want board members resigning in protest over a shoddy brief, an ill-considered lawsuit, or a flamboyant press release. The board reinforced my tendency to act in a lawyerly, respectable way.

I defined myself primarily as a lawyer, not a political actor. I wrote and spoke in lawyer-speak—cool, rational, dispassionate, avoiding arguments that rested only on my own instincts, convictions, and values. My writing avoided poetic expression and appeals to the emotions, making it a little gray and dull. Any claims we made to protect the environment were couched in public policy terms—no appeals to the glory of wilderness, the duty of stewardship, or the ecstasy of canoeing down a rushing mountain stream in spring.

The nature of our board membership also contributed to a subtle shift in the way we saw our venture. We had undertaken the project as an experiment. We were tentative in our claims of where it was leading or whether it would work. When important people began lending their prestige and reputation to help it succeed, we started to take ourselves more seriously.

Despite our discouraging debut at Harvard, we proceeded with the five law schools we had targeted—Yale, Michigan, Pennsylvania, Stanford, and UCLA. We chose schools inside the elite circle because we believed they would give the biggest boost to the CLASP reputation and were also likely to send us capable, well-trained students who could work effectively on our cases. We also chose schools where we had friends on the faculty who could open doors and vouch for us to their colleagues. Perhaps most important was Tony Amsterdam, a brilliant intellectual leader of the civil rights litigation efforts of the sixties, who was then in transit from the Penn to the Stanford faculty. He prepared a memorandum to both faculties, analyzing our concept and setting out the benefits to students. It was persuasive at both places.

At most of the schools we were invited to make a presentation to a faculty meeting. This was my first exposure to such meetings, and I did not find them places I would voluntarily choose to spend time. The atmosphere was heavy, freighted with a sense of institutional self-importance. We brought enthusiasm, energy, and urgency into our description of CLASP, grounded in our deep belief in the importance of the project. Most of the questions and comments we received were skeptical, cautious, and guarded.

"You want us to send students to CLASP for one semester. Which sixth of our curriculum do you suggest that we drop?" asked a crusty senior professor at Michigan.

"You have already adopted an elective program after the first year," I said, "so you have decided that a graduate need not take any particular courses."

"How will you assure sufficient uniformity of experience for the students who participate? How can you evaluate their work?" We answered their concerns as well as we could, though we were handicapped by our lack of experience in teaching and by the novelty of the enterprise.

We did well enough—in part because we tapped in to an underlying feeling of goodwill discernible among most members of these faculties. Even those who doubted that we would succeed seemed to hope that we would. They seemed to think that the existence of CLASP would be good for the legal profession and good for legal education. They knew that many law students were demoralized by the limited opportunities for public service careers.

By the fall of 1969, the five law schools had committed to send us their students for a semester's credit—if we were successful in opening our doors. It was an extraordinary achievement, obtaining commitments from these conservative institutions, especially because no law school had ever given a full semester's credit for clinical work, on or off campus. Moreover, CLASP had no track record and none of us had ever been a law teacher. A full semester's credit for work in a nonexistent institution, from the point of view of the law school, was a large commitment, and the fact that five major law schools were willing to entrust us with their students lent us respectability and the appearance of solidity. In retrospect, the success of our clinical program helped pave the way for the wide variety of clinical programs that have blossomed in the law schools in the intervening years, substantially enriching legal education.

These law schools may ultimately have been influenced by considerations that we hadn't even thought of. They liked the idea of being seen as educational innovators. And the program presented them with a chance to get some real troublemakers—activists who were at that time making life miserable for faculty and administrators—out of town for six months. Later, when we told the dean of the University of Michigan Law School the name of a student we had selected to come to Washington in 1970, he said, "Make sure that he brings his Vietcong flag with him." He was, of course, making a battle-weary observation about a problem that we had naïvely underestimated: we were going to attract many students who didn't like traditional law study or law practice, and who, indeed, didn't much care for authority at all.

Abe Goldstein, then dean at Yale Law School, referred to this period as the Dark Ages. Student critics were loudly raising issues of race, complicity in the Vietnam War effort, and corporate domination of the law and the law schools. It would be challenging to try to deal with such students at CLASP, to define ground rules and decisional processes. I was, after all, a person who didn't much like authority myself. I had been inclined to challenge authority my whole life, and I had little experience or enthusiasm for exercising it. So leading an institution with a mission of confronting authority was certain to be an important learning experience and a source of internal and external tension.

Having pulled together trustees and affiliated law schools, we were in a position to make a more credible approach to the foundations. I had had some early successes with two activist foundations, after persuading them that we were not too cautious, lawyerly, and elitist for them, and that we could really be effective in promoting social change.

But we could not begin the student program with so little money. At the eleventh hour, the Rockefeller Brothers Fund gave us a grant of $75,000, permitting us to accept students beginning in January 1970. The grant, which gave us enough money to run for four months, affirmed that it was not only the left fringe of the foundation world that would support a venture like ours. But it created some tension for us, because this money would not quite carry us through to the end of the semester and we would be assuming litigation obligations that would last much longer.

After we had raised $100,000 in foundation grants, I arranged a meeting with Paul Porter to discuss CLASP. We met late in the day, with the afternoon sun slanting through the large windows of his opulent office. He offered me a drink from his private supply, and we sipped bourbon on the rocks while discussing the new project and my future. I liked Paul and I think he liked me. He might have seen in me a shadow of Ben Cohen or some other idealistic Jewish kid who was around Washington in the thirties, during the early days of the New Deal. He seemed to like young idealists, but also thought they were funny.

I had decided to ask for a leave of absence from the firm, rather than resign outright. I thought that we would know within a year whether we were going to be able to sustain this new venture or not. The leave of absence was an insurance policy. If the whole thing collapsed, I could return to the firm and not disrupt my life totally. Paul happily agreed to my taking a leave. He seemed to think that this was reassuring evidence that I had not gone completely mad.

I asked him about the experience that he, Thurman Arnold, and Abe Fortas had had when they were setting up their own firm. I imagined at that point the energetic young man he must have been in the 1930s, when he was appointed by Roosevelt to be the first chairman of the new Federal Communications Commission. As he spoke about their establishing the firm in the late forties, I could sense some of the excitement and energy that must have animated their venture—three New Deal veterans setting up a high-energy law firm in the staid world of Washington law practice. It was the firm that would carry forward New Deal ideology into the postwar era. I felt a sense of connection with that new firm. I also wondered at what point along the way Paul's last vestige of idealism had sunk below the waves of cynicism.

I believed that we could create a mirror-image law firm, representing people who couldn't afford to pay for Arnold & Porter advocacy. As it developed, CLASP was far from a mirror image of Arnold & Porter.

I didn't foresee how moving out of the legal establishment would open up new possibilities for community, institutional forms, and creative advocacy. More important, I didn't realize that my new professional direction would create the opportunity and necessity for personal growth in every dimension of my life. At the time I felt this was simply a career move, but it proved to be much more than that. In retrospect, I see that I was taking charge of my life, abandoning the linear path of academic success and professional ambition. At some risk, I was aligning my work with my values, assuming leadership in a complex situation in which difficult choices would be a regular part of my work, in a world that was in flux and where few rules stood unchallenged. There were no maps to guide me through the legal issues, the institutional innovations, or the personal, psychological complexities.

As Paul and I rattled the ice in our bourbon glasses, I told him, "I'm reasonably confident that the country is on a progressive trajectory and that we can help to move it. I'm gambling that the country is moving in the direction of a deeper commitment to shared well-being."

Paul looked at me for a minute. Then he said, "I hope you're right. My crystal ball has grown cloudy, and I don't try to make predictions. But good luck with it." He took a long drag on his cigarette and added, in his husky rasp, "Go ahead and pursue truth, beauty, and justice. You may fail like everybody else. Just make sure you don't look too ridiculous in the process."

CREATIVITY IN
THE COURTROOM

W E BEGAN on a sweaty August day in 1969, in a row house on Swann Street, a street well-known for its high crime rate. Geoff Cowan had rented the house from friends of his who were in Paris on assignment for the *Washington Post*. "I have the whole house to myself," he said, "and I only need one bedroom."

Oddly, I worried about legalism, not about crime. "We are running an office in a place zoned for residential use. That's a hell of a way to start a new public interest law firm."

"You think too much like a lawyer. No one gives a damn about the zoning," Geoff said. "The District of Columbia government doesn't have it together to arrest the heroin dealers selling on the corner of our block in the middle of the afternoon. They certainly don't have the resources or the interest to come after us for violating the zoning laws. If you are going to worry, you should worry more about getting mugged after a long evening working on a brief."

I let go of my legalistic scruples, and we moved in. We paid no rent—which is what we could afford. Geoff assured us that his landlord wouldn't care about the use we were putting his house to. "He'll be proud of it," Geoff said. We took over the house, except Geoff's bedroom, and put our Xerox machine on the kitchen table.

The place had the secondhand look and casual maintenance that was characteristic of the activist, nonprofit organizations we expected to represent—different from the interior-designer offices of the corporate firms or establishment charities.

We also decided that we did not want to dress like conventional lawyers. We would wear khakis or jeans with bell-bottoms and save our conservative ties and pin-striped suits for court appearances. It may seem a small matter, but our clothes helped establish our identity. And rewriting the rules in small ways made it easier to think about rewriting them in larger ways—about the roles of the courts, about the way lawyers use the press, about the legitimacy of unconventional advocacy strategy, about the definition of a successful legal career.

The dress question made me conscious of the shifts I was making from my old identity and of the compromises that I was now compelled to negotiate. I was living between two worlds, with a suit hanging on the back of my office door to put on if I had a court appearance or an unexpected visit from a foundation officer. My effectiveness lay, in part, in my ability to change clothes at the right times, keeping alert and flexible, sensitive to subtle signals in the environment. As I traveled the distance from our laid-back office on Swann Street to the federal courthouse, I could feel my face falling into the earnest, purposive mask of the young professional. I was developing the skills of a tightrope walker.

In the months after we began CLASP, we had a wonderful sense of possibility. In our makeshift offices, sitting on worn-out furniture, we played with ideas for novel lawsuits and hypothetical clients. We talked over articles from the newspapers, reviewing outrageous situations that seemed to have no remedies—the takeover of the media by giant corporations, the failure of the Nixon administration to carry on Lyndon Johnson's War on Poverty. We discussed the power of corporations to shape the agenda of government. We spun out legal theories that could permit us to intervene in these massive problems, demanding that federal agencies exercise their rarely used powers to protect the public good. We made contact with nonprofit groups that might be able to use our legal advocacy.

Nothing seemed impossible. We had been in jobs where our choices were severely restricted. I had felt it sharply at Arnold & Porter, where my time was accounted for in six-minute segments. I thought of a conversation I had had with Dick Sobol in New Orleans a year earlier. He had left Arnold & Porter to work in the civil rights movement in Louisiana, and we talked about my plans for leaving the firm and starting CLASP.

"You'll never know how good it is until you try it. You don't even know that you aren't free, that you aren't your own person, until you get out of there. Then you can see—feel, really—what it means to be free. It's not just that you're free from time slips and assignments to cases you don't care about. You can launch any new project you want to, without anyone looking over your shoulder. You have been in harness, pulling someone else's wagon most of your life—first as a student, then as a lawyer. Now you can try it on your own."

Dick was right. When we started the Center, I had an exhilarating sense of freedom. We had the opportunity to invent a new institution—its goals and governance, its internal role definitions, and its place in the legal world. We had the opportunity to identify social and legal problems and do something about them. We could choose our issues and cases, and carry them as far as our imagination, ability, and courage could go—with only the courts and the clients to shape our efforts.

In the mental health field, that meant trying to think about the next steps beyond the *Rouse* case, developing ways to promote the interests of mentally impaired people, who were unorganized and held in disdain. In the environment field, Richard Nixon signed the National Environmental Policy Act into law in January 1970, just as we were beginning our work. NEPA could support a powerful new way of engaging the courts in protection of the environment or it could become a dead letter, setting forth high-sounding principles with no impact on the way government or corporations did business. We might be able to participate in the process of giving meaning to the words of the statute, helping to turn it into an effective environmental charter.

We were taking the idea of entrepreneurship into new arenas. An *entrepreneur* traditionally had been identified as a person driven by a desire to get rich. We were *social entrepreneurs*, driven by a different set of values—a desire to make political and economic institutions work more fairly, to protect the environment, to encourage democratic participation, to build community.

Then I realized that I had a close precedent, in my own family, to support the entrepreneurial direction I was taking. My father had succeeded as an entrepreneur of the self—moving from the narrow horizons of his immigrant family into the highest reaches of a learned profession that was not hospitable to Jews of immigrant stock. He had created a new identity that would have been unrecognizable to his father, who had delivered laundry with a pushcart— a new self, comfortable and effective as a judge, a professor, and a dean. It was entrepreneurship of a high order, and his inspiring success buoyed up my confidence and supported my effort. It also reminded me of the high-risk subtext of my venture. I was not only creating a new kind of legal institution; I was becoming an entrepreneur of my self. I could already see some of the shifts beginning— my ambition shifting away from material success, a greater openness to the new culture, development of my leadership capacity. And I was open to further changes in the person that I was becoming.

As an entrepreneur I discovered that I had a number of relevant skills. I could pick up and synthesize ideas and give them institutional form. I was willing to take risks, trust my intuition, and put myself on the line. My enthusiasm and confidence drew other people to these projects, attracting able people to work with me. And I had enough resilience and confidence to bounce back—and learn—from setbacks.

The payoff for my entrepreneurship was, of course, negative from the financial point of view. At the outset I sacrificed about 15 percent of my annual compensation when I moved from Arnold & Porter to become director of CLASP for a salary of $25,000. But this was enough money for my family to live on in our modest suburban house, and we didn't worry about the future. The nonfinancial payoffs turned out to be much more significant: a sense of meaning in my work and the satisfaction of working with friends, people who shared my values. CLASP gave me the opportunity to cultivate latent capacities—leadership, imagination, and institutional innovation. It was both a framework for striking a balance between my work and family life and a vehicle for participating more fully in the deep cultural and social changes of the times.

The first group of a dozen CLASP students arrived at our new office on Hillyer Place during a cold, slushy January, a particularly distasteful surprise for the students from UCLA. It was the end of the first year of Nixon's presidency and the war in Vietnam was escalating. The Weathermen had gone underground to "bring the war home" with their bomb attacks.

The students came from law schools that were at the elite edge of legal education—well-established, comfortably set up, and

predictable. They had moved successfully through the orderly hierarchy of academia, taught by tenured professors, watched over by
deans, meeting ever more challenging academic hurdles. We welcomed them to a different world. We had not worked out the rules
about how we would learn and live together, and the content of
their studies was only beginning to emerge from the cases that the
lawyers were taking on. We invited them to participate in the
cocreation of an institution and a curriculum with us. This level of
openness and improvisation was foreign to their educational experience. The more progressive law schools were beginning to offer a
few credit hours for clinical work supervised by academic faculty,
within the ivy-covered walls. These adventurous spirits who came
to CLASP were gambling a sixth of their legal education on an
untried experiment with a group of lawyers who had never taught
even one hour in a law school.

Since we had more applicants than we could take, we had to
adopt criteria for selection. In particular, we had to decide how to
weigh outstanding academic performance in law school against
proven commitment to public interest work. With the dust of
Arnold & Porter still on my cuffs, I favored a heavy reliance on academic success, which at that time I erroneously identified as the
best predictor of successful performance in our odd setting and in
public interest law. "Twenty years from now," Geoff asked, "will you
want to point to CLASP alumni who are leaders in the environmental movement and are leading antismoking campaigns—or to
senior partners in Wall Street firms? They have all been admitted
to incredibly selective law schools. That should be good enough for
us. We are looking for qualities of heart and mind that the big law
firms and the law schools don't value." I backed down, startled at
the reflexive way that I had fallen back on the conditioning I had
assimilated in my years at Harvard and Yale, capped by my experience on the Arnold & Porter hiring committee.

The students we selected were an interesting mix—diverse in age, race, and politics (from center to left). They brought with them the powerful forces flowing through the universities at that time—the early manifestations of feminism, the struggle against racial injustice, rage about the Vietnam War, and an enthusiasm for experimentation with the texture of their lives, known by the shorthand—sex, drugs, and rock 'n' roll.

We wanted to develop relationships that were unlike the rigid hierarchies of the law firms and law schools. Our roles were fluid collaborations—students and lawyers bound together by common purpose. We were trying to interact as whole people, not just valuing the parts of ourselves that made us the quick, clever students who stood out in the stylized dialogue of the law school classroom. We adopted many of the nonhierarchical trappings that were being tried out in various institutions in the late sixties. Lawyers and students dressed alike, adopted an irreverent work style, called each other by first names, spent a lot of nonwork time together.

Nonetheless, despite our intentions, we were an institution with its own peculiar hierarchy. We lawyers, after all, would have to evaluate and certify the students' work to the law schools at which they were enrolled. We were being paid a salary while they were paying tuition. We signed the pleadings and briefs and presented the oral arguments. When there was conflict between getting the brief filed on time and carefully dealing with the sensibilities of a student who had done the first draft, we usually put efficiency ahead of kindness and participation.

I learned, with the students, about the limits on the ways in which we could imagine and create a new kind of legal and educational process. I learned that some kinds of hierarchy are extremely hard to dislodge, and that some stubborn realities of institutional life don't change significantly, no matter how worthy its goals. I discovered, to my surprise, that there were some aspects of hierarchy that I was prepared to defend, that I thought were essential to effective operations. Questions of hierarchy and authority were always up for debate—often confrontive, always irreverent. One of our students came from Michigan with a rubber stamp that read BULL-SHIT. He applied it frequently to my memoranda posted on the bulletin board.

Our educational endeavor took concrete form every Monday afternoon at four o'clock when the lawyers and students squeezed into our library/conference room for our weekly seminar. We had promised the law schools that we would offer this recognizably academic event each week, to give the students an opportunity for intellectual review and reflection on their work at CLASP. In fact, our most exciting seminars were about the experiment itself—the shape of the organization, the decision whether to file a particular lawsuit, the discussion of possible legal strategies and complementary public relations efforts. A different lawyer led each seminar, and all lawyers participated in all of them. The seminar became an occasion for teaching students, for working out our own ideas, and for understanding the meaning of the new kind of law that we were pioneering.

I led the first seminar during the week of the students' arrival. Before I began to speak, I looked around the room with satisfaction and excitement. The walls were lined with secondhand law books—treatises on administrative law and civil practice, and long series of tan volumes reporting federal court decisions going back to the beginnings of the Republic. It was a real, functioning law library. We were all here, lawyers and students mixed together around scarred tables, sitting on unmatched chairs. Five leading law schools had certified the educational value of our unique enterprise, and now it was time to deliver. The students had already begun work on their assigned cases.

I wanted to invite the students into this historic moment, to introduce them to the concept of CLASP and to the idea of public interest law, then turn to a specific issue—possible ways to follow up on the *Rouse* case. "CLASP is a new kind of institution in the legal world. We want to give the adversary process a chance to be more effective," I said. "Think about this as an experiment to test whether the courts might work more effectively if a broader range of stakeholders were given a day in court—if environmental advocates had the same right to seek judicial review as the corporations that are being regulated, if mental patients could get courts to review the nature of their confinement."

Kenny, a student from Michigan, who had indeed brought his Vietcong flag, sat slouching in his chair at the corner of the table, pulling on his scruffy beard. He interrupted before I had finished the sentence. "Isn't that a little naïve?" he said. "Corporations have the biggest and best legal teams in the country. They control the media, they control the political process, and they control the courts. I can tell you for sure that the auto companies run the show in Michigan. Nobody gives a damn what happens to people in mental hospitals, and they certainly don't want to pay more taxes to treat them. I look around this place and it seems a little unlikely— grandiose, in fact—to think that our efforts, four lawyers and a dozen students working in a crummy office, are going to balance things out."

"Look, this is an *experiment*," I said, a defensive undertone creeping into my voice. "No one says that we are going to be as effective on behalf of the Wilderness Society as Arnold & Porter is on behalf of the Tobacco Institute. Some people think the legal system is hopelessly corrupt and has to be worked around, then uprooted. Others simply work within the framework of old institutions, accepting the inevitability of the existing structures and doctrines. We're trying to explore the territory between them. We won't know for a number of years if our gamble pays off, whether a different kind of law practice can be invented that will significantly unsettle established ways of doing business. Until then, I think that it is too early to give up on the courts and the legal system."

Kenny didn't back down. "I don't see it. My friends who are opposed to the war are going to jail or to Canada. My classmates are lining up like sheep for interviews with pig law firms. And I don't see much hope."

"Well, I don't suppose you would have come here if you were totally hopeless. So let's see what we can launch in the few months before you have to head back to Ann Arbor. I'm not usually the one defending the old order, and I don't like it."

I told the group that we saw ourselves as a part of the new thing, the extraordinary wave of creativity in response to the crises that were challenging American institutions. An impressive number of nonprofit advocacy groups began in this fruitful period—the Children's Defense Fund, Common Cause, the Natural Resources Defense Council, the Puerto Rican Legal Defense and Education Fund, the Environmental Defense Fund.[1] All these organizations grew during this fecund period, supported by a few foundations that thought that law could be used to build a more just society.

My answer seemed to satisfy Kenny for the moment, although I knew that the issues he raised could not be resolved definitively. I wondered if we really were naïve, and foolishly optimistic, to think that our small efforts could make a difference. If I reframed his challenges and stripped them of their angry impatience, I would have to acknowledge them, live with them, and reconsider them as our experience and understanding grew deeper.

The pace and the crackling energy didn't slow down for the next two hours. By the end of the seminar we had canvassed the limits and possibilities of CLASP and developed two post-*Rouse* ideas to explore: the treatment of mentally ill juveniles in detention facilities and the right of children with mental retardation to a public education. In the course of the next two years, we were involved in lawsuits on both issues.[2]

A few months after our first students arrived, in the spring of 1970, Jim Moorman received a call from David Brower, the former president of the Sierra Club, then the founder of a new group, Friends of the Earth. Jim knew Brower from his Sierra Club work. I knew of Brower—heir to John Muir and Aldo Leopold, the great pioneers of the environmental movement—from John McPhee's book *Encounters with the Archdruid*.[3] Brower had the presence and conviction of an Old Testament prophet. He had fought fiercely against many of the great dam-building projects, which had threatened to flood magnificent river valleys and obliterate riparian landscapes. He had won some and lost some. The Grand Canyon is still available for awestruck exploration because of one of his most hard-fought and successful campaigns.

The fact that Brower called Moorman was a success in itself. It meant that Brower acknowledged that litigation could be an important new tool in the environmental advocate's arsenal, and that CLASP was the place to go. "I want to come see you at the earliest possible date," Brower said. "Nixon's Secretary of the Interior is about to issue a permit for the largest construction project since the Great Wall of China. It will be an environmental disaster of immense importance, and no one gives a damn."

"Well, I think we can arrange a meeting," Moorman said, looking over an appointment book that contained little besides staff meetings, seminars, and his wife's birthday.

To our surprise, Brower suggested that we meet at "his club"—the Cosmos Club, a bastion of Washington's elite, housed in a magnificent mansion on Massachusetts Avenue at the lower end of Embassy Row. None of us had ever been inside the club, which was best known at that time for its exclusionary admissions policy. President Kennedy had forced the club to break the color line; the current issue was its refusal to accept women members.

As we arrived at the Cosmos Club, we laughed about the incongruity of meeting the archdruid to plot a radical environmental challenge in the neoclassical embodiment of establishment Washington. We were stopped at the entrance by a liveried black doorman who told us that we would have to enter through the side door. We were surprised but polite. "Why?" I asked. He pointed to Barbara Williams, a black law student from UCLA, who was participating in the meeting.

"It's her," he said. We were astonished. Were we being sent to the "colored" entrance? "Women aren't allowed in the front door," he explained.

Barbara stepped forward, and with her face a few inches from his, said, "I've been treated like a nigger too many times. I'm going to come in the front door." The doorman stepped out of the way.

When we entered the inner sanctum and joined Brower and some of his senior lieutenants, we recounted the story of our confrontation at the front door and suggested that future meetings should be at our office. He agreed, but it was clear that he was less distressed by this incident than we were. He was anxious to turn the conversation to the Alaskan wilderness. He had no time for small talk, and the policies of his club regarding women and blacks apparently fell in that category. Sitting in the cozy bar of this exclusive club, Brower looked too big for his chair, as if his energy might explode and break the delicate glasses lined up behind the bar. I thought that he would be more comfortable pacing across the tundra of central Alaska in a snowstorm with a heavy pack on his back, discussing this environmental disaster over a chewy piece of dried seal blubber.

"A consortium of oil companies—Mobil, Exxon, Shell—calling itself *Alyeska* wants to build a pipeline across Alaska," he said, "from the shores of the Arctic Ocean south to the Port of Valdez on the Gulf of Alaska—eight hundred miles in all, parallel to a new road which in itself would open the last American wilderness to reckless development. They are about to start. The pipe sections are stacked along the route, and they are awaiting only a permit to begin construction. There has never been the slightest public discussion."

We knew nothing of the project. It had been negotiated between the oil companies and the Interior Department, without public participation or information. The negotiation had been particularly smooth and cordial because the Secretary of Interior, Wally Hickel, had been the governor of Alaska, where he had earned a reputation as a friend of developers with little concern for protecting the unique natural resources of Alaska. It was a big state, he believed, and one more pipeline wouldn't do much damage.

Brower wanted to make sure that we understood the enormity of the issues. "An impenetrable barrier cutting across the migration routes of the largest caribou herds in the Arctic. Hundreds of thousands of animals in jeopardy, unable to move from winter to summer pastures. The pipeline route crosses the third most active earthquake zone on earth. The permafrost tundra is so fragile that a single footprint can leave a scar that will take decades to cover over. The southern terminal in Valdez sits squarely on the earthquake fault, and the oil will be loaded into tankers to be hauled across the treacherous Gulf of Alaska, pocked by immense floating islands of ice. Oil spills along the pipeline route and in the Gulf are inevitable. An oil spill spreading and oozing across the tundra could blight the landscape for centuries."

Brower painted an impressive picture of environmental apocalypse, but I had no way of knowing how reliable his information was or how serious the risks were. It seemed amazing to me that the oil companies would proceed so recklessly in undertaking this massive project without carefully assessing the risks and taking all prudent safeguards against major environmental harms. Surely they didn't want to have starving caribou banging their antlers against the sides of the impassable pipeline.

We thanked Brower for bringing this matter to us, and told him we would get back to him. We left by the front door of the club and went back to CLASP, sitting down together in my office without turning on the lights, our faces deeply shadowed by the harsh fluorescent streetlights outside. The students waited expectantly, the tension palpable.

"I'm ready to sign up and start drafting the complaint tomorrow," Jim said.

"Jim," I responded, with lawyerly caution, "we only have enough money to run for six months. This case could go on for years. And we don't have the information or the expertise to assess the environmental risks. Brower is a great man, but he isn't exactly an objective expert or a neutral observer. He is a persuasive salesman and a true believer. If you will excuse the expression, he could sell a refrigerator to an Eskimo." In my mind I ran through the nightmare scenarios— our case dismissed with a stinging rebuke from the judge, our apologetic efforts to explain our failure to the foundations, our vain efforts to persuade new funders to invest in an appeal, losing our law school connections when deans were called on the carpet by angry alumni.

Jim's face darkened. "If we don't take this case on, there is no point in starting CLASP. We may as well close our doors."

"If we do take this case," I said, "we are betting the store on this one roll of the dice. And we don't know yet if the legal arguments are plausible."

For the next few hours, sitting in the semidarkness, we worked through legal and practical arguments. Would we sue the oil companies or the Secretary of the Interior? Should we invite other environmental groups to join? What about the interests of the native tribes in the area? We shared our strong, conflicting emotions— anger with the Interior Department, despair about the recklessness of the oil companies, elation about Brower's coming to us, and fear about our ability to deliver.

Finally, we agreed that we would have to look at the case more closely, research the law, solicit the opinions of people familiar with the factual and legal issues, and consult with Justice Goldberg. And we would do it quickly. A few days later, we called Brower and offered our services to file suit against the Secretary of the Interior. "Let's go for it," Brower said, as if we were about to scale another Rocky Mountain peak from an angle that had never been tried before. And with that we were counsel to Friends of the Earth, looking for other environmental groups to join a consortium of plaintiffs. If we were going to take on the largest oil companies in the world and the Nixon administration, we were going to need all the allies we could find.

Clearly, this was not merely a lawsuit, legal arguments to be presented in a courtroom. We could see ahead: before the end of our lawsuit we would be enmeshed in a political battle and a struggle for public opinion with global ramifications. In addition to law, we would need solid science, media savvy, and political muscle.

Our first move was to seek a temporary restraining order and preliminary injunction against the Secretary of the Interior, prohibiting him from issuing the final permits that would allow Alyeska, the consortium of pipeline companies, to begin laying the pipeline. The initial hearing focused on the likelihood that we would prevail on the merits after the case was fully argued. There would only be legal arguments and sworn affidavits, no live witnesses and cross-examination. It was the kind of case that courts like to avoid. The

bulldozers were in place and ready to start scraping aside the surface of the tundra. The pipeline sections, fabricated especially for
this project, were stacked by the right-of-way, beginning to rust.
Alyeska had intervened in the lawsuit on the side of the secretary,
and their lawyers would participate in the argument. We prepared
our court papers, stressing the high stakes involved and the
irreparable injury that would be done to the Alaskan wilderness if
the court did not take immediate action.

On the day of the hearing, Jim and I arrived at the federal courthouse half an hour before the scheduled argument.[4] Working our
way through the crowd of lawyers milling around in the corridor,
we entered the courtroom with a combination of dread and excitement. Neither Jim nor I had had experience in high-stakes litigation. I hadn't been in a district court since the *Rouse* case. The
courtroom galleries were packed with corporate lawyers and oil
company lobbyists in dark pin-striped suits. "We are the two low-
est-paid lawyers in this courtroom, except for the judge's clerks," I
whispered to Jim. "Maybe we can get all these lawyers to contribute
10 percent of their billings on this case to CLASP. By filing this
lawsuit, we are buying a lot of lawyers second homes."

"Let's focus on our argument," Jim said.

Our clients and students stood out in the crowd, people who were
not acculturated to the buttoned-up look of lawyers, whose necks
were chafed by tight collars and neckties, showing excitement on
their faces rather than a look of studied nonchalance. They carried
their papers in backpacks, not shiny leather briefcases. We greeted
our clients and wished each other good luck. I shook hands with a
couple of Arnold & Porter partners, many years my senior, and then
Jim and I moved through a low gate to the counsel table.

As we spread out our papers, I reflected on the fiercely combative process that lay below the civil surface of the courtroom. Jim was an uncompromising advocate, and I was confident that he would present our case with force and conviction. Still, I nervously reviewed the magnitude of the challenge and my doubts about taking this case when Dave Brower described it. I had been carried along by Jim's enthusiasm. But we were challenging some of the most powerful corporations in the world, and they had not undertaken this project without a green light from their high-priced lawyers. As Jim stood to present our case, I thought, if we blow it, our promising experiment is likely to be prematurely terminated. Then, I refocused my attention on the argument.

Jim argued that the Interior Department had failed to follow NEPA, which required that any federal action having major environmental impact must be preceded by a careful analysis of environmental consequences.[5] Yet the Environmental Impact Statement for the massive pipeline project was cursory and superficial. Since the law was so new, no one knew whether the courts would insist on a serious, substantive review process with public participation, or whether a pro forma nod to the environmental issues would be held to be enough. We were also aware that a district judge would be reluctant to go too far out on a limb in reliance on a new law when such huge economic interests were at stake.

Jim set out our second legal theory, less dramatic and eye-catching, yet more reassuring to a conventional judge. A little-known statute, the Mineral Leasing Act of 1926, limited the width of pipeline rights-of-way across public lands to twenty-five feet plus the width of the pipeline. The Secretary of the Interior was about to issue a permit for a much wider right-of-way. This was an easy way for the judge to rule in our favor without having to break new legal ground.

As Jim began his argument, with all those lawyers staring at his back and wishing him ill, the judge was obviously troubled by the right-of-way issue, by Interior's seeming disregard for a clear congressional instruction. When the Alyeska lawyer's turn to argue arrived, the judge focused his questions on the width limitations in the statute, and emphasized the clarity of the statutory language.

We held our breath for the next several days, listening with one ear for a telephone call from the judge's clerk telling us that the order had been entered and that we could come down to the courthouse to pick up a copy. When the call came, we learned that the judge had ruled in our favor because of the width limitation in the Mineral Leasing Act. *We had done it!* While we didn't get the broad interpretation of NEPA and the resounding endorsement of environmental values that we had hoped for, we had won a signal environmental victory, saving America's last great wilderness from likely destruction. We had protected the rare ecosystem, the animals and plants, the way of life of the Native American inhabitants, and stopped irresponsible corporate exploitation.

Moreover, the *Alyeska* decision helped lay the foundation for a new stage in the environmental movement. Our success in the courtroom gave advocacy groups a seat at the table in a broad range of environmental decisions. The Interior Department and the oil companies could no longer treat environmentalists as a bunch of impotent do-gooders. Environmental issues had to be taken seriously. We had done it through the legal process, by the force of our arguments, in the face of a phalanx of the highest-powered corporate lawyers in Washington and the immense political and financial power of the big oil companies. I reveled in the pure joy of our achievement.

We had also put the Center for Law and Social Policy on the map. The novel idea of a public interest law firm, which had seemed theoretical and ungrounded, became understandable and important. Aided by the element of surprise, we had made it impossible for the oil companies and their friends at Interior to do business in the same old way, with private deals disposing of public assets behind closed doors.

We had taken a big risk in bringing this suit, and it had paid off. I felt gratitude that I had followed Jim's lead in accepting the challenge. I could see a pattern of lawyerly caution in my responses, conditioned by my father and reinforced by my legal education. Identifying the pattern was the first step in overcoming it. My anxieties about the viability of our program dissipated, and I looked forward to continuing to build CLASP. I felt that I could relax a little, since I did not have to explain our project with theoretical arguments. I had dramatic results that I could to point to. We never made an official determination that the experimental phase was over and that the merit of the program had been established, but we began to think and act as if we thought so.

The next weekend we threw a party to celebrate. We cleared the tables and chairs out of our library, brought in a stereo system, and invited environmental activists and public interest lawyers from the Washington community to join us. There was an overwhelming spirit of new beginnings in the room. This was solid evidence that the Nixon regime was not stopping all progress, that corporate power could not despoil the last wilderness, that some victories would be possible. In the low light, the Grateful Dead and Bob Dylan reverberated through our law library. The CLASP students and staff, excellent dancers, let loose that night. At close to midnight, Ralph Nader came across Q Street from his office where he had been drafting his next week's congressional testimony. "Congratulations on the pipeline case," he said, and then added with dry disapproval, "I see you're having a party."

"Yes," I said, a little embarrassed, as if I had been caught slacking my duty on a battlefield by a superior officer. "It's Saturday night, and I think we should celebrate victories when we have them, since they don't come along so often. Come in and have a beer." Ralph seemed lonely as he stood at the edge of the party. I felt fortunate that I had more balance in my life and that I had the impulse to celebrate success when it came along. "No, thanks," he said. "I have to get back to work." He buttoned his shapeless tan raincoat and headed back to his office.

We enjoyed a striking series of victories in the early years of the seventies.

After the district court decision, we successfully defended our victory in the court of appeals,[6] then participated in the long administrative proceedings in the Interior Department while the oil companies did what they should have done in the first place— candidly assess the enormous impact that the pipeline would have and carefully design it so as to minimize damage to the ecological system. They designed crossings for migratory caribou to get past the pipeline. They adapted construction techniques to minimize the damage to the permafrost, the permanently frozen groundwater in the tundra. Most important, they added frequent cutoff valves, so the damage would be minimized if the pipeline ruptured. We engaged in the dialogue with the Interior Department and the oil companies, critiquing their proposals and pushing for maximum environmental protection. In the course of the process, they designed a much more responsible project, a pipeline that didn't have environmental disaster built into its design.

In parallel with the pipeline case, we took on another high-risk case. We successfully represented the Environmental Defense Fund in a suit to require the ban of DDT, translating the work of Rachel Carson into legal argument. For the first time a citizen group obtained a federal court order to compel the government to take action against a major environmental pollutant. The Court of Appeals for the District of Columbia Circuit required the federal government to institute a proceeding on DDT that ultimately led to the ban of all domestic uses of DDT, a ban that saved a number of species that had been on the edge of extinction.[7]

We also established the Project on Corporate Responsibility to develop nonjudicial strategies for challenging corporate indifference to the environment, to the interests of consumers, and to the interests of minorities. Under the name *Campaign GM*, we ran a slate of candidates for the board of directors of General Motors, to highlight the shortcomings of GM's performance in these three areas.[8] We nominated René Dubos, the environmentalist, to dramatize the company's poor environmental performance; Channing Phillips, a civil rights leader in Washington, to highlight their failures to address racial issues effectively; and Betty Furness, the consumer advocate, to focus on their opposition to product designs that would protect consumers from injury. We invited universities, churches, foundations, and other socially engaged investors to support our candidates in order to demonstrate to GM their concern about the performance of the company in these critical areas.

After months of highly visible debate, in which GM's clumsy efforts to exclude our candidates from the ballot gave them greater exposure, one of our students engaged the CEO of GM at the annual meeting in debate about GM's failure, over the lifetime of the corporation, to place even one person of color or woman on its board. Our candidates made a respectable showing, and because of our efforts, the next year GM elected Leon Sullivan, the first African American to join its board of directors. Sullivan used his position to assume leadership on corporate responsibility, including the promulgation of the Sullivan Principles, influential guidelines for American corporations doing business in apartheid South Africa.[9]

Our technique of mobilizing the voting power of socially responsible investors became the foundation of shareholder activism for social causes, from the antiapartheid struggle to opposition to environmental irresponsibility.

We took the *Rouse* theory and participated in a class action in Alabama, *Wyatt v. Stickney*, challenging the adequacy of treatment of mentally ill and retarded people in all of the state's residential facilities. We succeeded in establishing a constitutional right to treatment and obtained a detailed order from the court stating what would have to be done to bring the state's oppressive facilities up to constitutionally acceptable standards.[10] The *Wyatt* litigation had a massive impact on facilities in that state over the course of three decades, and also led to major reforms in other states.

In the course of the *Wyatt* case, we uncovered a number of important issues that highlighted the tension between medical autonomy and the rights of patients. For example, we obtained an order to stop scientific experiments on mentally retarded patients who were subjected to procedures that put them at risk with no hope of therapeutic benefit, and to prohibit the practice of involuntary sterilization. The *Wyatt* decision reverberated throughout the country, leading us to establish an affiliated public interest law firm, the Mental Health Law Project, to follow up on these important issues, including situations when scientists and doctors pursued their own agendas at the expense of mentally impaired patients.

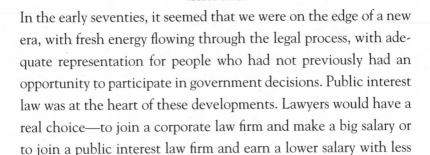

In the early seventies, it seemed that we were on the edge of a new era, with fresh energy flowing through the legal process, with adequate representation for people who had not previously had an opportunity to participate in government decisions. Public interest law was at the heart of these developments. Lawyers would have a real choice—to join a corporate law firm and make a big salary or to join a public interest law firm and earn a lower salary with less security, but do work that they believed in.

As CLASP registered some important victories, Victor Kramer, the man who had hired me at Arnold & Porter, called me for lunch at the Palm—decorated with affectionate caricatures of elite inside-the-Beltway lawyers, a kind of Lobbyist Hall of Fame. It was a wonderfully incongruous place to hold a subversive conversation.

"I am almost sixty, a good deal older than your group's median age," he said. "I wonder if you might consider me for the Center's legal staff." He clenched his pipe in his teeth and squinted his eyes in a grimace. I was familiar with this expression. It signified intellectual or moral strain. "I need work with soul. I am not even sure what I mean by that, but I know the work I'm doing doesn't have it. I think that you people are onto something. Your success in *Alyeska* has been remarkable."

I was amazed. Vic was a senior partner at Arnold & Porter and a legendary figure in the antitrust bar, known for his brilliance and crankiness. "It will take some adjustment on your part. We don't run things the way they do at the firm. It's all rather shaggy and diffuse. The Center isn't as orderly as you like things to be. Short on deference and respect."

"I am prepared to take my chances. The public interest bar is a bunch of people who resent authority and can't get along in any institution. I think I can be comfortable with that."

We invited him to join us, and his contributions to the early life of the Center were invaluable. He was a resourceful and imaginative lawyer, and provided a reality check on some of our far-out legal theories. "Remember that you are going to have to sell that to a judge," he would say. To the legal profession he was a guarantor of our seriousness and substantiality. For me, more than anything that was written about us, Vic's decision to join us was the most important affirmation of what we were doing.

In the heady days following our early successes, we thought about public interest law in a more ambitious framework.[11] We had begun CLASP as an experiment, hoping to survive for a few years. Our early successes and the newspaper analyses we read about ourselves led us to think that CLASP could become the model for the new law practices. We sent copies of our charter, bylaws, and basic policies to lawyers in Los Angeles and San Francisco who were establishing their own public interest law firms. We consulted with lawyers in South Africa and Latin America about adapting the American model for foreign settings. We offered advice on finding foundation support, and we discussed the possibility of developing other funding strategies.

The press began to give CLASP serious attention. CBS did a segment on CLASP for the evening news. Their people spent a full day at our office with cameras whirring. I realized, for the first time, how little control we had over how we would be presented—as uninformed, immature upstarts, or as a significant new phenomenon. Their story was quite respectful but, depending on how the videotape was edited, it could have gone either way.

I became modestly well-known. An enthusiastic early article on the *Washington Post* editorial page made me sound substantially more articulate and wittier than I am, and the line drawing that accompanied the piece gave me a formidable Jewish Afro and black

beard.[12] I learned how much of one's success is in the hands of journalists, and not to take my press notices too seriously.

I received some positive notice in books on the Washington bar
and the new generation of leadership emerging in Washington.[13]
Because of our success in public interest litigation, I was invited to
two coveted summer seminars, an Aspen Institute leadership program and the monthlong Salzburg Seminar in American Studies,
where I taught European lawyers about public interest law in America. As I described the pipeline case and the DDT ban in the
Baroque conference room at the Schloss Leopoldskron, I soared
into optimistic predictions about the future of the public interest
law movement. While we had accomplished a great deal, I see in
retrospect, after the Reagan and Bush decades, that a wiser assessment would have been more modest and tentative.

COMMUNITY AND CONSCIOUSNESS

S HORTLY AFTER the district court decision in the pipeline case, I sat down to lunch with my friend Ralph Siu and turned the subject to the case. I was full of our success and outraged by the oil companies' cavalier indifference to the environment. Ralph's calm offset my enthusiasm.

"It's important to plan your strategy with full regard for the long term," he said. "Your action was especially significant because you averted an action that could have had disastrous impact for generations. On the other hand, our country has an insatiable appetite for oil. Over time, that demand is going to drive resource decisions, and real progress will have to address that problem. The corporations will do what is necessary to meet that demand. I doubt if the corporate decision makers are bad people."

I realized that I had fallen into the habit of thinking they were bad people, the enemy. CLASP tended to run on polarized and adversarial thinking, and oil company executives had a high ranking on the list of villains.

I had met Ralph on the board of trustees of the Academy for Contemporary Problems, a nonprofit think tank in Ohio. A small, round-faced Chinese-American in his mid-fifties, he wore a shape-

less gray suit, a narrow dark tie, and a white shirt. The most striking thing about his appearance was the broad smile that almost
never left his face. He had been chosen by Attorney General Ramsey Clark to become the first director of the National Institute of
Law Enforcement and Criminal Justice, although his background
was as a research chemist and science administrator.[1] At the board
meetings in Ohio, he had a wealth of funny stories that he told—
to my considerable annoyance—whenever discussions became
heated and disagreements came to the surface. I often felt that he
was defusing significant disagreements that would be better left to
a more pointed debate and resolution by a vote. His self-effacing,
nonconfrontational style was simply not a way of being in the world
that I knew anything about. It's as if law schools screen out people
like this. I didn't know what to make of Ralph and I regret to admit
that I took him to be a lightweight, a little silly in fact, at our first
meeting.

I wanted to talk manifesto; he wanted to talk gentle exploration.
I wanted to sharpen the edges; he wanted to round them and find
points of intersecting interests. He did not seem rigorous or forceful in the manner that I had come to expect of brilliant and effective people. Always cheerful and relaxed, he listened with deep
concentration to what other people said and seemed to have no
overpowering ideological commitments. Still, I was intrigued by his
interest in integrating Eastern and Western ideas, and I enjoyed his
company.

When we were both in Washington I would call him for lunch,
and a pattern soon emerged. He would respond with great enthusiasm, inviting me to choose a date to come as his guest to the Cosmos Club.

I would often arrive a few minutes late, rushing and out of breath.
Relaxed in a large leather armchair in the lobby, he would greet me
with a radiant smile.

"I hope you haven't been waiting long. How are you?"

"Couldn't be better," he would say.

We would walk through the club's winding corridors to the dining room, past the wall of photographs of members who had received the Nobel Prize. We would sit down at our table, and he would write down my order, as members often do at clubs like the Cosmos, a nice gesture of hospitality. "Hmm. That sounds good, I think I'll have the same," he would say, and write a "2" next to each item. We would talk for hours. He was intrigued by what I was doing and asked questions of a kind that I had never thought about and that no one else had ever asked.

As we sat waiting for our food, I thought about my last visit to the club. I said, "Coming in here today reminded me of a meeting I had with David Brower. This same doorman tried to send us to the side door, because one of our students was a woman. She brushed him aside, and we all came in the front entrance."

A faint look of discomfort crossed his face. "Yes, it's a ridiculous rule, isn't it? But there are a few old members who joined the club during the Hoover administration, and they still cling to a Victorian system of propriety. In a few years they will be gone, and the club will be able to update its policies."

"And until then women will be sent around the side door?"

"Well," he said, "you have to choose which fights you want to take on. Which things are likely to change on their own in due course. And which changes can be moved along with a gentle nudge. Sometimes it is a question of timing. Think about opening the lens and looking at the widest possible picture. You can often get insights that are lost in a too-close attention to the problem of the moment."

I sat back to listen. These were novel ideas. I was troubled by what seemed like his excessive patience.

"There is a natural rhythm in things," he said, "and your work will be more effective if you bring your efforts into harmony with those natural rhythms."

I pressed him on this point. "How do you describe these rhythms? How can I be sure that I haven't just imagined them?"

"The rhythms are subtle and not easy to describe. They're more likely to be recognized by intuition than by analysis. You're more likely to recognize them if you are in silence and in repose, if your mind isn't busy and distracted. But that doesn't make them less real or worthy of attention."

His answer was interesting, but frustratingly unspecific, and difficult to implement in my busy public interest practice.

"When you approach a difficult problem, try to make your mind like the surface of a still pond—reflecting the world just as it is, without distortion, without highlighting any particular thing more than another, without flattening out the complexities. Don't let any political or ideological filters stand between you and the world. Make sure you see things clearly first, before you begin to think about the most skillful response."

As I walked back to my office, I thought about my conversation with Ralph. His gentle comments had put our success into a different perspective, reminding me of the complexity and importance of the work we were undertaking. I lived comfortably in the suburbs with two cars. I hadn't shifted my lifestyle significantly to use less oil or to conserve resources, and I knew only a few people who had. If the environmental cause was to succeed, it would eventually have to deal with these issues. And I would have to look at the way I lived.

Of course, most oil executives were not bad people. They lived in a milieu that rewarded them for ignoring the long-term consequences of what they did. The rules by which they played and their system of rewards would have to be changed, a task as formidable as reducing the profligate energy use by ordinary people—like me. The *Alyeska* victory was just a small step. My task, Ralph said, was to start, to choose carefully the right steps to take, and to move ahead forcefully, with full recognition that the final outcome was not in my control.

I found this insight difficult to follow in the overheated environment of a public interest law practice. I had, however, already learned to see some of the complex ways that CLASP interconnected with the establishment, through the foundations, our board, our professionalism. We were not in an "us-against-them" fight to the finish. Yet I sometimes spoke as if we were.

Ralph's comments set in motion a process that subtly affected the way I approached problems. Visualizing my mind as the mirrorlike surface of a still pond made it more difficult to jump to facile conclusions based on preconceptions. But it was a hard assignment. I had made a big investment in my identity as an activist, a public interest lawyer, a progressive. It was not easy for me to address a new problem—like the Alaska pipeline problem as presented by Brower—without immediately translating it into a legal issue and a challenge and opportunity for our public interest law firm. But there was an obvious advantage to understanding the facts in themselves, in their largest context, before putting them through the processor of legal-analysis and letting my understanding be shaped by what I wanted to see or hoped to accomplish. As I thought about the next steps in following up on the *Alyeska* success, I would do well to look closely at the complex, interlocking problems of energy use and to think about various strategies that might permit us to attract unanticipated allies in a struggle that was likely to last for decades.

Months into our relationship, I realized that Ralph had become my teacher, really the first teacher I ever had whose curriculum was not substantive content in history or law, but rather how to live my life. I edged into the relationship tentatively—simply conversations with a friend at first. Gradually, I realized that his lifetime of study of Eastern thought in Western contexts was filling our conversation with content, and suggesting to me a new way of approaching my life.

His subtle and sensitive way of teaching forced me to learn new skills as a student. I had been trained by my father, reinforced at law school, to learn by constantly challenging ideas, probing the weak spots in an argument. With Ralph, I learned in a different way—by restraining my impulse to critique new ideas, by listening more hospitably, by holding his questions unanswered and letting them echo in my mind in the days that followed our conversations. This new way of learning, patient and slow to make judgments, became a cornerstone in my cultivation of wisdom.

At the same time we were handling significant public interest cases and I was pursuing my dialogues with Ralph, we were trying to build an activist learning community that reflected a new consciousness—breaking out of hierarchical relationships and exploring the possibility of a broader legal education that integrated the personal and the professional. We tried to expand our lawyerly identities by engaging with the members of our community as full people who share each other's joys and sorrows. It was not easy, and the constraints generated by foundations, law schools, and my acculturated sense of appropriateness were considerable. Moreover, with each step away from the norms of law and higher education, I had to contend with my inner Woody Allen, the cynical, whiny voice in my mind constantly warning, "Don't be such a schmuck. This period of openness and exploration will end, and you will be better off playing safe."

Doing socially important work and challenging institutional authority—the David-and-Goliath aspect—fed the community spirit and supported our experiments in new relationships and structures. We were living at a time when inherited norms were crumbling. Many of our students were just a few years younger than I was, but they seemed to be on the other side of a deep divide, a barrier shaped by the sexual revolution, widespread use of marijuana, and their exposure to the Vietnam draft. Marijuana had been a normal part of the students' lives in college, and even in high school. They had grown up in the middle of the sexual revolution, part of the campus unrest that was shaking the universities. And they were eligible to be drafted to fight a war they hated.

Although my impulses in starting CLASP were primarily rationalist and lawyerly, I was also willing to experiment with consciousness, to try being less lawyerly, more open to new relationships and experiences. So I was receptive when our students brought their cultural innovations into CLASP, and I explored, somewhat randomly, the possibilities at the edges of my circumscribed, orderly life.

My horizons were expanded by my visits to California, at first undertaken with the earnest mission of persuading students at Stanford and UCLA law schools that they ought to entrust their legal education to CLASP (which had not yet opened its doors) and commit a full semester to clinical training in public interest law. While I was there, I also had time for a little exploration of the new California subculture. California was not just a place. It was the epicenter of a revolution, a new state of mind.

On one trip, I went down the Peninsula to Stanford Law School to interest students in CLASP and interview those who were interested. I was impressed that a dozen of them were prepared to take

the gamble on this untried experiment, after they had so successfully climbed the slippery pole of academic achievement and
reached this pinnacle, a jumping-off place to the prestige positions
in the legal world.

That evening, I went to Fillmore West to hear the Jefferson Airplane. The only person in the hall wearing a tie, I was shaken by
the face paint, the tie-dyed clothing, the stoned, grinning friendli-
ness. "One pill makes you larger/One pill makes you small/And the
ones that mother gives you don't do anything at all. . . ." After a
while, the light show and the loud throbbing music took me in and
I lost myself in the sea of undulating bodies. We were supposed to
hear the Grateful Dead too, but we left at 2 A.M., when they were
just setting up. I had a plane to catch the next morning, and I still
believed in getting some sleep before taking on the next day.

For the next several years I traveled to California to recruit students and to speak at conferences and meetings. The trips always
combined CLASP business with forays into the new culture. I went
to a Moroccan restaurant and ate honeyed lamb with my fingers
while reclining on pillows stacked on the padded floor. I hiked the
trails on Mount Tamalpais and in the redwood groves. I attended an
elegant party for law professors where the guests were offered a
choice of cocktails or joints neatly laid out on a silver tray. It wasn't
the deep California counterculture—no LSD, no trips to the baths
at Esalen, no Merry Pranksters—but it was enough for me to realize
that there really was something new going on. I found that my exposure to the California culture was loosening me up, creating a space
where I could bring some lightness even to the heaviest subjects. I
always carried a whiff of it back with me to my East Coast life.

Because I was at CLASP, I was continuously exposed to the new
things that were engaging students. We invited them to enter into
the Center's life with their whole selves. This was not a summer job
in a law firm where they had to accept the norms of the firm, put

on their dress-for-success suits and the masks of earnest profession-als. CLASP was still being invented, and issues of professional iden-tity were a subject for dialogue and debate.

I might have missed all of this, identifying with an older gener-ation, guided through life by the norms of the fifties—confused by the fierce attacks on established institutions, offended by the music, and reflexively opposed to the use of pot. I tried to find a way to learn from the counterculture, and to integrate the lessons with my Eisenhower-era skills and values in a way that would be useful in the new world that was emerging. CLASP was a place where I could work on that synthesis.

I found my own way outside of the mainstream, while continu-ing to hold on to connections in my old world. I tried to bridge the gap between generations, between the traditional and the radical, between those who defined success financially and those who were committed to a life of service. This meant that I had to develop a set of skills, some quite unfamiliar, that permitted me to stretch lim-its and open new directions—to listen carefully to people with whom I disagreed, to hold my own views less tightly, to present my ideas in a way that was open and inviting.

As I began to understand that being the executive director of the Center for Law and Social Policy was going to be a complex and demanding job, I decided to get some training in what it takes to head an organization. Although we were committed to a relatively flat hierarchical pyramid, I was the designated CEO, with admin-istrative responsibilities and obligations to manage our relation-ships with the outside world. I had a long history of challenging authority but little experience in exercising it. I thought that there were probably unique problems, too, in heading an organization like CLASP that had questioning authority at the center of its mission. It attracted staff and students who were doubtful of authority and willing to stand up to it, and in those egalitarian days we were committed to eliminating illegitimate hierarchy.

There was nothing in my education or experience to prepare me for these complicated tasks. I had never taken a course on leadership or led anything larger than a canoe trip. Like a good lawyer, I was trained to meet new situations with a confident demeanor and the brusque assurance that I was in control. I decided to try a different tack, acknowledging that I needed help and going where I could get it.

At that time, a friend told me about a conference on leadership and authority relationships that he had just attended. It was held by an American offshoot of the Tavistock Institute, a celebrated London center that brought a psychoanalytic approach to the study of group process. My expectations were modest and pedestrian—how to be more effective in running a meeting, evaluating employees, working with a board of trustees—and I decided to sign up.

The Tavistock meeting began at Amherst College on a balmy summer day in 1970. I had been extremely busy at the office, and had made travel arrangements to get me to the five-day conference just a short time after it was scheduled to begin. I thought there would be a couple hours of orientation, settling in, and introduction.

The atmosphere was decidedly chilly in the registration room, and I was the only straggler in sight. My registration packet lay alone on what had been a crowded table. The registrar urged me to go at once to the seminar room where my small group had been meeting for forty-five minutes. The work had begun. Everyone else seemed to know that being on time was crucial.

I walked into a simple room with a view out on the rolling greens of the campus, the mature oak trees in full summer foliage. Inside the air-conditioned room, under the fluorescent fixtures, it was chilly and silent. The tables had been pushed to the side and fifteen chairs were arranged in a circle, with one chair vacant. No one greeted me when I came in and no one identified himself as the person in charge. I took my seat quietly, surprised that no one made eye contact. I waited for something to happen. The people around me were, seemingly, as uncomfortable as I was. We were all there to study relationships and authority. I assumed that one of the people around this circle was going to make a presentation and lead a discussion. No one did. My anxiety was growing. Was I being hazed because I had come a little late?

As a discussion slowly began to unfold, I felt that everyone in my group knew a lot more about this process than I did, and I tried to be inconspicuous, sometimes attempting to defuse the tension with a joke—but my jokes were received with icy silence. We struggled to make sense of our Kafkaesque assignment, not even knowing at first who the consultant in our group was. Generally, I am a confident student, so I found my level of anxiety acutely unpleasant, causing sweaty palms and constant attention to my watch.

The consultant finally identified himself and began to probe areas that we were avoiding. Did the comments of men receive more attention than women? Were black people less likely to speak than whites? Did the same people keep trying to exercise leadership? What made their efforts fail? Did the same people try to cut them down?

The program was radically more difficult than anything I imagined. The Tavistock method applied a high-stress, high-return learning strategy to the understanding of authority in groups. We would not study in the usual cognitive way. There were no lectures, no texts, no summary of principles. We were going to learn experientially, by being placed in a high-anxiety situation where we had to figure out what the authority structures were and how we fit into them. We were given no instructions—and no task other than to study relationships in authority.

We were not introduced to each other, and the other participants knew nothing about me except my name. We were on our own, and we had to use our best intellectual, emotional, and intuitive resources to figure out what was going on and how to make the most of this unusual educational situation.

My first few days were full of fears and self-doubt. What had I gotten myself into? I hardly spoke to anyone, and I ate many meals alone. As the days wore on, I found that I began to function more effectively in this peculiar environment. I discovered that I was learning as much about myself—my own attitudes, fears, and expectations—as I was about groups. My training as a lawyer was relevant, but I found that I needed a lot of additional skills—an ability to read complicated relationships, to manage my own anxiety, to follow my instincts in threatening situations, to learn through reflecting on my own actions.

Being stripped of my identity and credentials created additional challenges. I had grown accustomed to leaning on my position and profession, the degrees I had earned, and the people I knew. When those props were swept away, I had to establish my identity in moment-by-moment interactions. In assessing the others in the group, I was also deprived of my usual stereotyping responses to people based on their status and rank; I had to evaluate my responses to people's race, gender, and age. Conventional, habituated responses were useless.

The experiential method demanded that I stretch my intellectual, emotional, and intuitive capacities. I learned the value of listening scrupulously to what people were saying, and what they were communicating without words, by posture, facial expression, and body language, things that were too subtle to name. I learned the value of keeping my mouth shut, and at other times, of acting even if it meant risking censure. Engaging the full range of my emotions and reflecting on them gave me a more profound learning experience than the purely cognitive, instructional lectures and seminars that had been the stuff of my education up to that point.

I didn't carry back to CLASP any of the concrete leadership skills that I had expected to learn. Instead, I brought back an ability to tune in to the underlying emotional dynamics in a group, a recognition of the importance and the limits of rational analysis. I understood at a deep level that educating the whole person is essential. In the complex swirl of group processes where lawyers spend much of their working lives, from courtrooms to client conferences, cognitive skills are important, but a well-honed emotional intelligence is just as important. That was also true of CLASP, and I would have to have the humility to recognize that we were all learning together.

My Tavistock learning was especially relevant when the secretaries at CLASP came together to protest the hierarchy of the institution that kept women in support positions and concentrated decisional authority in the hands of male lawyers. As the women's liberation movement was sweeping the country, CLASP obviously could not be untouched. We had started out with a legal staff of four white males. The support staff was made up of intelligent, conscientous women who chose to work at CLASP because they liked the ideology, the counterculture style, the promise of community. After my Tavistock experience, I knew enough to take their dissatisfaction seriously and to invite in a consultant to help us understand and respond to the problems.

A few of the secretaries who had been doing consciousness-raising and assertiveness workshops set the tone for the discussion.

"You lawyers call yourselves 'public interest lawyers,'" they said, "but we don't see much evidence of a public interest commitment. What we see is elitism and the replication of the forms of oppression that you would find in any corporate, male-dominated law firm in the city. You promised us community, but what we get is typing and filing and a chance to applaud the lawyers' successes. Why don't you try practicing what you preach?"

The Tavistock experience prepared me for the vehemence of the attack, but I did not have enough distance to respond well. Couldn't they see how much better we were than the corporate law firms? That accusation really hurt. They didn't know what real hierarchy and disrespect looked like—as if doing it better than a corporate firm was a sufficient measure of performance. In fact, I could have headed off this confrontation if I had been more alert and sensitive. I was defensive and slow at first, but I embraced their suggestions and moved ahead with them.

Once their grievances had come out, we had to respond. After a period of debate, we agreed to include the secretaries more fully in decision-making processes and to acknowledge the importance of their contribution. We hired two women to come to CLASP to build a women's rights agenda. With their leadership, we launched a Women's Law Project, later to spin off as the National Women's Law Center, which continues to exercise leadership in advocacy for women's rights.[2]

An important result of the "Secretaries' Revolt" for me was to understand more clearly that submerging myself in the role of lawyer was a mistake, that it limited my ability to see the problem clearly. I would have responded more effectively to the secretaries' challenge if I had been less lawyerly, less adversarial and polarizing, more open and responsive in hearing the secretaries' idealism, their hurt, and their desire to contribute to CLASP. I thought back to my conversation with Ralph Siu. He had advised me to confront any difficult or challenging problem without preconceptions, to try to see things just as they were and only then begin to frame a wise response.

At the same time this was going on at the office, I was dealing with the spread of feminist consciousness into my home. Susan had volunteered to work in the District of Columbia abortion counseling office of the National Women's Liberation Front. It was work that Susan believed in deeply. She was moved by the plight of the women she counseled, and she was committed to the work. The program also ran weekly meetings for their counselors to deal with the stresses of the work and to raise their consciousness of the oppression of women in a male-dominated, patriarchal society. They shared stories from their own lives—their personal experiences with date rape and incest, legal and illegal abortions, relationships with insensitive and oppressive men, efforts to assert themselves in male-dominated work situations. "You wouldn't believe what some of these women have been through," she said.

I wish I could say that I fully supported Susan's participation in the consciousness-raising sessions. I didn't. I felt that these sessions threatened to destabilize our quite traditional marriage. I was slow to recognize the merit of the feminist challenge and that we could not cling to old forms of marriage in rapidly changing times. I didn't see the ways that I could embrace the changes. Instead, I responded like a lawyer—logical, argumentative, and fierce. I objected, "You go off on Wednesday evening and sit around with this group of women you hardly know and talk about the intimate details of our relationship. And they encourage you to sharpen your sense of grievance. None of them are in happy, fulfilling marriages, and they invite you to put our relationship under a microscope, looking for oppression and patriarchal cruelty."

She hung in. The abortion counseling was important to her, and she liked the independence. Gradually, more slowly than I should have, I came to understand the importance of her growing autonomy and her participation in the group. She was right. And the powerful currents flowing through the society could not be ignored or fought. The women's movement became more familiar and less threatening. My most paranoid fears did not materialize. As I eased up, it became clear that Susan had no interest in pushing to the edges of feminist sensibility and action, and our marriage made an important transition to greater equality.

We were part of the de facto national experiment with the boundaries of the marriage relationship. Marriages were subject to an abnormal amount of stress in the seventies. We saw a great deal of divorce around us; other marriages persisted, but seemed to lose their resilience and joy. We came through this challenging time with a marriage that was full of love, vitality, and the capacity for growth. We had kept enough flexibility in the relationship to bend in strong emotional winds without snapping. Our commitment and love for each other gave us each sufficient space to participate in the exciting, energizing currents of the time without being torn from the roots that we had nourished together. I was able to get beyond a rigid clinging to male prerogatives and come to a vision of a marriage of sharing and equality, reinvention and renewal.

In order to build the sense of community in CLASP, I scheduled a retreat each semester for the new group of students to join the lawyers and secretaries for a weekend in West Virginia. We could get some distance from the stress of our law work, and build deeper connections. We took over the cabins of a summer camp two hours west of Washington, in the valley of the Cacapon River, which ran north to join the Potomac River west of Harper's Ferry. The camp nestled at the foot of rock cliffs at a broad point in the Cacapon Valley. The river's flow slowed at the camp's swim area, then increased as it dropped over a rocky ledge to a stretch of rapids below. It was a beautiful place, whether in the brilliant colors of autumn or the fresh greens of spring. Twice a year we went there, played Frisbee in the meadows, canoed on the river, and told stories around the fire late into the night.

These retreats built an easy connection among us, enabling us to engage with each other as whole people, not simply as finely honed thinking machines. On our walks through the woods and across the green fields we were able to delve below our professional roles to explore our aspirations, our doubts, and our ambitions. We talked about the ways that a lawyer's skills could be used to build a more just society, one more respectful of ecological realities, one more moved by compassion, and about the possibility of pursuing both a career of service and a family life. We touched a place behind the glib cynicism and lawyer humor that are cultivated in law schools and law firms.

Some of the students had never spent a night in the country. Together, we watched the moon rise as we sat around a campfire, listening for wolves howling in the hills. For many, over the course of a long weekend, their fears and doubts were replaced by joy in the silence and beauty of the place. On our long walks together, we slowed down to look at new spring leaves unfurling on bare branches and to listen to birdsong and the flow of the river. The peace and slowness gave us all some distance from our busy lives at CLASP and the urgently important cases on which we were working. From the perspective of this isolated valley in West Virginia, surrounded by deep woods and the drama of the turning seasons, the war in Vietnam and the depredations of the Nixon White House could be contemplated in a different way, more spaciously and with a larger time sense.

I treasured these West Virginia retreats for another reason. The camp setting resonated deeply with me, taking me back to a formative time in my life—my teenage years, when I had spent summers at a camp in the forests of central Ontario. At thirteen years old, it was a bold choice to go to an island in the middle of a large lake. I had learned to swim late, and I was nervous around the water. Neither of my parents knew how to swim. My father lived in his head; he viewed his body as a carrying case for his mind.

Although I had never seen a canoe before, my competence grew over the course of the summer, and I learned to paddle in the distinctive style of the Algonquin Indians who had lived on these lakes. I walked the same portage trails that they had and found my way across the trackless lakes as they had.

Far from my life as an ambitious and successful student, I met Susan. We began our lifelong, evolving romance in these idyllic surroundings, paddling canoes across clear blue lakes, stopping at sandy beaches for noonday swims, cupping our hands and dipping them in the lake water to drink. As I sat in the stern of the canoe, I loved watching the muscles in her back ripple under her smooth, dark skin with each stroke of her paddle. Our relationship deepened in those quiet hours, feeling the gentle movement of canoes through still waters.

In those Canadian summers I learned modest skills—reading the clouds to anticipate rain, building a fire with wet wood, carrying a sixteen-foot canoe across swampy, poorly marked portages. As I sat in the stillness of a golden sunset, listening to a loon breaking the silence with its wild laugh, I had an early intimation of deep connections and wordless relationships.

At the time I thought of this as merely a vacation, less important than my "real" life as a student. But, as I looked back from the West

Virginia hollows, I could see that this was the place where I first experienced inner stillness, and an emerging awareness of my place in the natural order, before I had ever heard the word ecology. My memory of those shadowy insights in my teen years made our retreats in West Virginia especially meaningful to me, an opportunity to reconnect to the part of myself that had awakened in a canoe on the northern lakes.

In our exploration of the new cultural landscape around us, Susan and I began taking a yoga class. Our instructor, Dorji, was an earnest young man who dressed all in white. He had a quiet, focused manner and a strong presence. His gentle teaching had me twisting my body in unimaginable ways, my arms knotted behind my knees, and my fingertips clutching each other behind my back. On his instruction, I began paying close attention to my breath, the symbolic point of connection between our physical being and our spiritual essence. At the end of class we would lie silently in *savasana*, the corpse pose, deeply relaxed and close to sleep, but awake and alert. I felt remarkably good after class, as if I had had a thorough workout, but I was grounded and cheerful, not tired. Problems that had seemed insurmountable looked more manageable, and tensions loosened their hold.

Sitting over coffee with a group of students one morning, I speculated about what it would be like if yoga were integrated into the training of lawyers. "People wouldn't live in their heads so much," I said. "They would learn to return to their breath and take a few full breaths before flying off the handle, cursing opposing counsel, or firing their secretary. And the experience of professors, secretaries, and students doing it together could help break down the status and rank order that gets between people and gums up the works. Who knows? Flexibility of the body may lead to flexibility in the mind. I am surprised that one of the California law schools hasn't tried it. I understand that just about everyone in California does yoga or something like it."

One of the Stanford students said, "At Stanford, they try to be like Harvard without the neckties and tweed sport coats. If there is going to be yoga for law students, you'd better do it here. My room-mate is a yoga instructor. I could invite her in for a class."

The next week Giselle arrived in a mauve leotard to teach yoga. We moved aside the tables in the library, closed the shutters at noon, and spread towels on the floor. For the next hour the library was off limits for legal research. We were a motley group—beauti-ful young women who had been college gymnasts and middle-aged men who drank too much beer and could hardly bend from the waist and touch their knees. The beautiful Giselle, lithe and flexi-ble as a bamboo wand, led us in *asanas*, breathing exercises and a deep relaxation that brought our minds to the edge of a spacious noncognitive awareness. "Don't judge yourselves," she said in a soft, smooth voice. "No comparisons with the person next to you. Just try to be friends with your own body, examine what it feels like to relax completely into a posture and let go of all tension." When the class was over, we walked out of the room relaxed and open to what-ever had come up. I went to my desk and leafed through the little stack of pink phone messages that had accumulated without my usual sense of dread and frustration. Work went a little better that afternoon, though the good effects had worn off by quitting time. I invited Giselle to come back weekly to carve out a little space of stillness and grace in the middle of our work. I never entered the library after that without my breath slowing down a little, sensing the musky smell of Giselle's incense.

"Aren't you afraid that CLASP will be dismissed as a bunch of flakes if word gets around the legal community about the yoga-in-the-library program?" one of our more cynical students asked.

"Some people already see us that way," I said. "I don't think this would make much difference. The key is to keep doing good cases and educating students." I believed that yoga helped with both—but I didn't highlight it when I reported back to the law school deans. Yoga helped us build our community and gave the students something important as they moved into their profession. Even in our busiest times, we took the time to take care of ourselves, to acknowledge the connection of the mind and body, and we did it together, in mutual commitment to each other. I relied on my inner sense of rightness in introducing the yoga; I hadn't fully worked out a justification and I wasn't ready to defend it to skeptics. Looking back, I think that bringing yoga into the law library was an early effort to introduce the practice of wisdom into my life and my work. It created a moment of balance and ease in our busy, purposive days and helped us connect with each other at a different level than during our sharp debates about the meaning of federal statutes.

As Susan and I planned a trip to Europe with our three young children, Winfield Scott, a man we scarcely knew, insisted that we stay in his house embedded in a medieval Italian village near the French border. "Fanghetto doesn't appear on any map," he said, "but I can assure you that it is there. It has been standing there among the olive groves for a thousand years. It is a bit primitive, but since you are planning on camping with three little children, I don't think it will be too primitive for you."

Our visit to Fanghetto that summer opened a new way of seeing the world for me. It started with the drive to the village. As we traveled north across the broad Mediterranean coastal plain, the road seemed to end at an impenetrable wall of mountains. Once we were closer to the steep granite slopes, the road slipped into a crevice in the mountain wall, and began its twisting course along the steep gorge carved out by the Roya River as it plunged down through the Maritime Alps. And then there was the village itself, a complex labyrinth of rooms, terraces, passageways, and staircases, all made of stone, perched on a steep mountainside above the river.

When our eyes had adjusted to the dim light inside Win's rooms, we saw that we were in an unfamiliar space. The walls of the rooms, made of white stucco, sloped into vaulted ceilings. There were no straight lines or right angles. No two steps were the same height, and each tread had been worn down in the middle by the passage of many feet. A non-Euclidian geometry governed. It was easy to imagine people living in these rooms for hundreds of years, harvesting the olives, watching the changing seasons. We found surprises at every turn in the streets, along every terrace in the olive groves, in every twist of the Roya River at the foot of the mountain. To swim in the river, we had to wind down through the olive terraces, across a bridge built by the Romans, and down across the rocks to the edge of the water. Nothing was predictable. Nothing corresponded to the world we knew at home.

One evening, Susan and I were sitting on our terrace in the evening glow, after the sun had dipped below the rocky ridge across the steep valley, sipping licorice-tasting Pernod and watching the swallows swooping through the air below us.

"This is a different world," Susan said. "And I love it."

I knew what she meant. We had grown up in Buffalo and Toronto, on the broad, flat plains near the Great Lakes, and we lived in Washington, where streets were laid out in grids. The geometry was clear, predictable, and simple. "We are flatlanders," I said. "We are accustomed to long, flat vistas. Life follows the geometry. In Washington, the parallel streets are lettered alphabetically. No surprises, everything rational and orderly. Mountain people couldn't possibly see the world that way."

"Too many cliffs, roaring rivers, contoured trails, unpredictable storms, porous borders, ecstatic vistas, and sudden catastrophes," Susan said. "No possibility of grids. Nothing is predictable."

After our visit to Fanghetto, we never were wholly flatlanders again. As we absorbed the perspective of the mountain people through our senses and in our bodies, we came home with a new understanding of the world's complexity, the long skein of human experience, and the joys of living without right angles shaping our consciousness.

Mountain people constantly experience the limits of what we can know and control with our minds. They would not expect the world to progress in a linear fashion. As a person with a newly acquired mountain perspective, I was impatient with the Euclidean geometry of the Washington streets and the classical analogue that dominated the legal system. We have returned to Fanghetto often, and our visits have been a catalyst, helping us overturn old expectations and move toward a more open, more exploratory, less predictable way of life.

After several years of retreats with the CLASP students, Susan and I bought a cabin in West Virginia, the Mountain State, downstream from the retreat site, on the east side of the river. The inconvenient fact that the road ran along the west side of the river and there was no bridge only added to its charm and lent an element of improvisation to our visits. Depending on the season, we could wade across, paddle our canoe, walk on the ice, or drive across. Our cabin reminded us of Fanghetto, where nothing was linear and reliable. We learned that the river could be powerful and unpredictable. It could be shallow enough to ford in our suburban station wagon on a warm summer weekend, but an upstream thunderstorm an hour later could turn it into an impassable inferno of dark brown water, running fif-teen feet deep, carrying full-grown trees uprooted from the banks. Then, the next morning, we might be able to drive across again and head home. As we went up to the cabin on weekends with the chil-dren and their friends in all seasons, the river was a tangible, living teacher about impermanence and the constancy of change.

Shortly after we began going to West Virginia, we picked up a couple of secondhand canoes, well-scarred before they came to us, and began paddling in the still waters and small rapids near our cabin. But we wanted to do more—to paddle the wilder sections of the river where it ran through rocky canyons, down boulder-filled rapids, and over steep ledges. Although we felt confident in canoes, we didn't know how to manage in a fast-moving river—to read the water, to locate hidden rocks, to ride the tricky currents where the river turned sharply at the foot of a cliff.

Susan and I signed up for lessons being offered by the Canoe Cruisers Association, a volunteer group of fanatical paddlers in Washington who were anxious to recruit and train new members. At our first lesson, we met with a group of other students on the edge of the C&O Canal, just beyond the Washington suburbs, and car-ried our canoe down a steep bank to the shore of the Potomac River, a mile below Great Falls, where the river runs swiftly, a half-mile across, around rocks and under low-hanging branches at the edges.

"Is this class for expert paddlers?" I asked, as I looked out at the river, deep and powerful, brown with runoff after the spring rains.

"Nope, for people who know the basic strokes," said Bill, the instructor, who appeared to be a teenager.

We tightened our life jackets and got ready to paddle out, fear-ful of being swept downriver into Chesapeake Bay.

"We're going to head upstream first," Bill said. "We'll work our way up to the foot of Great Falls and then ride down real fast on the current."

It sounded impossible and reckless. The water was still cold from snowmelt in the mountains. We thought about our small children. Perhaps we should haul our canoe up the hill and come back with wetsuits and a more mature instructor.

Bill gathered us around him for brief instructions before launching. "The main thing is to relax. Don't tighten up. Read the water carefully. At first, it looks like a giant, uniform flow, rushing downhill, with all the energy of Great Falls behind it. But look carefully." He pointed upstream, close to the shore. "There's a back current actually flowing upstream. You can ride that current for a couple hundred yards, then ferry across the main current to the eddy behind that rock. There's quiet water there. You can sit and plan your next move. When you come out of the eddy, keep the bow pointed into the current and you can actually make some progress upstream, moving from eddy to eddy. And don't push the river. It will flow by itself. Relax and pay attention."

Susan and I knelt in our canoe and pulled out into a sheltered pool in the river. Already we could see a complex dance of flows and currents in what had seemed to be an undifferentiated, overpowering flow of water. We found the currents that we could ride upstream, sat in still eddies and ferried across the main currents. With total concentration, we worked our way upstream to the bottom of the Great Falls, stopping the upstream movement before we entered into the foam, turbulence, and chaos at the foot of the falls.

"And now we go with the flow," Susan said, as we turned the canoe into the powerful downstream current for the quick and exhilarating ride back to our launch place, finding the channels between the rocks, avoiding the places where shallow currents flowed over submerged boulders.

We rejoiced in our new way to engage with fast-flowing rivers—without forcing, without trying to overpower the river, playing the shifts in current, carefully timing our movements. It would have been easy enough to tip the canoe if we had tensed up.

Canoes and small boats remain an important part of our lives. We paddled down the big rapids at Harper's Ferry, where the Potomac and Shenandoah Rivers merge and break through the last ridge of the Blue Ridge Mountains. Our skills at riding the currents served us well in kayaking in southern Alaska, the Yucatan, Crete, and the Sea of Cortez.

These experiences have provided a support for my work as a lawyer and social entrepreneur. When I am in a stressful situation, I can visualize myself in a canoe in fast water and reconnect with the physical sensation of riding the currents—giving clear, relaxed, and mindful attention to the needs of the moment. I can reconnect with my capacity to choose a course of skillful action in turbulent times.

When I was in my late thirties, the father of three children, I realized that I had never been alone for even twenty-four hours. In part because we married so young and were immediately engaged with child rearing, and in part because I inherited my father's gregarious personality, I had never taken a full day to myself. I decided to go up to our cabin in West Virginia on a cold wintry weekend and simply be alone, with nothing that I had to do. I had some misgivings about the project. I had so little experience of being alone that I did not know whether to expect a nurturing solitude or a frightening loneliness and isolation.

My weekend in the country was also undertaken in response to what I thought of as my *shallowness crisis*. The crisis grew out of a conversation I had with an old friend. Delighted by our chance meeting and feeling good about my life at that point, I said to her, "Probably, good things happen to good people."

"Oh, do you think so?" she said. "I think the story is more confused than that. The winds can blow from different directions. Four years ago, my husband and I were going out to dinner. He dropped me off at the restaurant, and went to park the car. He was crossing the street to the restaurant when he was hit and killed by a truck."

"Sorry," I said, trying to think of ways to back off from my incredibly shallow remark and express my sympathy.

"It was a long time ago, and I am doing all right. You don't have to worry."

She and I became friends again, and I raised the shallowness question with her when I met her next. At first, she was reassuring, then she added: "But, you know, you haven't suffered very much. Not many scars. And I'm not sure what you have put in place to hold you steady when strong winds blow. How deep are your roots? Trees with shallow roots get blown over in a hurricane."

She didn't mean to be unkind; in fact, she seemed concerned about me.

I took her words and the issue of shallowness with me to West Virginia. I felt that I was fortunate to have the shallowness crisis arise when I was doing work that I believed in, that gave meaning to my life. At least I didn't have to look at a career of defending lawn mower companies through the shallowness lens. Though my friends in the public interest law world were brilliant and dedicated, I didn't have the sense that they would do any better than I would in dealing with the shallowness problem. Being brilliant and dedicated is consistent with being shallow. Come to think of it, there was little in my upbringing or education about cultivating depth, building up the inner resources that would help me respond wisely to the really hard times—death, illness, profound self-doubt.

When I arrived at the Cacapon River, I found deep snow on the banks and the river frozen all the way across. The ice and the water were clear as glass, so that I could walk on the ice and look down below my feet at fish swimming, stones glistening on the bottom of the river in the sunlight, and twigs and leaves flowing with the current underneath the ice. I had never seen a sight like this, and it left me speechless. Gingerly at first, I walked across the clear, slick surface, enjoying an experience of a world that I had never imagined. I let myself into the wonder of yet another incarnation of the river I thought I knew so well, had seen so often from my canoe, whose warm water supported me during lazy summer swims. This was a new and different entity.

It heightened my sense of the possibility of unanticipated transformation, and made me think that some new insight into the shallowness problem might emerge from this weekend of solitude. I imagined that I might see the problem with a clearer vision, just as I was seeing the life of the river with an unimaginable clarity. I walked up the hillside through the virgin snow with the cold, dry air crackling, up to the cabin.

I lit the kerosene stove, and soon the cabin temperature was up to a tolerable fifty-five degrees, where it remained during my stay. I split wood, built a fire, drew water from the pump, cooked simple meals. The place was utterly silent with a special winter silence—no insects, no birdsong, no sounds from neighbors.

After a cozy night's sleep under a mound of blankets, I took a walk upriver through the woods to Loman's Branch, a little stream that flowed into the river. It was familiar terrain, but it looked different under heavy snow, and the silence made me aware of details that I would miss when I was with Susan, chattering and laughing. I settled into the solitude and became conscious of the quality of attention that I gave to the intimate details of the landscape—the faint tracks that small birds left in the snow, the crack of boughs giving way under the weight of the snow. I was simply moving through the woods with a bright, wordless awareness, without thoughts.

As I approached the banks of Loman's Branch, I heard an unearthly sound—like high bells ringing, softly and steadily, their sound merging and the notes harmonizing and shifting. I had never heard such a sound, doubly moving because it rang out against the silence of the winter landscape. I looked around for the source but didn't even know what to look for. As I came down to the edge of the creek, I noticed balls of ice suspended over the surface of the frozen water, hanging from branches low over the stream, vibrating as the branches shook in the light wind. This ethereal symphony was the voice of hundreds of glowing ice balls vibrating in the noonday sunlight.

I sat down in the snow, an audience of one, and gave my full attention to this remarkable concert. When my feet became uncomfortably cold and I began the long slog back to the cabin, a thought arose in my mind about the shallowness problem. I had a sense, a conviction actually, that there was a vital connection between the experience of silent solitude and the development of resources to handle misfortunes in my life. I had an intuition that I would be able to handle them as they arose, and that the experience of solitude would help me to do so. I stood still in the twilight, halfway across our neighbor's frozen pond, savoring this insight, as a light snow began to fall.

As I sat before the fire that icy winter evening, I felt a powerful connection to this valley and an enormous joy beside the frozen river. When I was quiet enough, I could feel it with my whole body. I hadn't figured out how to bring that part of myself into environmental advocacy. In fact, the legal discourse pushed it farther away, helped fence off my feelings for the natural world from the issues that we were framing for decision. The overlay of legal analysis left out the poetry and romance of wild places, the subtle and powerful relationship of nature to my health and well-being.

For me, personally, the Alaska pipeline case always involved a web of abstractions. At the time, I had never been to Alaska nor had I seen the Brooks Range or the Arctic Ocean. I approached the pipeline as a lawyer's task, with rules to be understood and applied, facts to be marshaled, logical arguments made, a specific result to be obtained. It was a creative piece of work, but it left me feeling incomplete.

I thought about the transparent river, flowing under the crystalline ice, which had given me so clear a view of the life of the river—the weeds bobbing in the currents, the fish swimming indolently upstream, the air bubbles sliding downstream, pressed against the ice. All of this was invisible when the surface of the water was ruffled by gusts of wind. I wanted to cultivate that clarity of vision, and to bring that sense of wonder to my work and to my life. I wanted to be able to touch back continually into such deep engagement with things as they are, and build my understanding and actions on that foundation, without distortion or distracting abstractions.

I began to understand that this clarity and connection flowed from stillness and silence, especially in natural surroundings. Later, I came to realize that such opportunities for reflection and introspection were essential to the cultivation of wisdom.

As CLASP's reputation grew, the circle of friends that had launched it began to disperse, with many of its lawyers leaving to spread the public interest law concept. Jim Moorman left to launch the Sierra Club Legal Defense Fund (subsequently renamed Earthjustice), later returning to Washington to head the Lands Division of the Justice Department. Geoff Cowan went to California to teach and practice public interest law, later becoming Director of the Voice of America, then Dean of the Annenberg School of Communications at the University of Southern California. Bruce Terris began his own environmental law firm, handling precedent-setting cases in the federal courts.

Former CLASP students moved into leadership positions in communications law, environmental advocacy, consumer protection, and public health. CLASP has had a succession of dedicated and creative leaders, gradually shifting its work into the area of poverty law and continuing to exercise strong leadership in the public interest advocacy community.[3]

I left CLASP in 1974 to establish the Council for Public Interest Law (a joint venture of the American Bar Association and three foundations). As the Council's executive director, I mobilized a coalition of public interest law firms, foundations, and leaders of the organized bar to assure the survival of public interest law and its continued expansion. We published a book-length report, *Balancing the Scales of Justice*, which analyzed the contributions of public interest law and proposed ways to foster its continuation and growth. Our recommendations were greeted respectfully—and widely disregarded.

In particular, we had recommended that courts award attorney's fees to public interest litigants who succeeded on the merits of their cases. We were encouraged by the court of appeals decision in the Alaska pipeline case in which we had been awarded a substantial fee, a decision that seemed to hold out the promise of a major funding source for public interest advocacy. But the Supreme Court reversed the decision in 1975 by a vote of five to two (with two justices not participating), limiting the authority of the courts to award fees in such cases, and eliminating the possibility that self-sustaining public interest law practice would become a viable alternative on a wide scale.[4]

After spending a year as a visiting professor at Stanford Law School, in 1978 I joined the Georgetown Law School faculty, combining traditional academic life with public interest practice as the director of its in-house public interest law firm, the Institute for Public Representation, which had been launched by Vic Kramer after he left CLASP.[5]

My Georgetown experience was influenced by what I learned in a two-week seminar held in the Colorado Rockies at Devil's Thumb in 1979. It was a program to introduce law professors to the insights of humanistic psychology in order to deepen their approach to law teaching and to make them more effective and self-aware law teachers.

After we had been meeting for a few days and felt that we had moved a good distance—becoming more open, more trusting, more connected to each other—Janet Lederman, a senior teacher from the Esalen Institute, arrived. Judging from her expression as she passed among us, Lederman seemed to think that we were just a bunch of uptight law professors. The first exercise she gave us is hard for me to even describe, much less imagine that I actually did it.

She brought us together in our main meeting room, assigned us a partner, and had each of us put on a blindfold. My partner was a small, rather proper woman who taught commercial law at George Washington Law School. When we were blindfolded, Lederman had each pair begin to discuss our strengths and weaknesses as law teachers. After ten minutes, she had us continue the conversations, still blindfolded, without using words. We did this at first, awkwardly and with embarrassment, through physical touch. "Try to understand each other," she said. "Get a feel for who your partner is, deeper than words."

Then she split up the pairs of partners and had us go to opposite sides of the rather large room, still blindfolded. "Now," she said, "I want you to find your partner using sounds but not words." I thought this was impossible, outrageous. We'd be here forever, doing this asinine and humiliating exercise. But I was willing to give it a try, and I started to make a quiet, tentative barking sound.

There was, of course, a cacophony of law professors making strange noises. My first reaction was that this sounded quite a lot like faculty meetings I had participated in. Then I started to sort out among the sounds a number of clear and recognizable voices. But my partner had a smaller, unfamiliar voice, so it took us a long time. We began a slow minuet, moving cautiously to avoid trampling each other. After about three minutes, people started to laugh hysterically as they found their partners, and within a couple of minutes we had all made the connection.

We sat in a circle, blindfolds off, to discuss our experience and what we drew from it. Naturally, I wasn't the only person who had felt insulted and humiliated by the exercise. All of us expressed our own surprise at the fact that we had actually done it. The angriest among us, an African American professor from the University of Pittsburgh, said, "Yes, I did this exercise and found my partner, but what the hell does this have to do with being a law professor?" There was a moment of silence. It was clear that Lederman wasn't going to say anything to explain what this was all about.

Joe, who taught civil procedure at the University of Iowa, said, "I can't say how this is going to affect my law teaching, but I'll tell you, it's changed me in some way. I did something that I thought was impossible, I did something that I thought was demeaning, I did something that leaves me with a slightly embarrassed feeling about having done it at all. But I contacted some parts of my brain and some skill at focusing my attention that I had no idea that I had. I'm going to listen differently in the classroom, more attentive to the music behind the words, and more sensitive to the nonverbal ways that I can make a connection to each student."

I resolved to draw on the techniques and insights from Devil's Thumb in teaching the course in Legal Ethics in order to introduce the students to the emotional component of the lawyer's complex ethical choices. Of course, it was easier to do this kind of activity in the high Rockies, below the towering peaks of the Continental Divide; and harder to do it in a sealed, air-conditioned room, under fluorescent lights, with seventy-five students sitting at tables bolted to the floor. But I tuned down the exercises to accommodate the different conditions.

I led a guided visualization exercise, calling on the students to shut their eyes and visualize themselves in a conference with an important client who asks them to forge a piece of evidence. I asked them to get in touch with their feelings when they hear this request, and with any sensation that they experienced in their bodies. Then I asked them to break into pairs to reflect on and discuss this experience. I emphasized that I wanted them to focus on their emotional feelings and physical experience, not analyze the legal and ethical issues in their client's request. After a few minutes, we opened a general discussion in the whole class. I was struck by the intensity of the responses some of the students gave—some felt outrage, some assumed that that this sort of thing was routine in law practice, some felt a physical constriction in their abdomen. One student said that she had never been asked about her feelings since she had entered law school. Then we discussed several possible responses to the client; I thought that the exercise had gone pretty well.

A few days later, I was called to the dean's office. Three of my students had gone to the dean to complain that I was not adequately preparing them for the bar exam. "I know that you are covering the black letter rules, too," he said, "but I think you might go easy on the guided visualizations." At first, I didn't quite know how to register this. Was this an official rebuke? Would a note of the students' complaint go into my file?

It seemed that Georgetown was not going to be a comfortable setting for my experiments in innovative legal education.

CLASP lawsuits had helped usher in an era when environmental activists and other citizen groups became a more important factor in governmental decisions. The concept of public interest advocacy was well established and a substantial literature was developing, analyzing its impact. It was even spreading to other countries. Some public interest firms, like the Natural Resources Defense Council and the Environmental Defense Fund, were beginning to morph into large membership organizations with a formidable expertise that enhanced their legal skill with scientific know-how and media savvy. Ralph Nader developed his own network of public interest law firms and helped secure passage of critical legislation to protect consumers, the environment, and workers.

But the public interest law successes were becoming fewer and less dramatic. And the victories could be frustratingly transitory. In the environmental field, our victories could be overwhelmed by the pressure of politically powerful corporations. In the Alaska pipeline case, for example, after our success in court, the Interior Department was overseeing the emergence of a more responsible plan, a pipeline that was not a short-fused environmental time bomb.

But the energy crisis of the early seventies gave the oil companies the opportunity to end-run the Interior Department process while the hearings before it were still under way. Using their political muscle, they sought passage of a special law that would permit the construction of the pipeline without further consideration of environmental issues and would waive the limitations on the width of their right-of-way. There was a stiff debate in the Senate. Oil company lobbyists applied maximum muscle to pass a provision to protect the legislation from judicial review. In the end the Senate was evenly split on this provision. It took the vote of Vice President Spiro Agnew—soon to resign in disgrace—to break the deadlock.[6]

The pipeline project went forward. It was a different and better pipeline for our efforts—better designed, more earthquake-resistant, and more respectful of the environment—but by no means foolproof, as the Exxon Valdez disaster in March 1989 was to demonstrate.

The early success of the public interest lawyers also helped generate a fierce and effective backlash. The conservatives' initial response to the public interest law firms' successes was to copy the form and establish their own network of "public interest law firms" devoted to the defense of corporate interests. They supplemented their law firms by creating conservative think tanks and setting out to make the federal courts less hospitable to government regulation and public interest litigation.

The Reagan revolution threatened to make the Washington environment toxic for the public interest law enterprise, closing the opportunities for public participation in government decisions that had opened in the preceding decade. The Reagan cult of individual accumulation made idealism suspect and cast doubt on the possibility of disinterested commitment to public service.

6

FACING A TOUGH REALITY

I was sitting in my Georgetown office when I received an unexpected call from Abe Chayes, with whom I had remained friends since we met at the Harvard Faculty Club. He got right to the point: "I've heard about the perfect job for you. They're starting a law school in the City University of New York and looking for a new dean. It's supposed to be a public interest law school, which means that you would have a chance to rethink what legal education ought to look like, and, perhaps, to build public interest law into a significant branch of the profession. The chancellor of CUNY called to ask if I had any ideas. I'd like to submit your name."

I thought back to a conversation that Abe and I had in a Japanese restaurant in St. Paul in 1976, as we swiped raw fish through soy sauce and wasabi with a group of public interest lawyers and professors. Chief Justice Warren Burger had convened a meeting of leaders in the legal profession to discuss his program of law reform, the core of which was designed to make the court system more efficient in handling corporate litigation. Our group was committed to the idea that poor people were inadequately served in the justice system and that this was a matter that should receive priority attention. I had persuaded the Chief Justice's lieutenant that it could be seriously embarrassing if a conference on the reasons for popular discontent with the courts included no participants who advocated for poor people and others unrepresented in the legal process. I was scheduled to speak the next morning, and Abe was encouraging me to be really tough, to confront the Chief Justice with some issues that he might not want to hear, about injustices embedded in the legal system.

I took his advice and gave a forthright speech, addressing the inadequacies of the legal process from the perspective of the people who are excluded, while Chief Justice Burger sat in the center of the front row, scowling, with his arms folded. Not even a gesture of polite applause after I finished.

"Let's go slow with this, Abe," I said, remembering the incident in St. Paul. "The last time you gave me advice, you told me to get up and spit in the eye of the Chief Justice. Now you want me to go to New York City, the cynicism capital of the world, to a gritty urban university that skates along the edge of bankruptcy, and invent a new kind of public interest legal education? You sound like the boxing manager pushing his man out into the ring and assuring him, 'He can't lay a glove on us.'"

Meanwhile, I began thinking about Abe's proposition. Even though I doubted whether his life in the Harvard cloisters and in the world of striped-pants diplomacy gave him enough information to know what it would be like to start a public interest law school at CUNY, I asked him to nominate me for the deanship. No harm in tossing my hat in the ring. I could check out the situation and decide later if I really wanted to pursue it.

Several weeks later, I met with Saul Cohen, the President of Queens College, a unit of CUNY, at the Shoreham Hotel in Washington, where he was attending a convention of educational administrators. Cohen had been entrepreneurial and effective in championing the new law school concept—shepherding the proposal through the state's education bureaucracy, assembling political supporters, and obtaining start-up money from the state legislature. The chancellor of CUNY had delegated to him responsibility for the dean search, and he apparently had concluded that I would be a good dean for the new law school. I had created new legal institutions and carried them from the stage of good ideas into real operations with lawyers and secretaries, typewriters and filing cabinets.

He was a flattering and enthusiastic recruiter. In full salesman mode, he offered a euphoric description of the opportunity awaiting me. CUNY and the legislature were solidly behind the venture. I could develop a unique program devoted to public interest law. A handsome facility would be provided in Queens. A core collection of law books for the library had already been assembled. I was in a mood to be flattered—and I wanted to believe that the law school project was broadly and generously supported. At CLASP I had launched a small program to educate public interest lawyers. Now, here was a university prepared to start a law school to carry that work forward on a grand scale. I would have the opportunity to put together the faculty and student body, as well as design the curriculum.

I was confident that I had the necessary tools to do this job. I was a different person from the Yale graduate who had begun as a corporate lawyer. I had rejected a career following the conventional path to wealth and prestige, created activist institutions to pursue a social justice agenda, and begun to explore the inner work that would nourish and deepen my work in the world. The deanship seemed a logical next step, one that would allow me to capitalize and expand on my previous work.

Nonetheless, before making a decision, I arranged to talk to Tim Healy, the president of Georgetown University—a Jesuit and a Renaissance scholar who had previously served as the academic vice president of the City University of New York. He knew the territory intimately. He was a jovial, cosmopolitan, and engaging person with a critical mind.

Tim and I had a long lunch together at the antique refectory table in his dark-paneled office in the Gothic building at the center of the Georgetown campus. Offering an excellent Chardonnay along with his advice, he reminisced about his role in CUNY, championing open admissions and low tuition, through the struggles of the sixties. He told me about the importance of CUNY's historic role as an avenue for generations of immigrants and poor people to get into the mainstream of American life. "There is no other university like it," he said.

And then, as his expression became more serious, he added the caveat: "This job will test you in every way possible—intellectual, physical, emotional, and—you may not buy this—spiritual. You will have to develop the capability to understand that remarkable city and that complicated conglomerate university. Issues of race and class are hidden behind every dispute. This is not a world of abstractions. It is grit, aggression, and concrete reality. You will have to see things clearly."

If I accepted the deanship, it would be a novel challenge for me. Even as a public interest lawyer, pushing against powerful corporations, I lived among abstract principles, bounded by the rules of civil procedure and the polite, ceremonial conventions of the federal courts. When I began CLASP, I had the back-door retreat option of returning to private law practice. This time, there would be no easy fallback if the venture crashed and burned. I would have to be more resourceful, move more quickly, rely more fully on intuition. I would have to jump the great and unfamiliar chasms of race and class on a daily basis, doing aerial flips without a safety net.

But Tim wasn't finished. "When you stand up in front of your first-year class—150 people who are gambling their careers on this new law school, whose friends and loved ones have told them that they are nuts to be going to an unaccredited law school in its first year of operations—they are going to be looking hard at you, not just listening to your words, but trying to figure out who you are. Are you someone they can trust to represent this fledgling institution effectively before the skeptics in the bar association, before the Albany politicians?"

He took a sip of Chardonnay and looked directly at me. "You have done a lot of jobs where you could succeed if you were smart, like a good law review editor. This isn't one of those jobs. You will need those skills, but they are only the beginning. I think you can do it—but don't underestimate what is being asked of you. Several new law schools were started in the New York area in the last few years. None of the founding deans were around to hand out diplomas at the first graduation."

It felt as if Tim were preparing me not only to get ready for a fight but to take on a dangerous combat mission behind enemy lines. He was telling me that I would have to be prepared to confront powerful adversaries who would be dubious of a law school with a public interest mission. They would have the capacity to destroy it or corrupt its mission. He was quite specifically reminding me that others with powerful minds and stellar credentials had failed, and that I could too.

He was right—I had succeeded as a public interest lawyer primarily because I was smart and focused. But that wouldn't be enough in this new position. It reminded me of the first time I tried to paddle a canoe in a fast-moving river. I had been a confident paddler on lakes in all conditions—strong winds, heavy rains, high waves. But that did not prepare me for the river's currents and eddies, or for the force of fast-moving water when the canoe spins sideways against a boulder. On the river I had to develop new skills—the ability to read the surface of the water quickly and precisely and to focus on the present moment with clarity, while at the same time anticipating the next set of rapids.

The deanship in Queens was going to require just as big a shift in skills and perspective, and the consequences could be much larger than a capsize and a swim through rapids. It would require some of the same clarity, focus, and intuition I had learned on the river so that I could find calm in the midst of contending forces and pressures, and be balanced enough to decide when to compromise and when to refuse to yield.

If I wanted to educate lawyers to be whole people, Father Healy, speaking to me as much as a priest as an educator, was telling me that I was going to have to be a whole person myself.

Susan and I sat together in our living room the night after my conversation with Tim. We added up some of the pros and cons. Phil and Ruth had already gone off to college, but Bob would be leaving his friends just as he was entering junior high school. Susan would be leaving her burgeoning career as a social worker and looking for work in a new community.

For the first time, I would be drawn out of the safe harbor of elite education and sophisticated law practice into a world of urban tension and underfunded public education. A municipal university system would confront my idealism with the reality of big city public education—scarce resources, low status, and many students who had struggled to reach law school, and were still contending with the burdens of poverty and limited educational opportunities. We talked about how big a risk we were willing to run. We could rent our house in Washington, and move back if things didn't work out.

The atmosphere in Washington made the decision easier. I would be leaving as the Reagan team was putting its imprint on the city, with their commitment to acquisitiveness and self-absorbed individualism, an environment in which it was hard to anticipate forward motion in public interest law activities. I had thought that the Nixon years were the low watermark for American democracy, for compassion and inclusiveness, but I had underestimated what was ahead. Reagan tapped into a different kind of conservatism. The worst abusers of the public interest became the government officials charged with protecting public values. James Watt, an alumnus of a right-wing anti-environment public interest law firm, a champion of wilderness exploitation, became Secretary of the Interior.

We decided that the move to New York made sense. The risk was great, but so was the payoff—creating a new kind of law school to prepare our graduates for work in public interest law. When Cohen called to offer me the deanship, I accepted. This law school would be a good place to work for social justice in the Reagan years, which I thought, mistakenly, were a temporary aberration. Training the next generation of public interest lawyers seemed like a worthwhile way to ride out these hard times.

My appointment was followed by a wave of good press. It was satisfying to see my picture in the *New York Times* with an enthusiastic article about the new public interest law school to be established within the City University system.[1] The American Bar Association and groups of legal educators invited me to give speeches at their gatherings and meetings. The fact that I would have thirty-five law teaching jobs to fill over the next three years made me a person of intense interest to many people who wanted to become law professors. People at other law schools who were frustrated by the rigidities of the legal education system saw an opportunity for innovation and growth in the new school. All of this was exciting, and it was easy to get an inflated sense of myself and the importance of the undertaking.

I had encouraging success in recruiting an outstanding team to plan and develop the school. In the spring of 1982, while I was still teaching at Georgetown and commuting to New York, I invited Howard Lesnick, a senior professor at the University of Pennsylvania Law School and an old friend, to join the faculty as the chief academic planner. I was asking him to give up his tenured position at a high-status Ivy League law school in order to join me at a new school that existed only on paper and had no solid assurances of ever opening its doors. I was amazed that he agreed, and I felt affirmed in my decision to accept the deanship.

Howard was a visiting professor that year at New York University Law School, and he was living in an NYU penthouse high above Washington Square. I sat with him, and the other members of our planning team, on his terrace for many hours, talking about the way the school would look and run. I was doing what I enjoy most: sitting with friends, spinning out new ideas, pushing the limits of possibility, and sharpening and clarifying our ideas. Howard brought to the venture a deeper dissatisfaction with the traditional legal education, and a more fully focused plan for how to replace it. His view was that we had an opportunity for a grand experiment, and that our options would only narrow over time. "We will never again be able to be as experimental as we can be now," he maintained.

I was more cautious, suggesting that taking on all of it at once might not be humanly possible: a wholly new curriculum; the search for physical space; developing criteria for students and faculty selection and then recruiting them; building the constituency for the law school in legal education, in CUNY, and in Queens. I

would have been content to leave more of the traditional curriculum in place. I found myself reining in the enthusiasm of my colleagues, insisting on the "reality factor." Howard, a strong-minded
and persuasive advocate, had a short fuse. "I never thought that you
would be the one with cement galoshes," he growled.

But Howard and I had much in common; he was a former CLASP
trustee and an alumnus of the Devil's Thumb program, and we
agreed on the core elements of our plan for the Law School. We had
an opportunity—to create a new law school from the ground up—
from admissions criteria, through curriculum design, to the place-
ment process. We would bring a new consciousness into law studies,
moving compassion and the public interest to the center. Our law
school would be a humane, integrated place where the emotional
complexities and the value issues that lawyers tended to slight would
have a central and honored place. We would teach the traditional
adversarial skills, along with the softer, collaborative side of lawyering—the strategies to find agreements between disputing parties,
and to assert forgiveness, generosity, and community as important
values in the legal system. Our graduates would bring this perspective into their careers and begin to influence other institutions.

We wanted to present the students from the first day with an
understanding of the lawyer's reality: that law is always practiced in
a human context, that the lawyer has to understand the clients'
problems fully and not immediately translate complicated real-
world dilemmas into legal categories that can be dealt with by filing a lawsuit or revising a contract. A dispute between husband and
wife that has implications for their children and community must
be fully understood, and may best be dealt with through mediation
or counseling rather than litigation. Even more radical was our idea
that the life experience of the lawyer is likely to affect the way she
responds to a client's problem—and that she should be conscious
of what she brings to the interaction.

Since they wanted to become public interest lawyers, our students would have the added challenge of sharpening and clarifying their goals in their professional and personal lives. What clients and causes did they want to serve? And what kind of people did they want to become? We wanted to encourage our students to take personal responsibility for their decisions and their consequences. Each decision should draw on the resources of the whole person— their values, emotions, empathy, sense of justice. Cultivating a humanistic perspective could nurture and deepen the lawyer's capacity for service.

It was an inspiring vision of a new legal education, well worth struggling for.[2]

When we came down from the penthouse terrace above Washington Square, we found that the world looked quite different at ground level. Euphoria and visionary planning quickly gave way to more pedestrian concerns and a sense of urgency as it came home to me that we were going to have to begin recruiting students in the fall of 1982, just a few short months away, if we were to have a first-year class that would begin the next year. We were scheduled to publish and distribute a credible brochure that described a new kind of law program with enough specificity and detail that serious students would think CUNY was the law school they wanted to attend. We had to list at least a few faculty members, present a coherent outline of the curriculum, and make a plausible prediction of what the building would look like and where it would be located.

When we rode the Number 7 train and the bus to our temporary quarters in a remote corner of Queens, we found a place that was truly unfamiliar. A couple of times each week, when the weather conditions were wrong, the roar of the planes taking off from LaGuardia Airport every few minutes made it impossible to talk or think.

The summer of 1982 was a sobering period for me, with a number of unpleasant surprises. There was New York City itself. It was hard to be in New York City and retain much confidence in public interest law—or in law itself. A layer of cynicism envelopes the city, making any kind of idealistic enterprise suspect from the start. The most frequent questions I heard when I arrived were "Who needs another law school?" and "Isn't *public interest lawyer* a contradiction in terms?" Lawyers who worked for citizen groups in the state legislature were known as "goo-goos," a term that suggests naïve do-gooders and gooey sentimentalists, people not to be taken seriously.

New York is a tough city, where no one expects to get an even break, not on the streets and not in the courts. As jaded as Washington was in those post-Watergate days, it was by comparison a city of idealists and utopians. When I thought of courts, I pictured the Grecian temple of the Supreme Court and the dignified courthouse in which I had clerked, strolling on the Mall—a far cry from the graffiti-spattered courthouse in Queens, where the judges struggle to keep the creaking and overloaded dockets ahead of the ultimate gridlock. The idea of public interest law assumed the existence of legal norms that had some vitality and courts willing to enforce those norms. In New York, as I was coming to understand it, these ideas seemed dangerously unrealistic.

I experienced the toughness of the city on a more personal level as I drove to the Law School on the Long Island Expressway, and saw the burned-out skeletons of cars lying by the side of the road. At first I assumed that people must dump their wrecks rather than undergo the expense and inconvenience of taking them to a junkyard. A taxi driver explained my error—these were functioning automobiles forced to come to a stop because of a flat tire or an empty gas tank. When the driver went for help, the sharks descended, stripping the car of anything of value—tires, doors, engine parts. Then they might smash the windows and set it on fire, leaving the shell standing on the side of the road, a reminder of the tenuousness of security, the foolishness of relying on the law or the social order to provide real protection. When, one sunny afternoon, I saw a group of men stripping the doors off a car on the LIE, it undermined my own sense of personal security. And it reminded me that students who had grown up in this reality might be skeptical about an educational program that asked them to let their guard down.

My sense of being in alien territory was enhanced by the remoteness of Queens, a place visited by people from Manhattan only if they were going to the New York airports. This was the place where Archie Bunker lived. The Queens College campus was far from the New York I knew—the subway system ran nowhere near it and the bus connections were slow and erratic.

Starting a law school in Queens had more in common with starting a law school in Schenectady than it did with starting a law school in Manhattan. Knowing that the NYU Law School was a hub of legal activity, I had anticipated making the new CUNY Law School a similar hub—with better connections to the community of public interest law activists. Little did I know that no program in Queens would draw Manhattan lawyers, even if the nine justices of the Supreme Court were all participating.

When I took the job, I thought I would be a colleague of the leaders of the Manhattan bar. Instead, my connections in the legal world were in the Queens bar. While I found a few lawyers in Queens who understood and supported our program, most of them were provincial small-town lawyers who happened to practice on the edge of one of the greatest centers of legal sophistication in the world. This realization heightened my sense of isolation and vulnerability. I discovered that the practice of law in Queens was closely aligned with the practice of politics. Success as a lawyer depended on a cordial relationship with the political machine, headed by Donald Manes, one of the last of the old-style political bosses. Lawyers who were close to Manes prospered. Any lawyer who aspired to become a judge was well-advised to stay on his good side, which raised problems for any lawyer who filed a suit alleging election fraud or challenging corruption in a Queens agency.

I first met Donald Manes (pronounced *Man*-ess) at a party held in honor of my appointment at Saul Cohen's official residence, a large Gatsby-like house with two-story Ionic columns overlooking a bay of Long Island Sound, on the high-income northeastern edge of Queens. Cohen introduced me to Manes with surprising deference. Manes was a short, heavy man, with thick features, crude manners, and a quick New York–style wit—irreverent and obscene, a political Don Rickles. His friend Joe Murphy, the former president of Queens College, told him that he could never run for statewide office unless he did three things: lose weight, take speech lessons, and read a book. He never took any of Joe's advice.

As soon as Cohen walked away, Manes grabbed the lapel of my suit jacket and drew me into a corner. At that time I had never heard of Manes, but people in the state with any political savvy knew he was a key man for getting things done in the city, and, often, in the state. Manes put his arm over my shoulder and pulled me closer to him. He looked me in the eye and said, "This law school exists because I want it. Queens has been shortchanged. Brooklyn has a great museum and music academy. The Bronx at least has a zoo." Almost a decade earlier, Manes had concluded that Queens should have a new law school. "But I was a practical person," Manes told me. "I realized that there were already a lot of law schools in the city, and that many of them—especially St. John's, which is in Queens—would not welcome new, low-tuition competition. I also knew that a new law school was going to cost a lot of money. So I decided to call it a public interest law school. Since it had a special mission, it was different from all the other law schools and not a direct competitor. No one knew what it meant, and I liked the sound of it. We could get the approvals we needed and the start-up funding, and then we would figure out what a public interest law school is."

So the public interest law school idea was a cynical gimmick to stifle criticism, I thought. This school is a patronage operation. I am a lieutenant in the Manes political machine! If I had believed that this new law school was simply a product of Donald Manes's political influence, I would not have accepted the deanship. It was a hard job anyway, and this open-ended obligation made it seem impossible. I was a good-government person, a reformer. I believed in the merit selection of judges. My past success had rested on my doing good work and producing results. Now I was facing a situation where my success might be determined, not by my performance, but my ability to keep Donald Manes happy. Even worse, it wasn't only my well-being that was at stake. The future of the school and its students depended on it. My desire to do good work in the world had led me to become a vassal of a man so cynical that he made it embarrassing to even talk about the public interest.

I began to speculate about the ways that the Law School would be expected to repay our debt to Manes. How could we start a public interest law school if Manes thought he owned it, if he saw it as an integral part of the Queens machine? I wanted to train lawyers to fight City Hall, to challenge the corruption and cronyism that Manes embodied.

"We want this law school to be a high-class operation," Manes said, as if he were reading my thoughts. "You don't have to worry about me looking over your shoulder and placing my friends on your faculty." Nonetheless, he took this occasion to urge me to hire one of his friends at the Law School as an administrator. "She will silence any critics who feel that the school is really a foreign institution being thrust into Queens by a group of outsiders."

A few days later he seemed surprised when I actually checked his friend's references and tried to make an independent judgment about her qualifications. I found that she was experienced and well-regarded, but sure enough, her husband was a political wheeler-dealer in the city and Manes's tennis partner. "She can be your ambassador to Queens," he said.

As he surveyed the room and whispered to me perceptive and funny comments, skewering some of the prominent guests, Manes told me that Queens was full of enemies of the Law School, waiting for the enterprise to stumble, and they would come forward angrily when that happened. "When you turn down one of their sons for admission, they will smile and say that there are no hard feelings and that you are just doing your job. And then they will look for their first chance to stab you in the back."

Yet I grew to like Manes. He was funny, lewd, and shrewd, and he had a keen ability to assess people's strengths and weaknesses. When we had an inauguration program for the school, addressed by Governor Mario Cuomo, the room was full of well-dressed women and men. Manes came in a polyester maroon blazer and a white-on-white shirt, as if he were going to dinner at a third-rate golf club. I found this endearing, a man who was doing it his way, making his own rules. Still, his relationship to the Law School was a constant challenge.

As we moved into the initial planning year, our time to prepare for the admission of our first class, I discovered that I could not rely on most of the commitments that Saul Cohen had given me. I viewed our letter of understanding as a contract; he considered it a statement of aspirations and a framework for negotiations. There was no building dedicated to Law School use. The funding of the Law School was tenuous and short-term. He had in mind that the Law School would be an integral part of Queens College and that the dean would be like the chairman of the English Department. He began acting on Law School matters unilaterally—such as the submission of a budget request for first-year operations—without even consulting me.

Because there was no building for the Law School, in the summer of 1983, only three months before students were to arrive, we had to scramble to renovate and furnish a rundown elementary school to house it temporarily in time for the opening. The books that had been purchased for the law library were out of date and moldering in a basement where they had been damaged badly in a flood.

More upsetting than any of this, Cohen had a fundamentally different vision for the Law School than I did. He wanted a traditional law school with only cosmetic modifications to tilt the program slightly in the direction of public interest law. He anticipated that the most successful graduates would go to prestigious corporate law firms and many of the other students would go into conventional bureaucratic careers in the city and state.

When I had originally discussed the deanship with him, I made it clear that I had something quite different in mind. I was candid in setting forth my vision before I accepted the position. Cohen had nodded his head with seeming approval, but he never gave up the ideal of a conventional law school that would be attractive to Nassau County suburbanites looking for a professional career.

After a bruising confrontation over my authority to choose my own administrative assistant, I wondered whether I shouldn't get out now, before our first students had been selected, while I still had my reputation and integrity intact, before I drowned in this swamp of broken promises and political corruption.

I had a moment of hope when Joe Murphy returned in 1983 as CUNY's new chancellor, its highest officer. This was the same Joe Murphy who had been the president of Queens College in the early seventies at the time the Law School idea was conceived. Cohen had opposed Murphy's return as chancellor, and the ill will between the two men was barely disguised. Murphy had a role in the early days of the Peace Corps and he retained some of the style and energy of the Kennedys and the New Frontier. He sometimes fell into the socialist rhetoric he had absorbed at the knees of his mother's Jewish radical parents. I thought he would be a good ally.

Shortly after his arrival, Murphy invited me to join him at the Association for a Better New York, a power breakfast of deal-makers, at the Waldorf Astoria. He was the featured speaker. I was delighted when, before the full ballroom, he described the Law School as one of the most important new CUNY initiatives. Then he invited me to stand, and after the polite applause had faded, he said, "If any of you have any contracts—any students you want to see admitted to the Law School—just contact the Dean directly. Don't come to me. Someone in this system has to have some integrity."

I stood for a brief moment gasping for breath, then sat down as quickly as I could. I could not believe what I had heard. The last thing we needed was the idea that anyone with political clout and a child who couldn't get into any other law school could find a place at CUNY. And, worse, they should call me directly with their "contracts." I felt like walking out of the room. I had hoped that this man would really understand and support what we were trying to do. But he seemed totally unreliable. He was playing his own game of political postures and power maneuvers that I could not even fathom.

Later, when I complained about his irresponsible comment before that influential audience, he shrugged and said, "We rescued the Law School from the clutches of these whores and hacks and now we have to negotiate the price of it. Running an institution is a sleazy business. If you're too pure for the job, you shouldn't be doing it."

One night Susan and I went down to Manhasset Bay after dinner to paddle our canoe in the still water and watch the sunset.

"I wouldn't have accepted the position if I had known then what I know now," I told her.

"Of course not," she said. "But it might be too soon to declare that the job is impossible. Why not talk it over with Ralph Siu before you do anything drastic."

I called Ralph and told him about my struggles, the political context, and the commitments to the new law school that evaporated as soon as they were examined. He suggested a lunch at the Cosmos Club on my next visit to Washington. When I arrived, he was in the lobby to greet me, with his usual gracious smile and his manner that suggested he had nothing else in the world that he would rather do than have lunch with me—an assurance that I would enjoy his undivided attention. After we were seated and I ordered, he said, "That sounds good, I'll have the same."

Before the food arrived, I launched into my litany of obstacles, grievances, and betrayals—Manes's cynicism, Cohen's interference, Murphy's glib indifference.

He responded with a question: "Do you know the game of Chinese baseball?"

"No, I don't think so. I know that the Japanese are good baseball players."

"No, Chinese baseball is something different. The game is exactly the same as American baseball but there is one rule that is different. When the pitcher throws the ball, anyone on the field can move any base—so long as the ball is in play."

I laughed. "So a person skilled at American baseball might do very badly at Chinese baseball. He could run to second base and find that it wasn't there."

Ralph joined me, with his deep and hearty laugh. "Yes, that's right. You have to be quick-witted, agile, and prepared to shift course in light of new circumstances. I hope that you are ready to play Chinese baseball in Queens."

I was accustomed to playing games where the rules were relatively static and predictable: statutes, rules of court, and the code of civil procedure. When we created CLASP, we created new results within the old systems of rules, inventing new interpretations and stretching the boundaries. But I never had to cope with bases that were in a different place on each play.

Ralph interrupted my reflection. "Impermanence is the only thing that you can be certain about," he said. "What if Cohen gave you the most concrete assurances in the world? If the New York economy failed, or he got an offer to go to another university, or the board of trustees decided to close the Queens College campus altogether, what would those assurances be worth? You are wise to learn as much as you can about the surrounding circumstances and get the best assurances you can, but do not mistake them for something they aren't. You should only stay in this job if you're prepared to live with uncertainty, if you are prepared to try your hand at Chinese baseball."

While Ralph spoke, the waiter cleared the table and the dining room grew quiet. Ralph continued: "In deciding whether to stay, learn as much as you can about the details, analyze the facts as closely as you can, compare the position to other possible alternatives, and then set all that aside. Step back from your analysis and make your decision based on an apprehension of the totality, listening to the voice of intuition. Once you have made up your mind, stick to your decision and—as Truman used to say—do your damnedest."

By then, we had finished our coffee and were walking out past the wall of Nobel laureates. I wondered how many of them were skilled at Chinese baseball. Although I didn't fully understand Ralph's words at the time, they gave me a framework to reflect on the challenges and problems that I was facing. If I saw my life in Queens as Chinese baseball, I thought that I could learn to play pretty well. Since I had left Arnold & Porter, I had made some risky choices, forging new paths, and things had worked out for me. The new law school certainly ratcheted up the risk level, but I thought I could manage it if I followed Ralph's advice—see the situation realistically, without illusion, and don't expect to play on a field where the baselines were fixed and the rules unchanging.

After talking with Ralph, I decided that I could continue to build this Law School. We had a reasonable chance of creating an important new institution. The program was one I deeply believed in, and I had not been asked yet to do anything that really violated my principles. No need to quit at this point.

As my relationship with Cohen deteriorated, I had an opportunity to assess where Murphy stood on the Law School. Cohen's challenge to the autonomy of the Law School came to a head with my submission of the names of the six new faculty members to develop and teach the program for incoming first-year students in the fall. We had received over a thousand applications for faculty positions and interviewed about a hundred candidates. There was a large community of people who felt themselves invested in what we were doing. We had an excellent pool to choose from.

I had kept Cohen informed in a general way about our selection process, but I did not invite him to participate as we sorted through the applicants, nor did I invite him to interview the finalists. Perhaps I should have kept him more fully engaged, but I was concerned about his excessive intrusiveness and about the core disagreement over the Law School's public interest mission. I also wanted to bring together a faculty that was diverse in race, gender, and prior experience and shared a demonstrated commitment to public interest law. We did not use the selection criteria we had used at Arnold & Porter and at Georgetown Law School, focused single-mindedly on outstanding performance in elite law schools.

When I brought the six names forward, I was prepared for some give-and-take with Cohen. The day after I submitted their papers, his secretary called me and summoned me to a meeting in his office later that afternoon, not a good sign.

"I find your recommendations unacceptable," Cohen said to me, even before I sat down.

"Which ones?" I asked.

"All of them."

I caught my breath, trying to pause long enough to get calm and centered. I went through each of our recommendations, explaining to Cohen our reason for thinking that each had a special contribution to make to our public interest law program. They were an accomplished and diverse group, but he had expected a more conventional slate of candidates. The underlying gap in vision between us now starkly came to the surface.

Fortunately, Cohen was not the last word on the matter. The Law School and Queens College were both units of the City University, and I succeeded in bringing Joe Murphy, as chancellor, into the process. I also took the precaution of calling on Donald Manes, to fill him in on the situation and try to gain his support or neutrality. I described each of our faculty selections and their qualifications. Manes agreed to stay out of the matter. Nonetheless, he gave me this cautionary advice: "Queens, despite its two million people, is really a small town. If you fill the Law School up with a bunch of Communists and lefties, I'll drive you and the Law School out of the County." The comment was delivered with a smile, but I believed that he meant it and that he could do it.

So it was up to Murphy, who first tried personal diplomacy, calling Cohen and me to his house for a wine-soaked, inconclusive dinner. When that failed, he decided to forward the Law School's recommendations to the board of trustees with his support. The board approved all of the candidates, giving us the opportunity to convene the faculty in the summer of 1983 and launch the challenging process of inventing a first-year curriculum.

The battle over faculty was critical in establishing the autonomy of the Law School and its role as a CUNY-wide institution. But we had survived only because Manes had not taken a position and Murphy had supported our decisions. This was a weak foundation on which to rest the new Law School. Since I didn't really know what had motivated their decisions, I felt insecure about the future. Cohen was still the CEO of the largest employer in Queens and a powerful player in the CUNY system. It would be touchy to keep this support together as we went forward. I couldn't play this game of Russian roulette very often. Neither Manes nor Murphy wanted to expend their political capital, time, and effort in resolving disputes between Cohen and me.

The battle over faculty catalyzed Cohen's subterranean efforts to have me fired, with whispered accusations about my indifference to academic standards, my excessive commitment to minority recruitment, my unwillingness to accept his decisions. I found myself fending off his attacks, trying to maintain a civil working relationship with him, and at the same time trying to press ahead with our mission. But Cohen never succeeded in pushing me out, and recurring rumors began to circulate that he was a candidate for other jobs. In the spring of 1985, he resigned from the University to become a senior executive in a national Jewish organization.

With Cohen out of the picture, my life became easier, and I took some satisfaction in having protected our vision of the Law School in the face of this assault by a consummate bureaucratic infighter. But in order to do so, I had been forced to become a skillful bureaucratic manipulator myself. Moreover, I still had to do what was necessary to stay on good terms with Manes and the other Queens politicians who were responsible for keeping the Law School intact and its budget growing. I was drawn into a world of unprincipled compromises around student admissions. One state legislator, in the context of a conversation about an applicant, told me about the way that he had cut the budget of a state-funded university program because the dean had been unresponsive to his admissions recommendation. Manes and Murphy double-teamed me on the admission of the son of an important Queens functionary. Sometimes I stood on principle. Other times, I settled for the best compromise that I could make. I hated this pressure and was uncomfortable with the deals that I struck to keep the train on the tracks.

Though I was the founding dean, I lived with the paradox that the survival of our public interest law school rested with Donald Manes, a man who thought that every person had his price. I continued to develop a public interest law program that was prepared to deal with a multitude of legal and governmental failures but resolutely overlooked the abuses that were occurring in our back-yard. In 1986, after his scheme for skimming money paid for parking fines was exposed, his name would be well-known , synonymous with big city corruption and violation of public trust. He committed suicide after the story reached the newspapers, before our first class had graduated.[3]

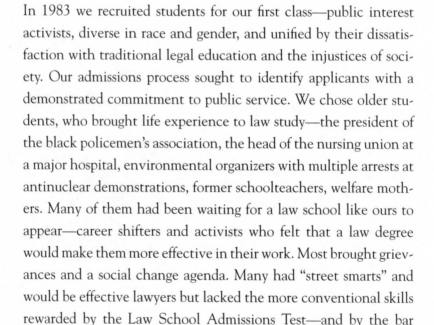

In 1983 we recruited students for our first class—public interest activists, diverse in race and gender, and unified by their dissatisfaction with traditional legal education and the injustices of society. Our admissions process sought to identify applicants with a demonstrated commitment to public service. We chose older students, who brought life experience to law study—the president of the black policemen's association, the head of the nursing union at a major hospital, environmental organizers with multiple arrests at antinuclear demonstrations, former schoolteachers, welfare mothers. Many of them had been waiting for a law school like ours to appear—career shifters and activists who felt that a law degree would make them more effective in their work. Most brought grievances and a social change agenda. Many had "street smarts" and would be effective lawyers but lacked the more conventional skills rewarded by the Law School Admissions Test—and by the bar exam. The students were an intense, involved group, full of anger and empathy, mutual regard and intergroup hostility.

I was thrilled with the diversity of the student body, a sharp contrast to the homogeneous, cloistered world in which I had been educated and employed. During the first week of classes, I sat down with a group of students who were eating lunch together. "Do you realize that we have in this class a woman who worked for twenty years as a typesetter, and another woman who's a nun?"

"Yes," said one of the women. "I'm the typesetter."

And another woman, dressed in jeans and a sweatshirt, added, "And I'm the nun. I never would have gone to a regular law school, but this promises to be something special." We began comparing notes on whom we had met in the first-year class—a sociologist on the CUNY faculty, several nurses, a man who had taken eight years to complete college because he was driving a bus at night to support his family. Many of the students had already held leadership positions in environmental action groups and in inner-city community action organizations. I could see why Tim Healy had been in love with CUNY. We looked forward to getting to know each other better. I often spoke of these early classes of students as our cocreators of the Law School, and in a fundamental sense it was true. I admired the courage and initiative that brought them to this new, unaccredited institution.

I had anticipated admitting some students with more traditional credentials, who could aspire to more established law schools but would choose to come to CUNY because of what we stood for, because they had a deep dedication to a public interest law career. In order to recruit such students, I called on my friend Stan Katz, who taught legal history at Princeton and advised the Pre-Law Club. He invited me to come and give a talk about the Law School and then meet over dinner with some students who he thought might be interested.

At the end of dinner, after a polite conversation, one of the students said, "I want you to understand why none of us is going to apply to your school even though it sounds wonderful. We have been climbing the greasy pole of academic achievement too long to quit now. We are Princeton seniors with excellent records. We couldn't turn down Harvard Law School and accept CUNY; we wouldn't be able to explain it to our parents who have invested in our education, or to our friends." We successfully recruited some excellent students who chose us over more highly ranked schools, but the greasy-pole phenomenon limited their numbers. I was discouraged by this conversation and sobered by the fact that I, too, would not have had the commitment and confidence to take a CUNY-like opportunity when I was a college senior.

The students arrived at the Law School on a day that was electric with excitement and anticipation. We opened our doors in that converted elementary school in north Queens, near Utopia Boulevard, remote from Manhattan and from any reminders that we were near a sophisticated urban center. The school had hurriedly been repainted and full-size furniture had been moved in. We left the basketball hoop in the space that we partitioned off for the dean's office. Despite our ambitious program and our high-minded mission, we had to persuade ourselves and the students that this was a real law school. It was impossible to take ourselves too seriously in this setting, which was a good thing.

The faculty shared with the students the gritty reality of the New York streets—the complexity and frustration of New York over race, class, and gender—and the staccato impatience of New York interactions. Their attitude toward the law was quite different from what I was accustomed to. For many of the students and faculty, the law was not their friend. It was more likely to be a source of trouble than of support. The life of a committed lawyer was one of struggle against the indifference and hostility of powerful social forces. It was not even conceivable for a lawyer to do a little pro bono work at odd hours while spending the day orchestrating corporate takeovers.

Their anger and commitment made CUNY a place of high energy and high stress. Disagreements easily morphed into all-out battles over principles. I learned what real class resentment and educational disadvantage looked like. I was accustomed to a lower decibel level, to reasoned debate over issues that did not have such an intense personal charge. The feminists I worked with at CLASP were concerned with equal pay for equal work, abortion rights, and stopping sexual harassment. Some of the feminists here were attacking the nuclear family as an engine of patriarchal oppression, and were skeptical that a heterosexual relationship could be anything but a mask for sexual exploitation.

We funneled this energy into our unusual academic program. Although we taught the students to carefully analyze judicial opinions, we tried to get behind the abstract legal reasoning to the human reality that lay behind the courts' decisions. In doing so, we invited the students to draw on their own life experiences and work through the emotional content, not simply to bury it and treat the law as an elaborate intellectual chess game. We wanted them to acknowledge the pain, suffering, and anger that the legal system had to deal with.

In our first semester we introduced the students to a series of simulations, inviting them to address legal problems of major social significance and personal importance. In one simulation we invented a group of actors who wanted to start a theater in a suburban community on Long Island and live communally in a single house. The local zoning code prohibited occupancy of a house by any group other than a "traditional family" and they were unable to rent a house.

We gave the students the local zoning code, relevant provisions of the U.S. Constitution and state constitutions, and some leading cases on housing law and discrimination, and then assigned the roles of various participants—the lawyers for the group of actors, the homeowner, the town attorney, members of the zoning board, and the reviewing judge. Under supervision by faculty members, the lawyers interviewed their clients and tried to understand what their real objectives were, researched the relevant law, and addressed the legal issues as well as the practical problems that the various groups would be confronting. They devised legal strategies, wrote memoranda, and offered practical advice. The students were given the opportunity to critique their own work, and to rethink how they might act more effectively. They were also asked to consider the ethical dimensions of their decisions, the ways that their actions might take unfair advantage of other parties, and to consider the extent to which their quick move into the lawyer's role might have polarized a situation unnecessarily and even undermined the goals of their clients.

Since these were not ordinary law students straight out of college, many of them had been in these situations—homeowners concerned with property values, people living communally who were excluded from neighborhoods by restrictive zoning, policemen who had been called on to defuse volatile neighborhood disagreements—and were able to bring their experiences and values into the work in the Law School. When we dealt with family law issues such as domestic violence and child abuse, students drew on their experience as social workers, rape counselors, and crisis intervention workers, as well as their own experience as participants in complicated and oppressive domestic situations.

Dealing with civil rights cases, we encouraged the students to go into their own experience of racism, homophobia, and gender discrimination. When they read the *Dred Scott* decision, which upheld the property rights of slave owners, our black students had to confront the Supreme Court's ruling that their ancestors could be treated as property.[4]

By the end of three years, our graduates had undertaken the work of lawyers with sufficient supervision and reflection that they could assess for themselves the complex mix of analytic clarity, ethical sensitivity, and emotional control that was necessary to function effectively as public interest lawyers.

The program was potent medicine, and educationally rich. And it made the Law School community edgy and prone to conflict. We had some impressive successes. Many of our alumni moved into leadership positions in the public interest bar and in government with unique skills developed in our program. One graduate became the director of the Gay Men's Health Crisis. Another is head of the ACLU in Michigan. Others are leading public interest advocates in the New York legislature. And many of them are engaged in poverty law practice—in legal aid and public defender offices and in their own private law firms.

Many of us opened ourselves to relationships with people whom we would never have met in other settings. The CUNY Law School became one of the rare places where people could mix openly across deep, normally impermeable borders. It was a rewarding and important learning experience for both faculty and students. Still, it was neither smooth nor easy, incorporating the forces that make the streets of the New York vibrate with tension and energy.

There was a downside to this mix of faculty and students that I quickly came to recognize. Many of them were suspicious of authority in general, and the authority of white, male academic administrators—like me—in particular.

The Law School was its own inward-looking universe, where faculty and students had little concern for the interface between the Law School and the world outside. Since I was the person who was responsible for the interface, I was under pressure from CUNY administrators and the board of trustees. The faculty and students were New Yorkers and activists, and they were distrustful of my claims that I had to respond to outside pressure. They had learned how to survive in an environment where only a sucker lets his guard down. As one feminist faculty member said, "When I hear the words, 'Trust me,' I immediately become suspicious."

I had anticipated being a leader in a cohesive community at CUNY, but my expectations were disappointed. Some members of the community even defined the community in opposition and resistance to me. It was not always this way, but to an uncomfortable degree this was a persistent undercurrent. I had swings between emotional highs and lows. When I was away from the Law School it was easy for me to be a convincing advocate for the school and its program. But when I was in my office, dealing with student protests over our grading system, it was harder to maintain my enthusiasm. It was a new experience for me to be part of a small white male minority. I became aware of the white male advantage that subtly and imperceptibly—at least to the beneficiaries—affects most institutions. Much as in the way women and black people often feel silenced in places where they are in the minority, I often thought twice before I spoke at the Law School.

Perhaps my informal style made the situation worse by generating a set of egalitarian expectations that were jolted every time I denied that each of us at the school had equal responsibility for decisions. I was a dean who insisted that I had the right and responsibility to make my own judgments about faculty appointments and curriculum policy, not always deferring to the majority views of the community.

In retrospect, I see that my failure to bring the practice of wisdom to the work of the Law School more explicitly and effectively was a serious omission, one that heightened the stress levels and reduced the capacity of the disparate elements of the community to come together with compassion and mutual recognition. I wasn't ready to do more, however, and it might have been more innovation than we could take on in a Law School that was already pushing up to the limits of what CUNY and the profession could deal with.

Frequently caught between intransigent students, hostile academic administrators, and corrupt Queens political leadership, my life as dean was full of stress, challenge, and confrontation at the same time that our fragile experiment was beginning to bear fruit.

By the time of our first graduation in 1986, we had succeeded in obtaining preliminary accreditation from the American Bar Association. There were, predictably, some tensions in the period building to the graduation. The Law School was entitled to make recommendations to the board of CUNY for honorary degree recipients. Most were uncontroversial—such as Judge Leon Higginbotham, an eminent federal judge from Philadelphia and one of the creative minds behind the civil rights movement's legal victories leading to desegregation, and Chief Oren Lyons of the Onondaga Nation, a leader in the movement for Native American rights and a distinguished scholar. But some of the students and faculty wanted to award an honorary doctorate to Michael Hardwick, a gay man from Georgia whose claim to distinction was that he had been the defendant in the case in which the Supreme Court upheld the Georgia sodomy statute against Constitutional challenge.[5] At that point the CUNY board of trustees was still closely and suspiciously supervising us, and I did not want to have an unnecessary fight with them over an issue that was not critical to our program. So I refused to recommend a degree for Hardwick, generating a nasty confrontation in the Law School and accusations of homophobia and political cowardice. Fortunately, we reached a compromise—Hardwick would not receive an honorary degree but would get a public service award from the Law School, which would not have to be approved by the trustees.

Our first graduation was a joyous celebration. Judge Higginbotham gave a moving speech, recalling the enormous progress made in civil rights through the courts, and encouraging the students to work at the tasks that remained undone. Chief Lyons, in full regalia with feathers and beads, received his honorary doctorate of laws and announced that he could now honestly say that he was a "doctor, lawyer, and Indian chief." The Hardwick award was deeply important to many of our students and faculty—and to Hardwick himself, who had never received recognition for the sacrifice he made in carrying his struggle to the Supreme Court. It is remarkable that the Law School recognized the contribution of a client, rather than his lawyer—recognizing the person who is actually taking the risks and putting himself on the line, rather than the professional who serves him.

Many families celebrated their first member to receive a professional degree. Single mothers came across the stage to collect their degrees carrying their infant children in their arms. After the ceremony, I met the spouses and parents who had made it possible for our graduates to obtain a law degree. As I spoke to the parents of one graduate, who acted as an interpreter, I heard about the child care that the student's mother had provided for three years and the sacrifices made by the whole family in order to permit the daughter to earn a law degree. I had a renewed sense of the community of effort that lay behind each of these success stories. It was a deeply moving event, and I felt lifted up by it.

There were these magical moments scattered through my years in the deanship that energized and validated my work. The recognition that our program received within the profession was important—an award from the Society of American Law Teachers for our innovative curriculum, for example—but my participation in our students' realizations of the American dream was the most gratifying.

7

BEGINNING MEDITATION

ESPECIALLY IN THE early years, I wondered whether the Law School would survive—and whether I would survive as dean, without being blown off course, without becoming a person that I did not want to be. I often thought of Tim Healy's caution—that I would be tested in every way, and that I would have to develop reserves of inner strength and wise judgment.

I was trying to lead a law school program that would train whole people, people who would work from their heads and their hearts, who would bring compassion, equanimity, and community to the core of their work. And I often found myself angry and frustrated—at war with the man who had hired me, appalled by the political corruption, misunderstood by the local bar, alienated from some of the students and faculty, frustrated by the uncomprehending bureaucracy, frightened by the lawlessness on the Long Island Expressway. I felt isolated, embattled, and over my head—emotionally, morally, and psychologically. Too many nights, I came home exhausted and dejected, falling asleep immediately after dinner with my briefcase full of unread memoranda and curriculum proposals.

I needed a way to live with it all—with the joys and the frustrations—to take it all in and still retain my goodwill and the ability to laugh and to lead. How was I going to find in myself the qualities that I wanted to teach in our program? It was not just a matter of improving my administrative skills or mastering some new concepts. I had to be less reactive, more flexible and open in my response to criticism. This was the challenge that Tim Healy had prepared me for.

More than once, I considered resigning. The job was not what I had been promised and the resources were not available to do it right. The backers were too sleazy, and the hope of creating a new public interest law paradigm in Archie Bunker land wasn't realistic.

I considered digging in my heels and slugging it out with Cohen and the political operators who supported him. I could have made an all-out effort to enlist allies against him—among the CUNY trustees and the other presidents of colleges in the CUNY system, mobilizing the people who distrusted Queens College's elitist pretensions.

While I did engage in limited political warfare, I decided to work for the vision that I believed in and at the same time push my own boundaries, to try to find resources in myself that would permit me to create a new law school in a genuinely new way—with integrity and decency. I worked as effectively as I could with Cohen, acknowledging my own part in our conflicts—my defensiveness, my sense of grievance, my self-righteousness—and working to change within myself what was contributing to our problems. I tried to honor the faculty and students in their desire to build a more egalitarian community. It was an uphill effort, but I had some tools to work with and a willingness to reach out to develop more. In retrospect, I see that I could have done better, that I could have clung less insistently to my vision in all its detail. But I could only do what I was ready for, to manage the challenges in a contentious environment with the best skills that I had at the time.

I started with small personal strategies to retain some sense of calm in the face of the crises that ran through each day. I began psychotherapy with a skillful Gestalt therapist. I felt that my relationship with Cohen might reflect some ingrained problems with authority that I might be able to understand and mitigate. I had never been in therapy before, and I found our weekly sessions useful, helping to release some of the emotional charge around my interactions with Cohen.

Another simple strategy was to leave my canoe on a dock close to home, on the edge of Manhasset Bay. After a long day of butting heads with bureaucrats, as the setting sun tinted the sky and water purple and orange, I took the canoe out onto the bay, paddling and releasing the tensions of the day, feeling the grace and ease with which the canoe slid among the moored sail boats. As the canoe glided through the water, I thought about trying to move through the next day at the office with the same confidence and mastery.

I also tried to find some daytime relaxation, joining friends in an informal lunch group that met monthly in Manhattan. Getting out of Queens and away from the Law School was a tonic in itself, but the Old Farts Club had special advantages since its members were some of the funniest people in New York—comedy writers, playwrights, a political cartoonist, novelists. Laughing for two hours on a Friday afternoon was a wonderful way to end the week, and I felt that I was able to hold my own in the group. I created a new genre of lawyer joke. The humor didn't flow from the rapacity, immorality, and greed of the lawyers as in most lawyer jokes—sharks with professional courtesy, "let us prey," selling out their own grandmothers. Rather the humor came from our earnestness, our unbending conviction of our own rightness, our suspicion of authority, and our rabid intolerance of people who had different positions on core progressive issues—in short, a humor based on my experience with some of my faculty colleagues and students.

Occasional visits with my friend Ralph Siu were also important to me. From time to time he would come to New York to take his wife to the Metropolitan Opera. Because he had no interest in the opera himself, he and I would walk in Central Park or sit in a coffee shop across from Lincoln Center until it was time to pick her up after the closing curtain. Our continuing conversations helped me view my work in a larger perspective, to see the humor in my dilemmas, and maintain my own integrity among the swirling currents of my deanship.

Ralph gave me some concrete advice. "Don't become totally committed to the Law School. Maintain some distance so every criticism of it doesn't seem to be a criticism of you. Keep the other parts of your life alive. You are the dean of an institution that could have many beneficial effects for the society, but always remember that you are more than the dean. There is a part of you that is separate from the law school, immutable, and deeply connected to the totality. Don't give the Law School 100 percent of your effort, because if you do, there will be no reserves left for crises that will surely arise."

While there were some things that Ralph said that didn't make sense to me at the time, like my "connection to the totality," I felt that he might be pointing in a direction that would make sense one day, and I was comfortable holding the idea without accepting it or rejecting it. Our conversations were a helpful reminder to keep balance in my life. Perhaps most important, his hearty laughter about my travails reminded me that, with a little distance, some of my problems were really funny.

And then, through a chance encounter, I fell into the world of Buddhist-inspired meditation.

When I began to understand the complexities of establishing the new law school, in early 1983, I thought it would be a good idea to talk with someone who had been through the birthing of a law school. I called David Hood, the founding dean of the Hawaii Law

School, who was then running the Carnegie Foundation's public interest law programs in South Africa. It had been rough going at Hawaii, where he lasted only a couple of years. He could probably tell me something about some potholes I might be able to avoid.

I went to David's office at the Carnegie Foundation in an elegant high-rise in the middle of Manhattan, a world apart from CUNY Law School. I had been to those offices many times before, since Carnegie had been an important funder of the Mental Health Law Project. The gray carpets and dark wood–paneled walls provided an air of quiet and restraint. It was a place where one did not raise one's voice, very different from our rundown, recycled public school. David's office looked down on the East Side of Manhattan, the East River that I had just crossed under, and a long, uninflected vista across Queens.

David was a tall man with long gray hair, blown dry and carefully combed across his forehead. He wore a well-tailored, European-style suit. We talked for a few minutes in his office, about people we knew in common, about public interest law in Johannesburg and in Washington, before he said, "Let's get out of here and go someplace where we can relax. Let's take my truck."

"Did you say truck?" I asked. We walked across Fifty-first Street toward a white van parked in a trucks-only space.

"Yes," he said, and we climbed into the van. On the side, it read in rather crude black letters: "Acme Corporation. We aim to please."

"You'll learn this after you've lived in New York for a while. It's a very tough place. You have to take every little advantage you can get. Because I have this van and commercial plates, I can park in many places where cars can't. Look, you have a tough job, starting a law school. You're going to have to look for things that will give you an edge. I don't have to hear the details to know how tough it is. Queens is like Hawaii in some ways: a neocolonial society and a multiracial population. Tensions that lie just below the surface come up when there is a new thing in town, new jobs to be handed out, new contracts to be let. And the CUNY Law School will be punching people's tickets, giving them a pass into a learned profession and the middle class. You're going to decide whose tickets get punched. Don't think people won't be watching you like a hawk."

He drove the van slowly and skillfully north through the rush hour traffic.

"You mean there is no Acme Corporation?" I asked.

"Not that I know of."

"Where are we going?" I asked.

"Let's go to my apartment. It will be quiet, and we can talk."

David's apartment was in a high-rise on the southern edge of Spanish Harlem. In the living room the main piece of furniture was a wooden platform, raised a foot above the floor, with a few cushions on it. On the walls hung softly draped painted cloths, pictures of Asian deities and demons, locked in combat, arrayed along the sides of fantastic cliffs and mountains.

"Take your shoes off and sit down while I warm up some sake," he said, leaving me alone in the room to try to figure out where I was and how to comply with his instructions. After taking off my shoes, I crawled around on the platform, trying unsuccessfully to arrange a few cushions so they were reasonably comfortable. I wondered if he sat here to read the *New York Times* with his morning coffee.

David came back into the room with a ceramic carafe of sake and two small cups. He had taken off his Saville Row suit coat and put on a silk robe embroidered with Japanese characters.

We lifted our cups and drank to new friendships and new law schools.

"I'm a Buddhist," he said.

I had never met a Buddhist before, and here was one who looked like a WASP investment banker.

"Oh," I said.

"These paintings on the wall are Tibetan *tankas*. They are traditional representations of the Buddhist cosmology, illustrating the
great struggles between good and evil that have shaped the universe
and the many planes of existence."

"Were you a Buddhist when you were dean at Hawaii?" I asked.

"I was," he said, "though I didn't talk about it much. In the racial,
ethnic, and religious stew of Hawaii, I thought it wouldn't make my
life easier if I was a *haole* mainlander and a Buddhist on top of it.
But my meditation practice and Buddhist principles really helped
me keep the boat off the shoals for a while, at least until I was
trapped in a riptide that I couldn't escape and it dragged me out to
sea." Then he added, "You might try meditation."

"Does it mean that I have to get into all of this?" I asked, pointing to the tankas and the statues of demons with their eyes popping
out and tongues coiling like corkscrews.

"No," he said. "Start with something simple. Get up a little early
in the morning. Find a quiet place. Light a candle. Sit comfortably
and pay attention to your breath. If thoughts arise, observe them as
they come and go. Then bring your attention back to your breath.
Do it every morning for twenty minutes. Simple, but not easy."

"What good will *that* do me?"

"Try it. You'll be surprised. This is the essence of Buddhist practice. They've been refining these techniques for twenty-five hundred years. You might find that the simple practice gives you a
wonderful, peaceful way to start the day, and a quiet place in your
mind that you can return to from time to time during your hectic
schedule. It can help you to avoid getting locked into polarized
arguments."

"And the rest of the stuff—the *tankas*, demons and all?"

"That's for a more serious spiritual exploration. You don't even
have to think about that. The simple meditation practice may

make that seem interesting to you at some point. But don't rush it. You're not at that place now."

I told Susan about this remarkable encounter. "I plan to get up a half-hour early to meditate," I told her. "I want to give it a try."

"Why not?" she said. "This job is driving you nuts."

I began meditating each morning. To my surprise, the meditative state seemed quite familiar to me. I sometimes had had similar mind experiences listening to the young Joan Baez sing, in Cambridge, before she was famous, when her voice was as pure as crystal. Or standing before a favorite painting, like Winslow Homer's *Canoe in the Rapids* in the Fogg Museum at Harvard. I would be fully present in that moment, and the rest of the world would disappear. Or sitting in the stern of a canoe, slouching over my paddle and effortlessly moving the canoe forward on a hot, windless afternoon, when my mind would be empty and still. Meditation seemed a way of systematically invoking a state of mind that was focused and reflective, relaxed and alert. When the world intruded during meditation, as it often did, I was able to return my attention to my breath.

My daily meditation practice seemed to buffer the knocks and crises that occurred each day. If I took time to touch into the place of stillness in the morning, I was less likely to be thrown as far off balance during the day. Sometimes, when I received a provocative phone call from Cohen, I would catch myself slipping into my angry, reactive mode, and I learned to pause before a confrontation could develop. A few deep breaths would reconnect me to the meditative space, and I would sometimes respond more thoughtfully—or at least the confrontation would be less venomous. Not all the time, but often enough to keep me engaged in my meditative practice.

The strategies I was gathering were nourishing my inner self and giving me a sense of balance—my Gestalt therapy, the canoeing in the evening, the Old Farts Club lunches, my conversations with Ralph Siu, my nascent meditation practice. Meditation, in particular, was heightening my receptivity to new possibilities. I remained alert, looking for other ways of staying grounded in my tumultuous life and of developing inner resources that would help me manage my deanship with more equanimity and grace, and to survive.

As I was anticipating the arrival of our first-year students in the fall of 1983, I thought it would be a good thing for me to undertake an exercise in empathy, to put myself in a situation where I would feel the way that many of our incoming law students would feel when confronted with a new, intimidating discipline. I wanted to immerse myself once again in the student role, in an area where my levels of confidence and competence were low.

Just at that time, I received in the mail a catalogue announcing the summer programs at the Omega Institute, up the Hudson Valley.[1] I had never been to Omega, but had been tantalized—and put off— by its catalogues for years. It was a "human growth center" of the kind that made me suspicious. Like Esalen in California, but without the hot tubs on the cliffs above the Pacific Ocean, Omega presented a smorgasbord of workshops offered by diverse teachers, holding out the promise of holistic, integrative growth of mind, body, and spirit. Few people I knew had ever heard of Omega, much less gone there. It seemed too ungrounded for me, home to too many teachers with none of the credentials that I relied on to certify competence.

Nonetheless, one weekend program caught my eye—Paul Winter, the creative saxophone player and his Consort of diverse, multitalented musicians—was doing a workshop on music improvisation, and the opportunity seemed almost perfectly designed for my needs. I had absolutely no skill in making music and no prior experience in improvisation. It sounded like fun—at worst, a good concert by gifted musicians. I headed north with the drum that a friend had brought me from Ethiopia.

We began the weekend with some instruction in improvisation, exercises to clear our minds, to keep us fully present and attentive in the moment, to rest in a noncritical, nonjudgmental frame of mind, and to listen deeply to the sounds around us. This quality of nonjudgmental attention was something new to me—especially being nonjudgmental of myself, because being critical of myself full-time was a basic part of who I was.

I had long been caught in what I considered the *success trap*. I had, ever since elementary school, engaged my time and energy in areas where I had been most successful—I had strong verbal skills, so that is where I focused my efforts. I avoided activities where I was less confident about my ability. This tendency stood as a barrier to developing myself as a whole person and undermined my capacity to get pleasure from activities in which I did not excel, a common enough malady in modern America.

When we began to make music, my drumming was awkward and I tried to keep it soft in deference to the sensibilities of my colleagues. As time passed, I became more confident, more assertive and experimental. On Saturday afternoon, after I had been drumming for about four hours and my fingers were aching, Paul Winter himself sat down with a group of four of us who were improvising on fiddle, tambourine, trumpet, and my drum. Paul listened for a few minutes with complete focus and presence, and then began to play with us. The next ten minutes were, for me, an experience of a pure flow state, riding the currents of sound, lost in the collective experience. The music seemed to me to be incredibly beautiful and absorbing, and I felt myself a contributor and collaborator. I realized then what a gifted teacher can convey to the student, simply by the attention he bestows and the empowering environment for learning he creates.

Driving home after the workshop, I felt that it had been worth-while and nourishing. I had dealt with my fear, finding satisfaction in performing at an acceptable, if not outstanding, level. I had made a friendly connection with the frightened learner in me, not allow-ing my behavior to be controlled by my fear of a humiliating fail-ure. This connection would help me to engage with the incoming students, and would allow me to manage my fear of failure in my high-risk job. It had paid off for me to suspend my skepticism and to try out a workshop that had seemed vaguely ridiculous.

There was a huge gap between my experiment with my fear of failure and the constricted world of Queens; my Woody Allen voice kept whining, "Get on with it, and forget this touchy-feely *mishugas*." Still, I was encouraged to push the boundaries more vig-orously, to get away from the law school and explore unfamiliar pathways that promised to help me manage my turbulent leader-ship responsibility wisely, with equanimity.

My need for balance was never greater than in the cold, gray days of winter. February 1986 was a dismal time at the school. The stu-dents and the faculty were getting short-tempered, and so was I. I was embroiled in unending struggles with the academic bureau-crats. The streets were full of slush, the snow lying on the ground quickly turning to a gray, icy soup. I parked my car by ramming it into a big plow-generated drift, hoping that it wouldn't be stolen, that the drift would not have turned to a single block of ice, and that I would be able to get out in the chilly evening. It had begun to seem that the school year was going to last forever. My hands were often cold and my feet wet. The old pipes in the building groaned as the steam passed through them. Most rooms were either like saunas or the students were taking notes with their gloves on.

A psychotherapist colleague of Susan's invited me to join him on a "Winter Quest" he was undertaking later in February—camping in the snow in the Adirondack Mountains in the far northern part of the state. My first reaction was that this was a truly terrible idea. Queens had plenty of winter right at my doorstep. Why look for more? But Susan encouraged me to think about it. She had grown up ice-skating on backyard rinks in Toronto, and she had good memories of treks across frozen lakes in northern Ontario on snowshoes made of bentwood and deer hide strips.

We mentioned the Winter Quest to our son Bob, the only one of our children still living at home. The idea appealed to his seventeen-year-old imagination. He said that if I was game for snow camping, he would be too. It seemed to me a good opportunity for the two of us to do something extraordinary together, and I appreciated his sense of adventure.

I phoned the trip leader, Joseph Jastrab, to learn more. I asked him a few questions—about the discomfort, the risks of frostbite and injury, the level of physical fitness, his prior experience. As he later reflected on our conversation, he said that he felt like a hostile witness under cross-examination. "Sorry," I said. "This is just my habitual lawyerly style, cranked up by anxiety."

Joseph responded to my questions with a calm authority that I found reassuring. He had been a wilderness guide for more than a decade, and had had special training for wilderness survival in extreme conditions. I felt that he knew what he was doing, and that I could probably deal with the physical challenge. "But why do you call it a 'Winter Quest' instead of a camping trip?" I asked.

He paused a minute. "I think of this trip as having a spiritual dimension too."

"Oh," I said, the single syllable carrying enough skeptical weight that he picked it up.

He responded slowly, choosing his words with care. "I don't think it is possible to go deep into the winter wilderness and expect it to be a wholly physical experience. Winter is too freighted for that. It is the time when nothing grows, when the bears retreat into the caves. In Native American traditions, it is the place of mystery, of death and renewal. The chill of winter can be terrifying—winds howling through the trees, blowing the snow in our faces and blinding our eyes. We will be going into the teeth of the winter. This isn't like the way we take on the winter in the city—creeping in and out of superheated rooms, wearing piles of down and wool to ward off the cold. Not even like skiing, with a mulled wine and Jacuzzi waiting when you come off the slopes. We are questing to learn something about ourselves as we deal with the primal reality of winter."

I didn't push this point any further. He might call it a quest. For me it was winter camping. And yet, I could see how this adventure could teach me something about myself—about ways to deal with fear, to see it clearly and not be controlled by it; to find pleasure in challenging, harsh circumstances; and to clean out my mind. Here was a chance to take some risks, but not crazy ones. I was willing to try things that were challenging, that seemed foreign, that required a suspension of my own entrenched beliefs. I sensed a possibility of insights that might open new doors for understanding the world and my place in it.

On a snowy day in February, Bob and I loaded our gear into the trunk of our car and headed north. We had special boots with removable felt liners that we could put inside the sleeping bag with us at night so that they wouldn't freeze solid. We also carried zip-lock plastic bags to piss in during the night without getting out of our sleeping bags. After we sealed them up and tossed them out of the tent, we would be greeted by them in the morning by a yellow ice brick ready for easy disposal.

We arrived at our Adirondack inn just as the sun fell behind the pines, and the snow glowed orange and purple, refracting the colors of the sunset. As the darkness came up, a few stars began to appear, then a profusion of stars pulsating through the crystalline, icy air. They were so bright that they seemed to be within reach. In Queens, you never can see stars, not even one. Too much city-generated light, and the air is too polluted. This starry sky was a revelation—a reminder of the universe that exists beyond our polluted atmosphere. I sensed that I was part of that enfolding universe too.

Our first night we stayed indoors at the inn. After dinner, we introduced ourselves to our fellow expedition members around a big fire in the stone fireplace. Then Joseph invited us to talk about our biggest fears in going on this trip. I found it a little difficult at first to identify my fears. I was accustomed to pushing fear aside when that was possible, not looking at it too closely, and certainly not talking about it with a group of strangers. As the discussion wore on, however, I was able to identify a very genuine and pressing fear—the fear that I would not be able to keep up and would be humiliated, or left behind in this frozen wilderness. I was the oldest in the group, and the most sedentary. As I spoke, I realized my relief at acknowledging the fear and not trying to present myself to the group as a fearless and confident venturer.

This sharing quickly turned us from a group of strangers into a community. Joseph took each person's fears seriously, sometimes identifying them with his own experiences. He was not without fear, but he did not let it control his behavior, and he carried on a continuing negotiation with it. As we talked, each person's fear dissolved into a shared pool of fears, less the personal property of any person than another part of the common baggage that we would all carry together into the forest.

The next morning we strapped on our snowshoes, loaded our packs on our backs, and took off for the woods. We started with light chattering conversation among us, but this fell away and we began walking without talking, appreciating the depth of silence of the winter wilderness. It was not like walking in the woods on a summer day. There was no birdsong, no crickets, no croaking frogs, no babbling brook. Occasionally a tree branch would groan under the heavy load of snow, and the snow squeaked under our snowshoes. The profound silence and the cold still air enveloped us, creating an almost tangible medium through which we slowly moved. The jangle of noise of the Long Island Expressway and the roar of the jets taking off from LaGuardia were an increasingly distant memory.

The blanket of snow radically simplified the landscape. Black, gray, and white replaced the rainbow hues of summer. The complex forms—the rocks, the ferns and grasses, the gullies, stumps, and hillocks—were smoothed out and transformed into graceful progressions of mounds and drifts. The snow simplified the mental processes too. My mind's stream of thoughts and plans, memories and associations, slowed down. My daily meditation practice gave me the same kind of mental respite and focus, but I had not expected to find it in the frozen wilderness. In the strangest way, I felt as if I was swimming languidly through a warm, windless pond, enveloped in the water. My life at Law School fell away, my obligations and struggles, my list of incomplete projects. My various identities—dean, entrepreneur, husband, skeptic—were replaced by a person who was slower, more focused on simple things—

warmth, food, and shelter—and no doubt less entertaining and amusing. I was interested in inhabiting this other person and getting to know him. I knew that this was just a short visit with him, but I thought it might return me to my other world changed in some way.

By midafternoon, we entered into a clearing in a grove of towering hemlock, where Joseph showed us how to build our sleeping caves. After an hour of steady work, Bob and I had created a cavern about seven feet round and three feet high. The floor was firm, and as the dome sat in the sun, it became extremely solid. We crawled easily into the cave through the low doorway. From the inside, the snowy dome was translucent with the brilliant light of the afternoon sun glowing through. The snow insulated the cave so that our body heat raised the temperature to a more comfortable level inside. It was a joy simply to sit in the cave, like sitting inside a luminous bubble, inside a form of ultimate simplicity and elegance—a cocoon, a womb, a blown-glass bud vase. We had built a primal dwelling of such practicality and beauty without tools, building materials, skill, or plan. When we crawled outside into the long shadows of late afternoon, we looked around at a landscape enhanced by our caves. The snow-covered hillocks and gullies beneath the hemlocks echoed the domes of the snow caves, curves intersecting curves, the swelling masses of our dwellings gently flowing into the hollows.

By the time it was too dark to work anymore, our group had established a small village in the depths of the hemlock trees, with common areas and private spaces. Bob said, "Our snow cave and our little village remind me of Fanghetto. Similar curving surfaces and enfolding spaces, and an organic connection to the land. Each room has a vaulted ceiling, no right angles."

"But in Fanghetto," I said, "there's the added mystery of its ancient, unknowable history, and its deep connection to the bedrock. This village has the opposite appeal—extreme impermanence. We built it in an hour and it will survive only until the next thaw, leaving no trace."

The first night, while the outside temperature fell to twenty below, we slept comfortably with dreams that were shaped by the magical space. I have never taken greater pleasure from any sleeping place, never slept more deeply in any bed. Nor have I ever seen a human-made structure so completely, so appropriately an organic part of a natural landscape. The next day, after a light snowfall, the dome was strong enough to walk on.

In our remaining days in the wilderness, we took hikes in the mountains, and ate hearty, fat-laced meals. In the evening we danced around the fire, to fill the hours between nightfall and bedtime, to bring our rhythms into synchronous connection, and to keep the blood from freezing in the arctic cold. I experienced moments of an almost religious ecstasy—in the silent woods, full of snow, and in the unexpected intimacy of our snow cave.

The learning gleaned from the experience stayed with Bob and me as we drove out of the Adirondacks, south toward Queens. We spoke of our surprise in being comfortable and at home in such a cold and isolated place. I was pleased that the spiritual side did not embarrass either of us. And I had found another way to connect to the natural world, to feel intimations of the human and nonhuman beings that have lived for millennia in such simplicity.

The discontinuity between that experience and my life in Queens came home to me the next morning in the rush-hour traffic tie-up behind a jackknifed trailer truck on the Long Island Expressway. When I finally arrived at the Law School, the faculty and students were in turmoil over the selection of honorary degree recipients for the spring commencement. Governor Cuomo had turned down our invitation to speak at commencement. I had an urgent call from the vice chancellor. And the roof was leaking.

Despite the chaos around me, I was able to hold onto something of the joy and tranquility of my time in the woods. As I fell into the fast pace of the dean's office and the incessant flow of decision making, I could still find moments of solitude and connect to the person who had lived so simply and with such joy in difficult conditions. I could suspend irony, and hold a vision of our Law School in Flushing inside a larger reality that included the wilderness as well as the city. Although the stars were not visible from Main Street when I left in the evening, I knew that they were still there, above the light and the smog. As I prepared to defend the Law School and myself in the swirling conflicts of Queens, I could draw on the incongruous ease and grace of my snowshoe trek across the frozen forests.

I brought back with me an altered sense of proportion—a reminder that the world didn't turn on our experiment, and that my worth as a human being was not a function of the success of the Law School. Now I understood the larger sense of myself that Ralph Siu had reminded me of. I was not just the dean of a law school or a householder in a Long Island suburb. I was a person who had a direct point of contact with the depth of the remote wilderness and the height of the winter sky.

My trip to the winter wilderness strengthened my meditation practice, the stillness of the wilderness reinforcing the inner stillness. Like practicing the piano or a sport, skill improves with faithful practice. Progress, however, was not linear or automatic. The benefits that I reaped from my practice were irregular, and sometimes my equanimity was overwhelmed by the stress generated by the work for days at a time.

By the next summer, I was exhausted from the semester's activities and feeling a need of renewal. It had been a successful semester in many ways, but extremely challenging. We had a visit from an American Bar Association accreditation team, a struggle over faculty appointments, a dispute over the way that we evaluated our students' work—with letter grades or narrative texts. I was ready for a new adventure that would take me out of Queens, perhaps leading me deeper into the inner space that I was exploring through meditation and the winter trip into the wilderness.

So I was intrigued when I heard that Joseph Jastrab was putting together a weeklong Vision Quest for men in the northern Adirondacks, drawing on Native American traditions. It began just after the end of the academic year at the Law School, and I liked the idea of leaving the struggles in the dean's office to enter directly into a radically different world. I was able to overcome my skepticism sufficiently to say yes, without demanding that Joseph define "vision" and "quest."

The skeptical voice, of course, reappeared. The image of a group of lawyers, insurance salesmen, and contractors leaving their comfortable homes and going off to the woods to act out Indian rituals sounded like a scene in a Woody Allen movie. I thought of Allen's famous quote, "I am at two with nature." I overcame the voice because of my experience on the snow-camping trip, because Joseph himself seemed so grounded and authentic, so deeply connected to the wilderness. It seemed worthwhile to continue to try to learn what he had to teach.

When I arrived at the campsite, a few hours late, I saw colorful tents sprinkled through the woods. A dozen men, lounging around the fire, introduced themselves by the names that they had taken for purposes of the vision quest. There were no references to where they came from or what they did.

"Heart of the Deer," one man said.

"Oh, shit," I thought. "My worst fear. Should I be Shank of the Lamb?" After searching my mind frantically for an alias, I introduced myself as Shining Pond. This name came to me from a conversation that I had had with Ralph Siu. He had encouraged me to cultivate my capacity to see the world clearly and without distortion, just as the world is reflected in a still, shining pond. I had often thought about that, about the screens of preconception, judgment, irony, and desire that stood between me and such clear perception.

One of the things I hoped for in this quest was to develop a clarity of vision that would resemble the clear reflection in a shining pond. For a person like me, who self-identified as an activist, the neutrality, even the passivity, of my adopted name gave me something to work with as I explored my capacity for passive vision—simply seeing things clearly, without feeling that I had to critique or change them. It was an excellent complement to the skills of a public interest lawyer.

On the first day Joseph led us in laying out a medicine wheel, a practice that he had learned from Native American teachers, instructing us to make a circle of stones about twelve feet across, with four large stones marking the cardinal directions. The cardinal stones were connected by two lines of stones that crossed at the center of the circle. It was a beautiful form sitting beneath the grove of hemlock trees. We sat around the medicine wheel while Joseph explained its multilayered meanings. "The medicine wheel focuses the energy of the four directions," he said, "and the axle running through the center of the wheel connects the earth below and the sky above. Each of the four directions has its distinctive characteristics, overlaying multiple maps, including the physical world, the seasons, the day, human psychology, and the life cycle." This seemed hopelessly abstract to me—and foolishly ambitious.

He sat down beside a large stone at the east side of the circle. The East, he said, is the place of the dawn, identified with the color gold.

It represents the high energy of early morning, the explosive trans-formative growth of spring, youth in the human life cycle, and the beginning of the in-breath. The animal of the East is the eagle—farsighted, visionary, and powerful.

Then he went to each of the other compass points and discussed the way that they integrated the daily passage of time, the flow of seasons, animal characteristics, the cycle of the breath, and the stages in a person's life. The South is midday, the summer, the place of maturity, and fecund growth; the West is the sunset, the autumn, the place of old age and wisdom, of ripeness and decay; the North is night, winter, the place of death and renewal. I was struck by the elegant and economical way the overlapping maps conveyed an evocative understanding of the many cyclical patterns that shape our experience.

After his introduction, Joseph invited us to sit by ourselves at the four points on the medicine wheel and reflect on its interlocking imagery. Often during the course of the next days, I would come back to the wheel alone, meditating on one compass point after another, and reflecting on its learning. Ralph Siu had been first to suggest to me that careful, thoughtful reflection on the stages of my life was something that I should begin early. When I was younger, I could hardly take in the idea of my own old age, with loss of strength and memory. I didn't see much point to thinking about it. However, my conversations with Ralph came back to me as I sat around the medicine wheel, and I began to feel a connection between the cycles of my life and the cycles of the seasons and the energies of the four directions.

It was more a matter of feeling than thinking. I tried to visualize integrating the different energies—carrying forward youthful energy into wise old age, connecting with the wintry energy of the North, old age, and death, while still in the fecund, generative sum-mertime of life. I could see that the cycles that seemed to organize so much of the life process also applied to the lives of institutions and nations. The medicine wheel created an integrative framework that could apply to every aspect of my life and thought. And as I sat beside it, I felt that the cycle of breathing—in-breath and out-breath—was a constant, ever-present reminder of the interlocking cycles within which I lived my life. The feeling arose from the silence of the place and the wisdom of the wheels-within-wheels.[2]

Midway through our week in the wilderness, Joseph introduced us to the sweat lodge, another ritual based on Native American traditions. We built a low hut out of tree branches, covering it with heavy tarps. Again, my skeptical voice was activated by this faux Indian ritual: You are a public interest lawyer and an academic administrator. What the hell are you doing out here in the woods building a sweat lodge, dressed in a bathing suit and sandals? Are you a self-indulgent adolescent nurturing fantasies about the life of the noble savage?

Nonetheless, we were in the woods together and I had made a commitment, so I overrode the skeptical voice as we gathered, sawed, and split immense logs for a huge fire. By the time it was dark, I had invested my labor in our preparations for the sweat lodge and these questions became less frequent and less importunate. We built a huge bonfire and placed large rocks among the logs so that they would be in the hottest part of the fire. The flames leapt high in the darkness, illuminating the trees that flickered in and out of the light. I stood transfixed by the fire, the largest I had ever seen.

We stripped off our clothes in the chilly night air and crawled through the low opening in the lodge, taking seats in a circle on the ferns, which we had laid to create a floor. A half-dozen of the superheated rocks, glowing red with inner heat, were brought into the lodge and placed in the firepit at the center of our circle. I was immobilized by the heat and the color. Joseph threw some sage on the fire, and we sat in the perfumed darkness as the heat in the lodge built. I had never been in a sauna that approached the intensity of the heat in the lodge, and my conventional defenses seemed to melt away with the sweat that poured from every pore of my body. The experience was heightened by the song of the crickets and by our isolation in the woods.

We sat for hours in the lodge, with the intense heat renewed from time to time by hot rocks brought in from the fire. As we began a slow chant, my sense of time began to fade. At times, the chanting took on a life of its own, for a few moments joyous, more often mournful, evoking a sense of the loss and suffering that we had experienced in our lives. Some of the men in the sweat lodge told stories of the pain they had suffered—the loss of loved ones, career failure, the death of hope—and the relief that they hoped to find. No one offered advice or verbal comfort, only a word of acknowledgment. I felt the speakers' pain with sharpness and intensity— and the pain in my own life, things that I had suffered seemed to merge into their suffering. In our shared experience, I sensed possibilities for forgiveness and hope.

Joseph invited us to bring our fathers and forefathers into the lodge, to share with them the healing and forgiveness. I laughed in the darkness at the ridiculous thought of my father slipping off his judicial robes and his custom-made suit to join me in the sweat lodge, in the depths and darkness of the Adirondack wilderness, and of his grandfathers, leaving their *shtetls* in Eastern Europe, bearded rabbis in *kepahs*, to join their descendant in the sweat lodge. My laughter lodged deep in my belly, then gave way to silent reverie, then reverie gave way to tears. I had never felt such an intimate connection to the generations of ancestors whose lives had made my life possible. My ancestors felt as real to me as the men who were sharing the space with me, and I felt myself part of their joy and suffering.

At times I put my head down on the ground where the air was slightly cooler. Time disappeared as I lost touch with past and future, fully focused on the intensity of the moment. In the heat and darkness, my various identities dissolved—dean, husband, father—and I melted into something more primitive, more universal, and less differentiated. After uncounted hours, we crawled out of the small opening in the lodge, into the light of the fire, pouring sweat. I dropped into the icy water of the stream that ran beside the lodge and floated facedown in the slow current, then rejoined the group standing around the fire, drying off in silent reflection. I assembled my clothes, walked through the darkness to my tent, and fell into a deep sleep.

The next day I spent much of the time sitting at the compass points on the medicine wheel, reflecting on youth/springtime, maturity/summer, aging/autumn, death/winter. I thought about keeping all four dimensions within consciousness at the same time, wondering if that were possible. I experimented with holding an awareness of my own death present in consciousness. I wondered how, as I moved toward the western, autumnal, sunset point on the medicine wheel, I might expand my capacity for wisdom.

I returned to the Law School during summer vacation, when most of the students and faculty were gone. Although I told few people about the experience, I spoke more slowly and I listened more attentively. It took several days before I had fully reassembled my old persona, and in some ways I was never the same. The out-breath reminded me that I was a part of an interlocking system of aging, death, and renewal, and the in-breath connected me to the energy of the East—visionary, energetic, and confident. While I would often lose track of my breath for days at a time, the medicine wheel teachings infused and enriched my daily meditation practice, offering me a pervasive sense of the cyclical patterns echoing through my life, through nature, and through human institutions—the reality of impermanence and the inevitable death that is contained in every birth.

Even in my office at the Law School, the memory of the sweat lodge took me to a more primitive place, a world of visceral, instinctual reality. It connected me to my ancestors and to the people over the millennia who found their common humanity through ritual, through surrendering the peculiarities of their personality into a collective awareness. On my daily drive to work, I reflected on the accumulated wisdom of the generations of Native Americans who had passed through similar experiences on these marshes and seashores for centuries before the invasion of the Europeans. I brought this additional dimension to my vision of our fragile new school, giving it a context that was larger, more complicated, and more ambitious.

In 1987, while we were preparing for our second graduating class, I decided to resign from the deanship, take a year's sabbatical, and then return to the Law School faculty. I was exhausted by the continuing pressures of the deanship, and I was ready to think about the next steps in my life. By this time I had come to think of myself as a person who started things, not a long-term, stay-the-course administrator. The Law School was well-launched, and it still had some formidable tasks ahead. I was prepared to let someone new lead it through the next phase of consolidation and adaptation. In particular, the relatively low proportion of our first-year class to pass the bar examination was going to impose an ongoing challenge; it would be necessary to rethink the admissions criteria and process, and to bring greater rigor to our internal evaluation. I didn't want to take that on. My successor as dean, Haywood Burns, was an old friend and a leading civil rights attorney. An experienced teacher and administrator in the CUNY system, he was committed to the Law School's mission and knew how to work effectively in that system.

During my sabbatical, I went to Yale for a semester as a Senior Fellow and worked on a manuscript reflecting on the CUNY experience and drawing some preliminary conclusions about our educational innovations. Some of that thought is reflected in this book. I enjoyed the comfort and ease of the cloistered life, sitting at my desk in a small office, looking out at the old elm and maple trees turning colors in the New England autumn. The world of problems that was so tangible and present in Queens seemed remote and abstract. While I missed the sense of mission and the energy of CUNY, I was happy to have quiet days and few visitors coming through my office door. I spent time with faculty friends and the gifted students who were drawn to Yale. But I felt that I was not likely to continue to grow and move ahead in this setting, that I could all too easily slide into being the person I had been before CLASP and CUNY. I didn't know how I would like being a CUNY faculty member, but I liked it better than thinking about teaching in a more conventional law school.

In the spring semester Susan and I began a four-month odyssey through Asia. I signed up with the United States Information Agency, which had a program to send American lecturers to foreign countries. I agreed to intersperse lectures and meetings with our travels. It turned out that I had the opportunity to meet some of the most interesting lawyers practicing in Indonesia, India, Pakistan, and China. In the course of our travels, we tuned our eyes and ears to the sights and sounds of a world that was radically different than ours, experiencing a unique mix of meetings with the public interest lawyers of Bombay and Karachi, a trek in Nepal, gamelan concerts in Bali, and dialogues with administrative judges in Peking. I was impressed by the courage and initiative of many lawyers who were trying to use their tools to bring the rule of law and the ideal of justice into areas where these notions were suspect and their work was dangerous.

Although I returned to the Law School faculty in 1988, teaching first-year students, I found the work frustrating. I was an impatient teacher, and I found it difficult to fit into the role of a faculty member with little capacity to deal with the problems facing the Law School. I was good at generating new ideas and organizing the people and the resources to make things happen. The teaching didn't give me these opportunities. It was an unhappy time, and I began to think about what I wanted to do next. I was a tenured member of the faculty, and there was some comfort in having that security. But I didn't want to let security keep me at a job I didn't find exciting or rewarding. I thought about looking into a public interest law job or going into state government or getting out of law altogether. I was turning fifty, and I was uneasy and uncertain about my future. Queens seemed even more isolated. Many of the faculty members retained their zeal and enthusiasm, but for me it seemed tired and limiting. I felt that I was at a dead end, and I didn't see the way out.

The Exxon Valdez sank in the Gulf of Alaska, causing a devastating oil spill—precisely the kind of disaster that we had warned of in our Alaska pipeline litigation almost twenty years earlier. It was a bitter reminder of the fragility of our public interest law successes. Though we had substantial success in opening governmental processes to public participation, in the Reagan and the two Bush administrations the doors were closed again.

In early 1989, I received another catalogue from the Omega Institute. I was more aware, as I thumbed through it, that I was looking into a parallel universe, across a vast uncharted space. The politicians, educators, and lawyers who surrounded the Law School in Queens were not looking through this catalogue, marking interesting programs. I knew that I didn't have to worry about meeting someone I knew if I actually signed up.

I was struck by the announcement of a five-day meditation retreat led by a Vietnamese Zen Buddhist monk, Thich Nhat Hanh, called Thay by his students. He had lived through the Vietnam War, a leader in the Buddhist peace movement, despised equally by the Americans and by the Vietcong. A poet and philosopher, he had been nominated for the Nobel Peace Prize by Martin Luther King.[3] The retreat would be conducted in silence for the most part. Thay would offer meditation instructions and a lecture once a day, drawing the connections between meditation practice and social action. *Engaged Buddhism* is what he called it. No frills. No elaborate Tibetan tales and no panoply of gods and saints with polysyllabic names. He taught *mindfulness*—wakeful attention to the present moment.

It sounded interesting. I had been practicing my own homegrown meditation for several years at this point. I hoped that a skilled teacher, a supportive community, and a period of prolonged practice might deepen my practice. Besides, a week in spring among flowering fruit trees on the shore of a pond with canoes sounded like a good escape. Susan had not yet begun meditation, and she was interested in trying it.

When we assessed the housing options Omega offered, from private double rooms to tent sites, we decided to heighten the camplike experience by pitching a tent. We had just upgraded our equipment to a spacious dome tent suspended from three long golden wands that formed intersecting arches. We pictured ourselves camped beside the lake, plunging into its chilly water each morning, the rising sun reflected in its still surface. We felt that the natural connection would complement the meditation experience, literally grounding the meditation practice by actually sleeping on the earth.

It worked pretty much as we planned—except that the sun never shone, and we struggled continually with wet raincoats and muddy boots. Yet we were surprisingly comfortable and happy.

At the core of Thay's teaching was cultivating mindfulness, being fully awake and alive in the present moment, whether that moment holds joy or misery. All phenomena are transitory. Nothing is permanent. The meditative state is one of watching things closely—ideas, physical sensations, emotional states—as they arise and disappear, without attachment or aversion.

Our wet tent was a laboratory for this work. We were disappointed that there was no sunshine and swimming, but we let ourselves experience our disappointment and then we watched it disappear, to be replaced by a new feeling, often the feeling of pleasure at being warm and snug under the elegant dome of our tent. Clinging to no particular feeling or idea, we brought awareness back to the moment, to the in-breath and the out-breath. A constant process of letting go, of seeing our thoughts flowing through our minds without claiming them or holding onto them.

This was, in essence, the same process I had learned from David Hood and had been practicing each morning. It was different at Omega, however, surrounded by a hundred other people committed to the same process, their commitment helping to strengthen mine. The meditation went on for hours each day. At first, this was a big problem for me. What could be more frustrating than sitting for hours, watching my breath, harassed by an unceasing flow of thoughts, memories, anxieties, and plans for the future? I wanted to free my mind of outside concerns but, of course, my mind did not cooperate, throwing up one anxiety-generating issue after another.

But the endless stream of Law School business began to slow down. And I was able to suspend the steady flow of negative judgments about myself as an inadequate meditator. Thay taught, "Meditation is about starting over, again and again." Cultivating a nonjudging mind. Being fully present with whatever arises in each moment, whether it was pleasant or not, letting go of the characterization, of the judgment.

Thay's gentle teachings helped guide Susan and me into this unfamiliar thought terrain. He was a man of striking presence. Small, brown-skinned, with close-cropped hair, dressed in a rough brown robe wrapped around his slight body, he had a serene expression, a gentle half-smile that often appears on the lips of sculptures of the Buddha. Of course, I knew he had survived as a peace activist though the Vietnam War, so I understood that this serenity was hard won. It was not forged by avoiding difficult situations—violence, rage, and misery—but by immersing himself in the full catastrophe of the Vietnam War. He had witnessed the destruction of his country and here he was, teaching Americans to meditate, be kind to ourselves, and relieve the suffering of others.

I was accustomed to a different kind of teacher. Short on equanimity, most of my teachers had taught with a hard-edged, assertive intellectual style and a single-minded focus on technique and subject-matter mastery, lessons that I found congenial at the time. They encouraged us to live in our heads. Thay, in contrast, taught softly, bringing us into our bodies, into the world of sensation.

At first, I was put off by the apparent simplicity of his teachings. I had been trained to thrive on complexity, on making fine discriminations, on isolating reason from emotion or feeling. This was something new, and in a quiet way, exciting. A teacher with a limited vocabulary, a humble but confident presentation, introducing us to a technique of inquiry that was almost embarrassingly simple.

At the end of a long day of meditative silence, Susan and I crawled into our tent, lay in our double sleeping bag, listened to the rain drumming on the dome, and tried to make sense of this experience. We laughed about the incongruity of it. Eating our meals in meditative silence, with close attention to each bite of food, reflecting on the food's texture and flavors. Looking at other people across the table slowly and attentively chewing. Giving full, undivided attention to ordinary activities. We found ourselves in a state of heightened sensitivity to the sights and sounds around us. Our normal anxieties and commitments fell away, while a quiet, reflective part of the brain that had been accessible only sporadically gradually became more available.

Thay was a learned Zen priest who offered teachings rooted in Buddhist doctrine during the course of the long silent days. Coming to his lectures out of my place of meditative silence, I was able to temporarily suspend my usual habit of critiquing each new idea as it was articulated, almost in midsentence. Perhaps because of this unusual receptivity, I found myself drawn to some core Buddhist principles—impermanence and nonattachment, compassion and the commitment to relieving suffering, the interconnection of all beings. These concepts resonated with the ideas that had been emerging in my conversations with Ralph Siu and in my wilderness quests. Although I was not interested in becoming a Buddhist, I was drawn to these simple and profound concepts, presented with depth and humility, which seemed to have so much to offer in my work and my world. And I listened with interest to some of the more esoteric teachings—rebirth across species and many lifetimes, full enlightenment, karma that extends from one life into the next— feeling no need to accept them or reject them.

As I listened to Thay and observed him, I noted that he had much in common with Ralph Siu. Despite the obvious differences between a robed Buddhist monk and an eminent research scientist, I was struck by the qualities they shared—the fullness of their presence; their precise, unwavering attention; their calm, easy, and unhurried movement; their empathy and kindness; their cheerful good humor.

I began to explore the idea that wise people are most easily recognized by the way they live their lives, not by the books they write, the ideas they teach, or the movements they lead. Wisdom is a quality of their whole being, expressed in their words, their actions, and their relationships. Their ability to bring wisdom to the solution of problems is an outgrowth of the way they live. The respect that they enjoy as problem-solvers and advisers is grounded in their personal qualities, which are recognized and valued. They speak with modesty and hold their opinions lightly. Their wisdom is apparent, but only to people who are attuned to wisdom and have the ability to recognize the qualities of the wise person.

Wisdom is undervalued today because most people move too fast and too blindly to even recognize the wise person when she appears. Glib self-confidence and substantive mastery are mistaken for wisdom. We rely on credentials and advanced degrees to certify that a person deserves our respect and attention rather than make our own judgments. We mistake expertise, which can in some cases lead to the growth of wisdom, for wisdom itself.

The experience of extended meditation practice and my exposure to Thay's teaching of the basic Buddhist insights awakened my interest in exploring the connection between meditation and wisdom. Could I undertake to practice wisdom, living the wise life that would generate wise actions and decisions? Could this be a new way to approach activism, to start from the place of wisdom and compassion rather than the place of anger and insistence on legal rights?

I could imagine shifting the balance between reconciliation and polarization, between resolving disputes and sharpening conflict. I could envision a vigorous advocacy that avoids demonizing people who disagree—an activism nourished by meditation and infused by wisdom.

My exposure to Thay also demonstrated to me the connection between wisdom and a commitment to social transformation. I thought of other people who brought wisdom to the work of social justice—the Dalai Lama, Nelson Mandela, Gandhi, Martin Luther King. Their lives were lived with courage and depth, and they grounded their work in generosity of spirit and compassion.

Meditation, wisdom, and the commitment to social transformation could flow together. Thay had figured out how to do it in a way that fit his culture. I might be able to figure it out in mine.

8

CONVERGENCE

IN 1989, while I was thinking about what to do next, I took the private elevator to a spacious suite on the thirty-fifth floor of the Waldorf Astoria, where I was greeted by several members of the family of the late Nathan Cummings, the Sara Lee cheesecake king. The hosts were Cummings's elegantly dressed, silver-haired son and several of his adult grandchildren. His daughter, Buddy Mayer, who was not physically in the room, participated actively in the conversation from her hospital bed in Chicago via the conference telephone that sat on the coffee table beside the silver tea service. We sat informally on the overstuffed sofas, spreading marmalade on flaky, fragrant croissants as we talked. They welcomed me with unaffected cordiality into their circle.

A few weeks earlier, I had run into a friend on upper Broadway who told me about a new foundation, endowed in his will by Nathan Cummings with more than $300 million in assets. So far, his descendants had chosen four areas for grant making—arts, health, environment, and Jewish life—but they didn't have a clear idea about what they wanted to do and were looking for a president to help them figure it out. The foundation would give away about $15 million each year. She asked if I would like to be considered.

It sounded interesting. When I was looking for money to launch CLASP, I had believed that most people who worked in foundations were passive in their work style, arrogant in their interactions, and cautious in their responses. While there are some foundation people who fit that description, I have had enough experience in raising foundation money to know that a foundation officer with courage and imagination can do enormous good, supporting new ideas, convening meetings to explore solutions to pressing problems, helping grantees assemble the resources they need to be effective. I liked the idea of opening to a broader world where beauty, spirit, and intuition were not inherently suspect, of spending time with a mix of artists and rabbis, environmental activists and health advocates. The prospect of working as a foundation president sounded like it might be a welcome respite from the adversarial, argumentative lawyer's world—and it might be an opportunity to explore the practice of wisdom.

I asked her to put my name forward. "But I'm not hopeful," I said. "I've never even worked for a foundation before."

"True," she said, "but you've raised a lot of foundation money, so you obviously know how to play the game. And they'll like your start-up experience."

A few weeks after preliminary conversations and reference checks, I was invited to meet with the family. When I received their invitation, I reflected on the fact that I never would have been invited to the preliminary interview if I had stayed at Arnold & Porter. My decision to leave had opened more doors than it had closed, although I had no way to know that at the time.

After some small talk with the Cummings family, I raised the issue that was uppermost in my mind. "I know that there are few foundations that are willing to take controversial positions and to commit to a social justice agenda. Those are the foundations that have supported my work in the past, and that is the kind of foundation that I would be interested in building."

Ruth Cummings Sorensen, a granddaughter who was actively engaged in the downtown arts world, replied, "We want to create that unusual kind of foundation—cutting-edge grants and social justice, rather than grants to well-established art museums and research universities. Enough buildings have already been named in honor of our grandfather, from the Stanford campus to Mt. Sinai Hospital on Central Park."

Her cousin, Rob Mayer, the family member with an M.B.A. and experience working with his grandfather at Sara Lee, seemed less comfortable with my orientation and unconventional résumé. He was good-humored about it, but he obviously valued order and businesslike administration, and was troubled by my lack of financial and managerial experience. "Cutting edge is fine," he said, "but I want to be certain that the foundation takes only prudent risks and carefully measures the success of its grantees against objective benchmarks."

"You can see we have some strong opinions and disparate views," said the elegant Herb Cummings, the founder's son. "This is not going to be an easy start-up."

"Every family has its dynamics," I replied. I could see that the corporate, managerial faction of the family, with Rob as its spokesman, would be aligned against the more risk-taking, venturesome branch that Ruth had spoken for. But, when I remembered the intensity and anger of the arguments at CUNY over race, class, and gender, this fault line and the family's other disagreements—splits among family branches, intergenerational tensions, and shadows of ancient grievances—seemed manageable.

After I finished my café au lait and was in the oak-paneled elevator going down into the streets of Manhattan again, I had a sense that I could be comfortable with this family. They had much in common with my own family of origin, Eastern European Jews arriving in a foreign land at the turn of the twentieth century, with no money but great ambition, who in one generation moved out of poverty. Their connections to Judaism were all over the map, from pious observance to militant secularism, and some of them had explored other spiritual paths; still, they retained a traditional Jewish commitment to social justice. I liked their unpretentiousness, their willingness to acknowledge what they did not know, their openness about their search to find meaning in their own lives. Buddy Mayer, the voice over the speakerphone, told us that marching in Mississippi in the civil rights movement had been one of the most meaningful events of her life. I thought back to my own brief stint in Louisiana and was impressed by the impact that her civil rights work had on her sense of herself. The others in the room had obviously heard her story before; I respected her for underscoring the responsibilities of wealth: "the duty to give back," she called it.

There was much about this foundation that sounded attractive to me. It was large enough so that its grants could make a real difference, yet not so large—like the Ford or Rockefeller Foundations—that its grants were on the scale of a small country's annual budget, which made them more visible, cautious, and vulnerable.

On the other hand, I was concerned about becoming a retainer to a rich family, the person who doled out their money to the nonprofit world. I disliked that part of the philanthropic enterprise, which was at its root an exchange relationship—philanthropists negotiating over the size of the sign that recognized their generosity, making large contributions to their children's prep schools and to the hospitals at which they anticipated being treated.

I discussed my concerns with some people I knew from my years of foundation fund-raising. Waldemar Nielsen, whose books on foundations had become standard texts, told me: "If you take this job you will have had your last bad meal, and your last honest compliment." Still, he advised me to take the position. I thought of the New Yorker cartoon showing a man shoveling money out a window; his disapproving supervisor runs up behind him and says, "Just a minute, young man! That's not the way we do things at the Ford Foundation!"

I reflected on Nielsen's light remark. There was a real question about how I could take a job like this and not be seduced by the power and money. I would move from our law school in a converted junior high school on Main Street in Queens to the thirty-second floor of a Philip Johnson building on the Upper East Side; from lunches at the kosher pizzeria across from the Law School to the latest Thai/French fusion restaurant off the lobby of our building. The paradox of working for the poor in this setting would become a tension in my new life. The large sums of money we were dispensing would pose challenges to my balance and humility. Everyone was a potential grantee and everyone would want to be my best friend.

At the same time, this foundation definitely presented an opportunity to direct substantial new resources into the solution of important issues. I liked their four program areas: environment, health, arts, and Jewish life. Among them, Jewish life was probably the only one that I would not have chosen myself. As a secular Jew who had not received much nourishment from the rationalistic, desiccated Reform Judaism in which I had been raised, I had never thought deeply about the Jewish spiritual tradition, but I was open to learning more.

The foundation would also present an opportunity for me to learn about artistic creativity, deep ecology, a more just and effective health system—things that interested me but that I had not fully explored. I knew that I had changed greatly in my past career moves, and I anticipated that this would move me further along. When the family invited me to become the first president of the Nathan Cummings Foundation, I accepted, thinking that this foundation would be an ideal place to work to bring social transformation and the practice of wisdom together.

The announcement of my selection in the *New York Times* landed on the desks of hundreds of fund-raising professionals.[1] As soon as I moved into the NCF office on Third Avenue, I began to receive requests for meetings from prominent people—university presidents, museum directors, symphony conductors, hospital directors. One of my first visitors was Teddy Kolleck, then the mayor of Jerusalem, who had known Nathan Cummings and was always looking for American Jewish investors for his projects. Until we were able to develop and publish grant guidelines, any fundraiser with imagination could frame an argument for why his or her program fell within one or more of our four program areas. I moved quickly to hire a staff to manage the foundation's assets and four directors to work with me and the foundation's board of trustees to develop each of the program areas.

As the foundation president, I became accustomed to the flattering attention of people who thought that all my ideas were good and all my jokes were funny. Especially in the beginning the contrast with CUNY, where every word I spoke was subject to a criticism that could be harsh and unforgiving, was stark. I had to remind myself that the response at Cummings was conditional on my being so close to a large amount of money. I was not entirely successful in resisting the temptation to take it personally.

In developing NCF's programs, I drew on my experience in law and advocacy and the Cummings family's willingness to take on controversial issues. In the arts, for example, the foundation had opportunities to exercise leadership on the issue of arts censorship.

Shortly after we began, I learned that the director of the Cincinnati Museum of Contemporary Art had been arrested and was being criminally prosecuted under pornography laws for an exhibit of Robert Mapplethorpe's photographs. Although we had not yet established our grant guidelines or hired the program director, it seemed to me that the use of the criminal justice process to censor artistic expression should be a matter of fundamental concern to a foundation with an arts program. I flew to Cincinnati, saw the exhibit, and met with the director and his board chair. Although the story of the criminal prosecution had received national attention, they had not received support from any foundations, museums, or arts organizations, and they felt entirely isolated in facing criminal charges and taking on the conservative establishment in an important skirmish in the culture wars.

As I sat down to lunch with these people who were on the firing line, I realized how grateful they were that I had come to look into their situation and offer support. The director said, "I am actually facing criminal charges because of an exhibit I installed in the museum. I can't believe that I have not heard from any other museum director or any of the established foundations that have supported the arts." It seemed clear to me that Mapplethorpe's exhibit fell within the protection of the First Amendment and that the prosecution was unjustifiable.

My first grant recommendation to the board was to establish a legal defense fund for the museum and its director. The board approved the grant, additional supporters came forward, and the defendants were acquitted after a trial.[2]

We made a number of grants to resist art censorship and promote public support for accessible and public art. When the Brooklyn Museum was under attack from Mayor Giuliani for displaying paintings that the mayor considered impious and indecent, we organized a small group of foundations in the arts area to support the museum, financially and through our defense of their right to display controversial art.[3] I was surprised that many foundations and museums failed to come to the aid of the Brooklyn Museum. I attributed it, in part, to their unwillingness—and the unwillingness of their trustees—to stick their necks out and risk the wrath of a famously vindictive mayor with whom they had multiple, complicated relationships. This was a reminder for me of the extent of the interconnections between the world of politics and business, on the one hand, and foundations and art patronage, on the other.

I also drew on my experience in advocacy when I began to explore the creation of a new think tank that would develop a public policy agenda for the new century grounded in social justice, sustainability, and community values. After a long gestation period, we located foundation partners and established Demos: A Network for Ideas & Action.[4] Now in its sixth year, with offices in four cities, it has become a leading center for research and advocacy for democratic renewal, effective government programs, and economic equality.

Robert Redford, a serious environmentalist as well as an actor and arts entrepreneur, came to the foundation to discuss his planned conference on global warming, which was at that point a still-controversial hypothesis, bringing scientists and policymakers from around the world to his conference center at Sundance. Arriving at our office in a cream-colored suit and a lime green silk T-shirt, he created a considerable stir.

I agreed to participate in the conference, the first meeting I ever attended where my presence was justified by the money I had access to rather than my knowledge, insight, or experience. There were times when people genuinely wanted my advice, my input, my partnership on a project; I had, after all, some relevant experience and a capacity to develop creative responses to hard problems. But for as long as I remained at the foundation, I was always valued, at least in part, for the checks that I could sign. And some people could never look at me without seeing a flashing dollar sign on my forehead.

Redford's Sundance conference was a wonderful opportunity for me to be educated on global warming by some of the most knowledgeable scientists and policymakers in the world. I became an early convert to the view that global climate disruption, a more accurate term, is a serious problem that poses a great threat to planetary well-being. I returned to my office from the conference to face a dilemma of how a foundation could use a relatively modest amount of grants—perhaps $500,000 per year—to deal with a problem of such enormous dimensions.

With the leadership of our environmental program director, we decided to focus on transportation, a sector where the greenhouse gases that cause global warming are generated in large quantities. It also was an area where innovations in technology and public policy could dramatically reduce the amount of carbon dioxide emissions. It was a large problem but small enough that we could have an impact. The transportation issue was a good one because it required us and our grantees to see an environmental issue not in isolation but embedded in a complex political, economic, and cultural matrix. We funded transportation specialists in environmental advocacy organizations and technological innovation to reduce fossil fuel consumption.

We drew together a coalition of other funders and created the Surface Transportation Policy Project, with an office in Washington, D.C., to coordinate the work of the environmentalists and provide a steady, well-informed capital presence on transportation issues, from highway construction to mass transit.[5] I was pleased by the connection between this project and the environmental advocacy we had done at CLASP. The public interest law pioneers had developed the skills to influence key environmental issues—through the courts, the administrative agencies, the media, and Congress. Their accumulated knowledge and experience meant that there were committed and sophisticated advocates to work on transportation policy and other aspects of global climate disruption.

The environmentalists' alliance to develop a more energy-efficient transportation policy won some major victories. But it could not catalyze the major shift in American life, especially alternatives to the gas-guzzling automobile, that will be necessary to reduce our generation of greenhouse gases. There has not been any fundamental move toward a green transportation policy, and few Americans have changed their lifestyle to reduce significantly the amount of greenhouse gases they generate.

Our Jewish Life program officer, Rachel Cowan, was a rabbi, a convert to Judaism, and a veteran of the civil rights movement. Like the members of the Cummings family, she had an unusual background for a leader in Jewish philanthropy, and our grants reflected their unconventional perspectives. A few years before she joined the foundation staff, her husband Paul, an influential writer, had died of cancer. She had been disappointed by how little the Jewish community had to offer to support their spiritual needs during his illness and as his death grew near. She brought to the foundation an interest in building the field of Jewish healing, developing and promoting a distinctively Jewish way to provide support for the nonphysical suffering that is a dimension of serious illness both for the sick person and for those who are close to the sick person. With the enthusiastic support of the NCF board of trustees, she and I worked together to create the Jewish Healing Center, which has catalyzed a Jewish healing movement in communities across the country.[6]

Our work led us to think more generally about supporting the movement for deepening Jewish spirituality. With the inspiring leadership of Rabbi Zalman Schachter, Jewish Renewal communities were springing up around the country. Rabbi Michael Lerner and *Tikkun* Magazine were energizing spiritual activism. Rabbi Jonathan Omer-Man was leading a revival of Jewish meditation.[7] Jews who had found the religion spiritually arid were returning to their faith. As yet, the highly structured and traditional Jewish philanthropies had not acknowledged this shift and were not supporting it. We felt there was an important opportunity for the Cummings Foundation to have a significant impact.

I found myself in rewarding dialogues with rabbis and other spiritually engaged Jews. The foundation made grants to support their efforts to bring Jewish insights to modern problems, from environmental protection to feminism and the role of women. NCF grants supported the spiritual growth of rabbis and congregations. After the foundation's trustees visited Russia, meeting with Russian Jews who were just learning what Judaism was, we began programs to support Jews who intended to stay in Russia, at a time when the organized Jewish community was insisting that emigration was the only viable policy.

The foundation was able to support this renaissance in Jewish spiritual life and to develop new institutions to encourage Jews to pursue their commitments to ecological wholeness and social justice in a Jewish context. Rachel was an inspiring guide, and many

of the Cummings family members found their own ways to reconnect with their Judaism, finding personal growth in their engagement with the foundation's work. I also found myself going more
deeply into my Jewish connection. My exploration of other spiritual paths enriched my participation in the Jewish work.

When I received a letter soliciting foundation support to bring a
group of rabbis together with the Dalai Lama for a conference about
points of intersection in their traditions, I was immediately
intrigued. Unprecedented in the long history of the two religions,
the dialogue held promise of being a significant exchange. We made
a small grant to support the meeting.

I went to Dharamsala with the rabbis and observed the rich conversation and the ways in which a deep mutual respect for the spiritual traditions emerged from their interaction. I was absorbed by
the relationships with the rabbis and intrigued by their dialogues
among themselves, across denominations. Most of them seemed to
open to the wisdom of the Dalai Lama's perspective without feeling that they had to constrain their engagement because of the chosen people rubric or a special Jewish relationship with God. I had
never felt so connected to my Jewish roots. I was also impressed by
the Dalai Lama—his wisdom and presence, and the compassionate
way that he held the suffering of his people and the Jewish people.

I persuaded Rodger Kamenetz, a poet who attended the gathering,
to write *The Jew in the Lotus*, a book that chronicled the interchange
and reached a large audience, continuing to enrich the understanding of both Judaism and Buddhism.[8] He described the American Jews
who had found spiritual enrichment in Buddhist practice. I felt that
I was part of that community, and that my exposure to meditation
and Buddhist ideas had opened the Jewish world to me.

The Cummings Foundation developed a unique blend of grants, integrating support for forceful, cutting-edge advocacy with support for meditation and other inner work. This grant-making perspective came, in part, from my experience in Dharamsala and my evolving understanding of inner work as a way to support and deepen good work in the world, as I drew together the poles of my previous work.

It became increasingly clear that Jewish Life was more than just one out of four grant-making areas. Since the foundation had declared that the Jewish heritage was central to its mission, it opened up the sphere of spiritual inquiry in all the areas of our program. In most secular environments such inquiry is, by tacit understanding, foreclosed. Secular institutions leave little space for spiritual dialogue; the language of secularism is a barrier to introducing the language of the heart and the spirit. Because we had a religious identification, we were freed from that rigidity. Once we were liberated from the secular limitation, we were not bound to exclusive reliance on the Jewish perspective. We could range more broadly. We had the advantage of the rich Jewish tradition—but we were unlike many other insular Jewish foundations by virtue of the secular dimensions of our mission. We had an unusual opportunity to deal with issues of life and death, illness and health, human responsibility for the ecosphere—in all their dimensions, secular and spiritual.

Since the foundation had a Jewish commitment and a rabbi on our staff, we were an unusually receptive place for the dialogue between spirit and social justice. Because several of the trustees and most of the staff were not Jewish, we had an incentive to speak about spiritual matters in an ecumenical manner, to find a language that allowed us to find the wisdom that lies at the heart of Judaism, many

other religions, and secular humanism. It was this institutional culture that led the foundation to make the initial grant for the
National Religious Partnership for the Environment. At that point,
there was no systematic effort to encourage religions to bring the
weight and depth of their traditions to bear on issues of environmental protection. Cummings saw the importance and potential power
of such an initiative, and we stipulated it must reach out to the more
conservative religious groups as well as the liberal denominations.

Many of the trustees welcomed this direction in the foundation's
work. Rob Mayer, with his more managerial orientation and analytic clarity, would often raise probing, skeptical questions about
some of our grants to promote inner exploration and spirituality. I
became accustomed to his challenges on these matters—and I tried
hard to think about outcome measures, even for grants where outcomes were likely to be uncertain, subtle, and unpredictable. But I
insisted that our grants could not be limited to projects that would
yield measurable outcomes over a short period of time. Other members of the board were open to my view, and Rob was always willing to support the board's decision. His tenacious probing created
a dynamic tension on the board that made our program more rigorous and effective, while it made our process more stressful.

As we were thinking through our health program, I invited Daniel
Goleman to the office for a conversation. He was a *New York Times*
reporter on psychology and health, and later became the author of
the global best-seller *Emotional Intelligence.*[9] He had written his
Ph.D. thesis at Harvard on meditation and Buddhist psychology,
after doing research in an Indian ashram.

The entrepreneurial Goleman was delighted to be drawn into
the NCF conversation about our health program. "The relationship

between the mind and body is an area of growing therapeutic importance," he said. "Scientists are investigating the many ways that mind states affect physical health. High stress causes heart attacks. Pain can be reduced by meditation practice. Suffering at the end of life can be managed by treating dying people with a compassion that is grounded in meditation."

His comments intrigued me, and I thought about the connection between my own experience with meditation and the emerging therapeutic applications he described. I began to see the way that my work in the foundation could draw on and reinforce my meditation practice. Through Dan, I came to meet some of the pioneers who had studied with Buddhist masters, in Asia and the United States, and began teaching meditation in the West. Among them were Joseph Goldstein, Jack Kornfield, and Sharon Salzberg, who spent years in southern India, Thailand, and Burma, then established the Insight Meditation Society in Barre, Massachusetts; Joan Halifax, a Zen priest and anthropologist in New Mexico; Paul Gorman, a senior vice president at the Cathedral of St. John the Divine in New York, who collaborated with Ram Dass on their classic book, *How Can I Help?*; and Mirabai Bush, another collaborator with Ram Dass, on the book *Compassion in Action*.[10]

I met Ram Dass himself. He was living in a cottage in Marin County, where we sat together in his hot tub while he reviewed his incredible journey from a brilliant academic career at Harvard through a complete spiritual reorientation. As Richard Alpert, he had been the youngest tenured professor in the Harvard Psychology Department; then he began his experiments with LSD, left Harvard, and traveled to India, where he met the guru who put him on the spiritual path. "He told me that my life should be given to helping others, to relieving suffering. There are different spiritual paths. Mine is the path of service." Consistent with his understanding of that mission, he was happy to help me think through the ways in which we might bring the wisdom of inner work to the world of social action.

I began to meet with these wisdom teachers and others, an informal and shifting group, with people coming and going, as I worked with staff and trustees to shape the foundation's program. Sometimes we called ourselves the Compassionate Action Working Group, sometimes the Spirit and Action Working Group, sometimes, whimsically, the Wisdom Party. As we met through the early years of the nineties, we talked about our desire to be of service in these unsettled times. We asked ourselves hard questions. How could we have the courage to confront the underlying structures that led to deep injustice in our country and in the world? What fear of failure or isolation held us back from making the sacrifices necessary to address the deepest challenges? We acknowledged our attraction to the world of power, and our reluctance to give up our connections to people in power. Longtime meditators and respected teachers, their modesty and commitment to service gave me a new model for a way to be in the world—committed to serving others, cultivating wisdom, being open to changing themselves, and exposing their own vulnerability.

I found that our conversations helped me resist the temptations of power inherent in my work, and also helped me bring the spiritual dimension forward among my foundation colleagues, where there was a strong tendency to be secular, pragmatic, and cautious. I sometimes discussed Cummings Foundation programs in the Working Group, but more important than addressing specific projects, these sessions helped me stay devoted to seeking the deepest wisdom available to me and bringing it into the work of the foundation.

I had stumbled into an extraordinary circle of wise and dedicated people. The Buddhist term *sangha* refers to the community of people who support each other in their meditation, study, and effort to bring wisdom to their service in the world. We all need such support. Some of the Cummings Foundation's most creative initiatives were nourished indirectly by the Working Group's free-floating conversations.

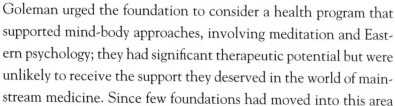

Goleman urged the foundation to consider a health program that supported mind-body approaches, involving meditation and Eastern psychology; they had significant therapeutic potential but were unlikely to receive the support they deserved in the world of mainstream medicine. Since few foundations had moved into this area and the science had begun to look promising, it seemed a natural area for our support. This was especially important because research efforts and treatment resources were increasingly moving in the opposite direction—toward biological explanations of illness, and treatment of the patient as a collection of symptoms, not as a whole person with emotional and spiritual needs.

The NCF investigation confirmed Goleman's enthusiastic assessment. In addition to making grants to the explorers who were developing this work, we drew together a small group that met at the NCF office to share information and think about ways to develop the field. One critical issue was that the mind-body interventions had not received the recognition and legitimacy that was due. There was too little public understanding, and the medical establishment was skeptical.

The Fetzer Institute, a foundation in Kalamazoo, Michigan, headed by Rob Lehman, shared our interest in mind-body healing.[11] NCF and Fetzer became decade-long partners in the work, developing ways to bring the subject to a larger public. Rob and I brought the project to Bill Moyers, who had a unique place in American television journalism and a skill at getting below the surface of current events, finding the story that hadn't yet broken, often exploring the connections of spirit and public policy. Lehman, Moyers, and I met for sandwiches around Moyers's conference table. He had a lot of questions: Was there really enough to report on? Was it solidly grounded? Were there articulate, compelling people working in the field? We made a small grant to his nonprofit production company to permit him to investigate these questions. He decided to go forward, and prepared a proposal for a five-hour series for public television, *Healing and the Mind*.[12]

Cummings and Fetzer jointly funded the series, highlighting the work of some of the leaders in the mind-body field, people who were treating illness and health disorders as a complicated challenge to the mind-body organism, not simply a biological matter. Cancer, pain management, and heart disease were all illnesses being effectively dealt with. Moyers's sensitive treatment of these matters was a turning point, leading to a popular television series and a best-selling book; in large part because of his presentation, most doctors today are exposed to mind-body thinking as a part of their medical education.

The most important outgrowth of the Working Group meeting was the Center for Contemplative Mind in Society. Mirabai Bush, a senior meditation teacher who had been a charter member of our Working Group, agreed to take the leadership in developing the Center, a new organization to bring the contemplative dimension to mainstream institutions in order to build a wiser and more compassionate world. A number of meditation centers had been created around the country, teaching meditation in a particular tradition, most often Buddhism, but they did not focus on the general benefits of meditation if the practice were more widely diffused in mainstream institutions. The Center would build on their work and present

meditation in a secular form, permitting people who were not interested in a new religious commitment to explore the benefit of meditation in their lives. This was a natural extension of my inner work.
I had discovered in my own experience the benefit of meditation in
making my work more effective, and helping me cultivate clarity of
vision, compassion, and a sense of balance.

Over the past ten years, the Center has conducted meditation
programs for lawyers, social activists, corporate executives, and journalists. Together with the American Council of Learned Societies,
it has awarded more than a hundred fellowships to permit professors
to introduce contemplative practice into their teaching in a variety
of disciplines—from architecture to literature, from law to philosophy. During this period, meditation has become more widely
accepted and understood, and significant scientific findings have
indicated that it can have important health benefits and a dramatic
impact on brain function. As chairman of the Center's board of
trustees I have been actively involved in its programs, which in turn
has deepened my commitment to my own meditation practice.[13]

Global warming and other major environmental challenges will
respond only to a shift in the deep structure of values, a fundamental shift in consciousness—toward the recognition of interdependence among people and with all living beings—leading to changes
in the way we live in the industrialized countries. The leaders of
the environmental movement and others will have to reach a new
level of consciousness if they are to be able to imagine and inaugu-
rate the dramatic changes that will be necessary to respond effectively to the massive challenges ahead.

I thought that meditation was a technique that might open environmentalists to a new consciousness, to looking into the connec-

tions between human beings and the natural world—more deeply than at the level of intellectual theory or legal doctrine. Contemplative, slow inquiry could drop down to a level at which interconnections could be felt more in the body than understood by the mind. I went to see Joan Halifax, an environmentalist, a Zen priest, and a member of our Working Group. I proposed to Joan that we work together to offer a meditation retreat for environmental activists.

At the retreat I had attended with Thich Nhat Hanh while I was dean of the CUNY Law School, I had been moved by his vision of a world held together in a network of mutual dependence that he referred to as interbeing. He highlighted the reciprocal relationships of all elements of the natural world—the connections that unite the dying flower, decaying to nourish the soil, to newly sprouting flowers. I heard his teachings framed in a meditative silence that permitted me to take them in at a deep level. Many hours of focused silence had heightened my receptivity to new concepts and points of interconnection.

I thought that a meditation retreat led by Thay could have a deep influence on many people in the environmental movement. Joan agreed to take the lead in the venture. She developed the plan, and we funded it. More than three hundred people attended the five-day retreat, led by Thay, Joan, and Peter Mathiessen, the writer and Zen priest. It was an inspiring event.

The teachings invited contemplative attention to interbeing—our reliance for life and health on clean air and water, the inevitable passage from birth to death, the joy we can take from the natural beauty of the world around us, the need for respect and stewardship, the literal understanding that the human body is the aggregate of water and small amounts of other natural substances.

The participants were people who lived in the world of words, committed to advocacy efforts to protect the environment. Here they were together, with their primary commitment to looking inward in reflective silence. Only after they had spent days in this inward process did they begin to build bridges back to their ordinary lives, between their meditative insights and their advocacy.

I met Grove Burnett at the environmental retreat. An environmental lawyer in New Mexico, Grove returned home encouraged to start a meditation retreat for activists on a ranch in the Carson National Forest in northern New Mexico. He wanted to bring environmentalists together to retreat in silence, to restore their energy and deepen their connection to the natural world. It was just the kind of thing that I had hoped to see emerge, and the foundation supported it financially.

When Grove was ready to hold his first retreat for environmentalists, I decided to make the pilgrimage despite the daunting trip to get there. The Vallecitos Mountain Refuge was northwest of Santa Fe, and the last fifteen miles were over unpaved mountain roads.[14] There was no electricity or telephone. I was particularly drawn to meditation in the wilderness. It connected for me with my experiences of nature in the lakes of Ontario, the valleys of West Virginia, and the Adirondack Mountains. Here was an opportunity to deepen my connection to the natural world without distraction. It was a place where the human imprint was hardly visible and the magnitude and grandeur of the land would fill my consciousness completely—the rocky cliffs, high grass meadows, ponderosa pine, and the wild, unpredictable weather.

We slept in tents and met in the old log ranch house. Joseph Goldstein, the lead teacher on the retreat, was a tall, loose-jointed man who had grown up in his parents' bungalow colony in the Catskills. I found his talks about the Buddhist teachings, incongruously punctuated with Borscht Belt humor, accessible and engaging. It was interesting to receive teachings from a contemporary, someone from my own culture. I was struck by his presence and his wisdom.

The retreat was a profound experience. I had never been so long in so wild a place, maintaining a mindful awareness that made the silence and beauty more tangible. I was alive in my senses, seeing the sun rise and set day after day, feeling the afternoon heat and the frosty cold of the high-altitude nights.

Joseph's teaching focused attention on the present moment. At first, I was slow to give up familiar thought patterns—letting my mind wander, planning for the anticipated future and reliving past memories, but after a time, past and future fell away. When thoughts entered my mind, I let them come and go, without attachment or evaluation. I had heard these instructions before, but I was able to respond more fully as each day passed in this remote and overpowering place. The uninterrupted passage of time and the grand, unfamiliar surroundings made it easier to leave my traditional modes of thought and behavior.

Each evening Joseph gave a talk, introducing some of the wisdom teachings of the Buddhist tradition. We gathered in the log house that was the center of the ranch and watched the light of the setting sun slowly fade from the deep green meadows and the rocky cliffs in the distance as he spoke. A skillful teacher, he left aside the exotic elements tied to the specific Asian cultures in which these teachings had first appeared, cutting directly to the more universal core. The teaching about impermanence was reinforced by my own experience of the thoughts that passed through my mind and then disappeared, and by the never-ending changes in the high-mountain sky. The teaching of the interconnectedness of all beings was easier to understand when I was so deeply embedded in a wild place, far from the noise and hurry of my hyperurban life in Manhattan. My life was close to the essentials.

Joseph advised us to settle into the practice and observe what came up next, to refrain from making judgments of the experience that would interfere with the direct experience itself. I found that the stillness of the place was generating an inner stillness in me that made me more receptive to his gentle suggestions. I was able to suspend my critical faculty for much of the time, and simply be present in the experience, observing what was happening without judgment.

After a week in the stillness of the retreat, I took an early morning walk among the immense ponderosa pines as the sky was just beginning to glow in the East. I walked beside the Vallecitos River, at first a little stream that meandered through the meadow. After a half-mile of walking upstream, I was at the point where the river turns to frothing rapids as it comes roaring out of a narrow canyon, between two rocky cliffs. I sat down in a grassy spot beside a deep pool, savored the solitude, closed my eyes, and connected with my breath.

The roar of the flowing water blocked out all other sounds. I found myself in a place of deep inner peace, fully present in the moment. I felt myself a part of this place, not as a tourist or observer but rather as integral a part of the moment as the river or the fallen trees, the boulders or the grasses. It was a wordless space, and I felt myself taking it in more through my body than through my mind. It was a genuinely new experience—total presence, clarity of awareness, an uncritical sense of being at home, nothing to be done. Time fell away, and I sat without any sense of its passage.

Sitting there, I was exactly where I belonged; all my decisions had been right, though some had seemed doubtful at the time—to begin my meditation practice, to stick to it even when it seemed pointless, to accept the job at the foundation, to come on this retreat in a remote corner of the world, to get up this morning in the predawn chill and find my way to this isolated spot. It all seemed perfect. And I had the sense that I could trust my inner knowing to guide me in the future, that I had access to a wisdom that was a powerful and reliable ally to the finely tuned intellect that has been so potent a guide and asset in the past.

On the last day of the retreat, I took my notebook up to a high meadow and let myself reengage my analytic mind while I was still vibrating from my early morning experience by the river. I began to write down some thoughts about the role of meditation practice in cultivating wisdom, about the way that meditative silence can clear a space for wisdom to arise, and about the core of wisdom that Joseph's teachings had exposed—impermanence, interconnection, and compassion. These did not feel like lessons that came from the outside; rather it seemed that he had helped me connect with things that I already knew but had somehow forgotten. I realized I had a need to embrace the solitude that allowed wisdom to emerge. Our foundation could be the right place to work on this project. I felt confirmed in the thought that I now had begun to walk a wisdom path, and that the cultivation of wisdom would become central to my life and work.

When the foundation moved its office to a nineteenth-century industrial building facing Lincoln Center, we had an opportunity to renovate a large empty space. It is significant that we placed a meditation room close to the heart of the offices. It was a room for silent reflection and renewal, where some staff members would come together midafternoon for a period of silent meditation. Spatially and temporally, we were opening a space in which wisdom could arise. In renovating the building we also made a decision to leave the immense concrete support columns open and visible, a reminder of the reality that supported our lives and of the beauty in simple things. The treatment of space was sufficiently startling and open so that people coming into the place were challenged to think outside of their usual patterns. When our grantees or applicants were in the office at meditation time, we invited them to join us. It was a novel experience for many of them. Both staff and grantees received a creative jolt from the space where we met and the fact that we made a significant commitment to silence and meditation.

The members of the Cummings family entered into the creation of the foundation with a willingness to go deeply into the process, to embrace the possibility that they would be changed by their partici- pation in its activities and in their interaction with grantees. They were not simply analyzing social problems and allocating grants to support solutions. They were prepared to let their experience in NCF affect the shape of their own lives. I was not surprised that many of them underwent profound spiritual shifts: one entered rabbinical school, a second emigrated to Israel, a third undertook a deep medi- tation practice, a fourth enrolled in a series of in-depth programs designed to develop his full human potential. Even Buddy Mayer, the secular doyenne of the board, was willing to sit gamely and patiently in the studio of a senior Jewish meditation teacher and push her own capacities to look inward and find a place of inner peace.

Unlike the eminent and successful members of many foundation boards, they did not enter the process with the confident assump- tion that they knew the answers, that their knowledge and experi- ence were adequate to shape and guide an effective grants program. Some of the family, individuals who would not have been selected to join a nonfamily foundation board because of their relative lack of worldly recognition, were extremely effective board members precisely because they were open to new learning. Some had emerged from their own life crises with a deep interest in spiritual matters. Others had gone through the changes of the sixties with an openness that led to spiritual exploration. They were pleased to be in a foundation setting where this experience could be honored and expressed.

The foundation's early success in its grant programs integrating the inner and outer dimensions had created something distinctive and important in the foundation world, with few precedents. And it was exciting for me personally to see the different pieces of my life come together; my early explorations—yoga at CLASP, winter camping in the Adirondacks—formerly tangential to my real work, were now being seamlessly woven into the most creative part of my work life.

Our work in meditation and contemplative awareness was not greeted with uniform enthusiasm by all trustees. Some objected that our support for inner work was ungrounded and unconnected to the other program objectives. Their objections were also tied to the rising enthusiasm in the philanthropic world for clearly articulated corporate-type decision processes and evaluation standards. A frequent claim made in the philanthropic world was that foundations would be more effective if they made themselves more like corporations. Corporations had an easy way of judging their effectiveness, by their bottom line, by their profitability, by their financial return to shareholders. Philanthropy obviously had no such bottom line. But if a philanthropy had clear and quantifiable goals—the number of poor children going through a specific program, or a certain number of exhibits by new artists to be shown at a particular museum, for example—there could be a relatively simple process for evaluating success.

NCF was in a less concrete area, trying to change people's consciousness about the environment, bringing a deeper meditative reflectiveness into the professions, or alerting young physicians to the complex interrelationship between mind and body. We could establish evaluation criteria, but they inevitably would be diffuse, long-term, and unpersuasive to doubters.

The philanthropic sector, I felt, was fundamentally different from the corporate sector. Foundations should be home to wisdom, compassion, and interdependence. The norms of aggressive, competitive, and materialistic behavior that dominate the corporate sector could easily overtake foundations, but it would be a great loss. In a world that is becoming increasingly dominated by free market ideology, it is important to have a sector in which a different set of norms holds sway.

I remembered a conversation I had had with Ralph Siu during a visit to Washington, D.C. I told him about our transportation program at NCF. I was frustrated that our grantees weren't having more success. They were on the defensive, trying to protect air quality standards from dilution. We set benchmarks in our grant agreements, and our grantees weren't meeting them.

"Well, these are hard times," he said. "You can't be too attached to specific outcome measures, and you don't want your grantees to be. They should be flexible and responsive to subtle shifts in their relationships. They should be supple and able to flow with the currents. This is a long-term effort. You can't be too attached to outcomes that are measurable in the short term."

At that time, when some foundations were calling themselves "venture capitalists of the nonprofit sector" and asking nonprofit organizations to prepare "business plans," I was under that kind of pressure from some of my trustees. I was happy to have different advice from someone who had managed billion-dollar research budgets.

This debate frequently surfaced in our board meetings, explicitly and implicitly, with Rob Mayer taking the lead. There was never a conclusion to the discussion. We all agreed that we would evaluate our grants as effectively as possible while resisting the temptation to limit our grant making to those areas where hard-edged evaluation would be possible. The general thrust of the board was to continue our probes into the spiritual dimension of life and to draw together the connections between those explorations and the vigorous commitment to social justice and sustainability that characterized the foundation's grants.

I brought to these debates the fruits of my inner work, a growing capacity to listen receptively to people with whom I disagreed, a willingness to question and let go of my own dearly held beliefs. I thought back to my days at CLASP, how easy it had been for me to demonize the people who disagreed with me, to identify fully with my current causes, to grow impatient with delays. I had come a long way, and I felt that my meditation and other inner work had helped me respond to difficulties and challenges with equanimity and grace. I still had a long way to go—practicing wisdom is an unending voyage, not a destination.

I discovered that an advantage of being in a family foundation is that the crises of ordinary life—death, illness, and divorce—were never far from our experience, and these crises were dealt with and discussed. One turning point was the diagnosis of Herb Cummings, one of the senior members of our board, with a serious cancer. As the family struggled to cope with his illness and rapid decline, it deeply affected the way we thought about our grants programs. The health program, for example, undertook to look at the way death and dying are treated in America and made grants to support efforts to handle them more humanely. It made grants to address the extraordinary burdens that serious illness imposes on family caregivers.

Midway through my decade of leadership at the foundation, I was called one day to join Susan at her doctor's office. A lump had appeared in her left groin. The doctor tried to be reassuring and positive. Two weeks later we went early one morning to Lennox Hospital for a surgical biopsy, and the doctor told us that Susan had Non-Hodgkin's Lymphoma. Suddenly, we were ourselves at the center of a health crisis—the grants we had been making in the health area were close to home. We were living in the middle of the emotionally fraught world of cancer.

Susan's cancer was a slow-growing type that did not constitute an immediate threat to her life, but it was resistant to cure. During the next years, we went through alternating periods of radiation and chemotherapy, bracketed by long periods when she was symptom-free and we had only to deal with our anxiety. Altogether, her illness created a fundamental change in our lives.

I thought about the poignant Woody Allen story, "The Shallowest Man."[15] Lenny Mendel, the protagonist, was so frightened by his friend's cancer that he could not even visit him in the hospital. I was afraid that I would be unable to engage Susan's disease and become a full partner in dealing with it. I had never been much of a caregiver, and I was going to have to develop a new set of emotional skills.

But I found that Susan and I were able to draw on our shared experiences of contemplative practice, and we became closer as we joined in the management of the disease—in its physical, emotional, and spiritual dimensions. We went together to doctors' appointments and slogged across town in the midwinter slush for daily radiation treatments. Later, I sat with her during the long hours while chemicals were dripped into her arm, lived through the nausea and exhaustion that followed the chemotherapy. And we developed strategies to celebrate and rejoice during those periods when she was feeling herself, strong and energetic. When it was time to buy a wig, we went to the wig store with our grown children, and we all tried on wigs, clowning and improvising comic sketches. And when it turned out that Susan preferred to be bald most of the time rather than wear the wig, she looked beautiful with no hair, and we felt a kinship with the men and women who were bald by choice, a fairly common fashion statement in Manhattan.

Susan, who had been meditating since our retreat with Thay, found that meditation practice helped her face her new reality, the periods of uncertainty and the debilitating treatment, with less despair and anxiety—and so did I. Meditation practice starts from a recognition that suffering is an inevitable component of the human condition, and we had been reflecting on that reality for years. Our pain and anxiety were reduced by staying fully present with what was happening and not exacerbating the situation by clinging to a particular way that we wanted things to be. I was inspired by the thought of the Dalai Lama in Dharamsala, confronting the suffering of the Tibetan refugees with compassion and good cheer. Susan was part of a supportive community, people who had the capacity to deal with her crisis with love, clarity, and generosity. I was able to reach out, acknowledge my need, and accept their support, without any pretense of autonomy or strength. We were both able to rejoice in her periods of vitality and strength, when the disease was dormant.

Susan's cancer became a central part of my reality during my last five years at the foundation. It made my inner work more essential—morning meditation practice and annual ten-day retreats at Vallecitos. It made the work at the foundation more precious. The Nathan Cummings Foundation was an important leader in drawing together the elements of wisdom and compassion in a foundation's grants and work, and I was fortunate to be there to promote it and to benefit from it.

9

THE NORTHWEST PASSAGE

S USAN AND I moved to Berkeley in 2001, when she was still weak from her latest round of chemotherapy and the walk up the steep stairs to our rented house in the Berkeley hills left her panting. We wanted to be close to the children if she had to undergo further treatment. A few years later, through the kindness of a friend, I found myself across the table from the playwright Tony Kushner at a dinner sponsored by the Berkeley Repertory Theater at a French bistro near the Berkeley campus. Kushner, who was in town for the opening of his play, *Caroline or Change*, was remarkably gracious in engaging the strangers assembled for this dinner.

I was introduced as the former president of the Nathan Cummings Foundation, perhaps with the hope that I could be helpful to him in financing his next project. But I had no help to offer—being a former president is radically different from being a president, with direct access to the foundation checkbook.

I told him about my decisions to leave the presidency of the Cummings Foundation, to pack up our Riverside Drive apartment, and to move to California. "My wife and I were ready to slow down and to live closer to our children and grandchildren. I was worried that I was starting to believe all of the subtle flattery that was aimed in my direction—it can be disabling. I thought that the community in Berkeley was likely to be more supportive of my peculiar mix of activism and meditation." I had anticipated continuing to make waves and ride the currents, with a shift in the balance toward more ease. I looked forward to being relieved of the burden of responsibility that rests on the shoulders of a CEO.

"How has the move worked for you?" Kushner asked.

I started on the positive side, describing the joys of California life—magnolias and camellias blossoming in February, canoeing in mountain lakes, sleepovers with the grandchildren.

Then I got to the harder part. I told him that I missed the foundation and the work that had been at the center of my life. My phone rarely rang, and I was on my own to handle phone calls, email, and correspondence. I missed the dense flow of people and issues, and the opportunity to support important and promising projects with money, ideas, and introductions to other funders. I had vaguely thought that I would work as a consultant in Berkeley, and I did some informal consulting with nonprofit groups, but it was a pale shadow of my former engagement. I had been accustomed to making waves on a large scale; now I was making ripples.

I had anticipated a challenging transition, but it was more severe and prolonged than I had expected. I missed what I had come to take for granted—the special attention given to me and my ideas because I was the president of a large foundation. I reflected, with greater empathy, on the "ex-great-man" syndrome that I had identified when I was a young public interest lawyer dealing with former presidential cabinet members. I missed the "foundation bounce," the added energy that flowed my way by virtue of my ability to give away large sums of money. This was the first time since I was twenty-nine that I did not have the status and identity of a prestigious position.

"So you're having trouble with retirement," he said.

"Not exactly retirement," I said. "I'm not working at a regular job, but I continue to be involved, and I am open to seeing what new opportunities arise. And I am still engaged in some projects I started at the foundation, especially the Center for Contemplative Mind in Society. I co-led a four-day meditation retreat for lawyers recently, and I lead a weekly meditation group for law students at the University of California, Berkeley, School of Law."

He seemed puzzled by the idea of lawyers in meditative silence. Then the crème brulée came to the table and he turned to another conversation. As I broke through the crust of my dessert, I thought about the lawyers Kushner had created in *Angels in America*—Roy Cohn, ruthless, manipulative, and immoral, and the young Mormon in the prosecutor's office, cerebral, repressed, cut off from his emotions. I didn't suppose that he could imagine lawyers in meditation, sitting in contemplative silence, looking inward, opening to wisdom and compassion.

As I left the Berkeley Rep dinner, I thought that this stage in my life was full of opportunities for practicing wisdom. The shock of a phone that doesn't ring is actually an opportunity for reflection and growth. I recalled the medicine wheel in the Adirondack wilderness. I was sitting at the west side—the sunset, the time of harvest, aging, and physical decline, the time for letting go. I was shifting through the northwest, toward the north, the place of night and winter, death and renewal. This was my "northwest passage," and I had the opportunity to enter it mindfully and consciously, a profoundly important application of my practice of wisdom.

I found myself at the front edge of a large wave of aging baby boomers who would be entering the northwest passage, the new life stage that comes between departure from the regular full-time workforce and actual retirement. Because of longevity and prosperity, there will be a growing cohort in this interesting stage, full of vitality and trying to decide how to use their time and energy. We don't have a cultural model for it or a vocabulary to talk about it.

I had been uncomfortable introducing myself as the former this or that, who had done so many interesting things some decades ago. I have found that my meditation practice helps to cushion these problems, helping me relax into the new situation. Practicing wisdom has become the key to my dealing with these unsettling circumstances, and it is something that I can share with the growing communities of "northwesters." Sharing the practice of wisdom—writing, teaching, and mentoring—could become the core of my new life, bringing forward the values of reflective stillness and compassion.

Wisdom has traditionally been associated with advancing age and accumulated experience. Much of the new scientific inquiry into wisdom has analyzed that connection.[1] It seems totally appropriate to offer the practice of wisdom as an organizing principle for people leaving their full-time careers, to give their activities in the next phase weight and a deeper meaning.

In the spring of 2003, seventy lawyers gathered in the modern, Japanese-inflected buildings at Spirit Rock Meditation Center in Marin County, living in spare, monastic cells and spending eight hours each day in silent meditation, with some time for discussion of law-related topics, tempered and modulated by the stillness and beauty of the place. The spring rains had turned the hills a vivid green.

The principal teacher, Norman Fischer, had been the abbot of the San Francisco Zen Center and taught Jewish meditation as well.[2] A poet and translator with a son at Yale Law School, he had been meeting with a small group of lawyers in our living room monthly, exploring the ways that meditation practice affected the way we lived and worked as lawyers. I led the planning committee for the retreat, and had particular responsibility for teaching Qi Gong, a form of moving meditation that I had learned from an itin-erant teacher at a meditation retreat a decade earlier at Vallecitos.

The lawyers assembled for Qi Gong in the early darkness on our first morning, walking under the luminous, star-filled sky to the meditation hall, a large square building with enormous windows and a roof that soared to a peak in the center, a modern adaptation of the temple architecture of Kyoto. I imagined that many of them were wondering what they were doing in the predawn chill, echo-ing the doubts and ironic judgments I entertained when I had first been invited to learn Qi Gong. "I never felt a 'flow of energy' in my body," I had thought, "and I don't believe that exercises can mirac-ulously cure illnesses that antibiotics can't. It sounds like a lot of New Age hooey." Nonetheless, my first exposures to Qi Gong left me feeling remarkably good, in a way that I could not exactly put words around, and I have done these exercises most mornings since then, as well as teaching them to hundreds of people.

"Qi Gong," I told the lawyers at Spirit Rock, "is meditation in motion—an ancient Chinese system for working with the body's energy—integrating movement, breath, and the flow of energy." I stood in the center of a large circle of lawyers—professors, public interest lawyers, partners in corporate firms, students—in the dim light of the hall. "It helps you become centered in your body, and it supports focused attention and mindful presence in the moment. And it complements meditation, keeping the joints limber and the body relaxed and grounded. They say that masters are able to cure diseases that are not curable with Western medicine."

I was surprised that I took so much pleasure in sharing this ancient practice, so remote from the world in which I had grown up, unconnected to the skills that I had prided myself on and built my career around. I was actually quite comfortable teaching Qi Gong to this group. These lawyers had, after all, voluntarily signed up for a silent meditation retreat, so they were not likely to be as rigid and tight—physically and intellectually—as I had been when I was young. They probably would accept the teachings more easily because I was not a lithe and flexible sprite, but a somewhat stiff and lumpy older lawyer, like many of them.

With gentle instructions I encouraged them to focus their awareness on the body's energy center, the *dantien*, to plant their feet solidly on the floor, to be attentive to their breath, and to feel the flow of energy as they slowly followed me through the movements. "Waving Hands by the Side of the Lake," I said, and slowly raised my hands up the front of my body, fingers relaxed and pointed to the floor, while I drew in a long in-breath. Half an hour later, after the sun had risen, revealing the steep hillsides around the hall, I led the Marriage of Sun and Moon, and we bowed deeply to each other, sharing a surprising sense of connection to ourselves and to each other.

Late that afternoon, after hours of meditation, the silence framed a contemplative discussion of the tensions of the lawyer's life. Successful partners in big corporate firms shared their frustrations about careers that left them no time for quiet and reflection. "I am tired of acting like a pit bull every time a client comes in with a scheme to attack a competitor or stave off a government investigation," said one lawyer who had fifteen years of corporate practice. "Perhaps the meditative perspective can help me deal with these pressures."

"I need something more fundamental," said one law student, taking the conversation to a deeper place. "I have to figure out how I can practice law. I spent three years in South America before going to law school, and I was appalled by the way the big oil companies despoiled the jungle and abused the natives. Of course, I could never represent such clients or the banks that finance them. But I don't feel good about participating in a system that makes their abusive behavior possible." The conversation circled through the hall, people listening to each other respectfully, and allowing a few moments of resonant silence between each speaker's comments. I was surprised by the level of intimacy and trust.

The substance of the conversation was familiar to me, although I had rarely encountered such candid and undefensive reflections or such a flow of empathy, tangible in the room, as people heard each other and allowed other people's reflections to illuminate their own experiences and emotions. These people are practicing wise dialogue, I thought.

On the drive home from Spirit Rock at the end of the retreat I reflected on my career in law. I recalled my own unhappiness with the pressures and moral ambiguities of corporate practice, and the joy with which I entered public interest practice. I took great pride in the continuing success of CLASP and the other public interest groups that I had helped to launch. I was proud of the CUNY Law School, and the thousands of public interest lawyers who had studied there and gone into law practice to serve the poor and disadvantaged.

But something had been missing from my public interest work and the institutions I helped to create. I had been dissatisfied with the institutionalized self-righteousness and aggression of the public interest law firms, and disappointed by the harsh and unreflective anger that often divided the CUNY community.

I had found my work as a foundation president a relief from the lawyer's world of argument and competition. And yet, how much worse things were now in law practice—the huge firms where partners do not even know each other's names, a business ethic that has undermined the sense of professional independence, immense salaries paid to young lawyers to practice corporate law, a scarcity of public interest law jobs, difficulty in getting a hearing for the poor and powerless before increasingly conservative judges.

I was intrigued by the idea that the practice of wisdom could make a different kind of law practice possible—a wisdom practice. It is not so long ago that wisdom was considered the highest virtue for lawyers and judges. The quotation from Justice Benjamin Cardozo emblazoned above the entrance to Boalt Hall of the University of California, Berkeley, School of Law, admonishes students to "study the wisdom of the past" so that they can order human affairs "with wisdom." Yet the word wisdom has virtually disappeared from the legal classroom. Our retreat at Spirit Rock filled me with the inspiring hope that the practice of wisdom might return as the core of the lawyer's commitment, beginning in law school and running through a lifetime of practice.

At that moment, I didn't suspect that I would soon be reentering the world of legal advocacy and facing the challenge of integrating the meditative perspective into real-life legal encounters.

In November 2004, California voters passed Proposition 71, authorizing the sale of $3 billion in state bonds to fund stem cell research. Prop. 71 was generated by entrepreneurs who supported it with a $37 million advertising campaign. In large part, a vote for Prop. 71 was a vote against President Bush and the limitations he placed on embryonic stem cell research in deference to the views of his Christian fundamentalist constituency.

When I rolled up my sleeves and addressed the tangled legalese, I concluded that the short-term medical benefits of stem cell research had been dramatically oversold. Moreover, I discovered that Prop. 71 had launched an unprecedented political experiment, in addition to its scientific experiments—billions of dollars of state money would be spent with virtually no oversight by the public, the governor, or the legislature. In the small print of the text, the normal checks and balances of democratic government were suspended.

Perhaps, I thought, I might play a useful role in assuring that the vast sums of money would be well spent and that the difficult ethical issues involved in genetic manipulation—the commercialization of women's eggs, cloning embryos, and designing babies—would be subjected to searching public scrutiny and debate. This area of scientific research called for great wisdom in its oversight and management. The passage of the proposition in a flood of extravagant medical claims was not an auspicious beginning.

My response grew directly from my work as a public interest lawyer. I had spent years trying to assure democratic oversight of medical and scientific enterprises—issues ranging from the abuse of patients in public mental hospitals in the name of therapy, as in the *Rouse* case, to participating in the adoption of federal regulations to regulate experimentation with human subjects. In the *Wyatt* case, we stopped an experiment that involved giving electric shocks with cattle prods to mentally retarded inmates. In another case at the intersection of science and public policy, we helped obtain an injunction in Michigan against experimental brain surgery to affect the behavior of nonconsenting mental patients. It was this work that helped secure my election to the Institute of Medicine of the National Academy of Science. While I was committed to the scientific enterprise, especially when there was promise of significant therapeutic benefit to sick people, I did not think that the fact that a project was undertaken by scientists meant that it rendered democratic oversight unnecessary.

The lack of concern with democratic process was reflected in the agenda for the first scheduled meeting of the oversight committee.

I saw that the planned meeting was in clear violation of the state's Open Meeting Act—inadequate public notice and no opportunities for public comment on the issues being presented for decision. I sent a letter to the members of the committee, and to the attorney general's office, requesting them to follow the open meeting law and adopt a more open, democratic process.

I dusted off my gray pin-striped suit, which had been hanging untouched in my closet since our move to Berkeley, and went to the auditorium at the UCSF Medical School. I found that the committee had acceded to my request that it comply with the state's open meeting law; and nine-tenths of the agenda items had been omitted in order to comply with the law. But there was little interest in opening their processes to full democratic dialogue. The committee members, who included five medical school deans and various CEOs of biotech firms and research institutes, wanted money to flow to their institutions as quickly and as generously as possible. They didn't want a seminar on bioethics. They wanted to build new buildings and fund high-tech science.

Bob Klein, the principal draftsman and promoter of Prop. 71, was elected chair. My intervention on the open-meeting issues attracted a good deal of attention in the press, and made it worthwhile for Klein to get to know me. He called me the next week with an invitation to have lunch in San Francisco.

Before the lunch, I took a walk at Point Reyes with my old friend Gary Friedman, a convenor of the Devil's Thumb gathering, a member of our lawyers' meditation group, and a leader in nonadversarial dispute resolution. As we walked out the Bear Valley Trail toward the Pacific, through forests glistening from the rains earlier that day, I talked about the upcoming lunch. "I can feel all my old adversarial energy arising, waking up in the middle of the night thinking about arguments to show just how undemocratic their governance structure is. It's rather exciting, but it feels incomplete.

I want to draw on the wisdom perspective to shape my conversation with Klein to increase the chances of our dealing with each other productively, with respect and goodwill."

"That sounds great," Gary said. "You've come a long way from your kick-ass days as a public interest lawyer. I don't remember you talking much about mutual respect or avoiding polarization. But Klein isn't going to feel too good about you, since you slowed his process down by insisting that they comply with the open meeting law."

"Yes," I said. "But perhaps I can be sufficiently anchored in my own meditation practice that I can retain some flexibility and modesty that will be contagious. Meditative skills aren't worth much if they just work when you are on retreat or are talking to other meditators. It might take the conversation to a different place."

"It's certainly worth a try," Gary said, just as the gray skies opened. We rushed back through the pelting rain to our car.

The lunchtime conversation didn't go well. I took a few deep breaths, trying to stay centered in my intentions. Klein turned the conversation to the stem cell initiative and the urgency of making grants as soon as possible. Soon we were engaged in a lawyerly discussion of the conflict-of-interest issue—edgy, precise, focused on scoring points.

After lunch, I walked out into the warm midday sunshine and crossed over to the Ferry Building. I found an empty bench looking over the water and the soaring towers of the Bay Bridge, and pulled out my cell phone to call Gary.

"It didn't work out the way we had hoped. He didn't seem interested in anything but proving to me what a good guy he was. 'Just trust me'—that was his message."

"Yes, but how were *you?*"

"Actually, I felt pretty good—clear, but not aggressive. I listened to him carefully, stayed centered and flexible. I didn't feel the same messianism that I used to feel when I was a full-time public interest lawyer, and I held my ideas more lightly. It didn't seem to do any good, but who knows? It may have done more good than I can see now."

"The benefits aren't going to be linear or obvious," Gary said. "Here you are on the phone with me, in a reflective frame of mind, thinking about what you learned, how you might do better the next time. You and he have some serious disagreements, and they aren't simply going to disappear."

I continued to track the developments with Prop. 71. As I have delved more deeply into the issues of biotechnical advance, I have become more persuaded that we are in the middle of the most serious ethical issues. We are at a point where no humans have ever been before, capable of taking over the evolution of the human species, designing the traits of babies, and altering the genetic package that children carry forward into life. Some enthusiasts say that we are on the threshold of a "transhuman" future, and they are anxious to push forward into the new era. If ever there has been a cluster of issues that demands the highest level of attention and care—wisdom of a high order—this is it. Instead, it is being treated like a political football, with Republicans playing to the fundamentalists and many Democrats mindlessly championing the unfettered discretion of scientists to do whatever experiments interest them, regardless of their social consequences.[3] The recent spate of books demonizing all religions, in the name of science and reason, seem to be calculated to heighten polarization and decrease the likelihood that wisdom will enter the discussion.[4] It would be a tragedy if the voices of wisdom aren't heard on these matters.

In 2006, on a chilly February weekend, I flew to New York for a conference on meditation in higher education at Columbia Teachers College. As the chair of the Center for Contemplative Mind in Society, I welcomed the 250 participants, mostly professors, and began to frame the discussions. I described the Center's fellows program, which we had begun a decade earlier in partnership with the American Council of Learned Societies. "We have supported a hundred professors on campuses around the country who have brought contemplative practice into their teaching in diverse disciplines—from English literature to music, from architecture to sociology. These are the first fellowships for contemplative studies to be offered in universities since the Renaissance. They may point the way to a new wholeness in the way we think about education. At a time when life and study on campus are speeding up and looking outward, we are holding a space and a scholarly justification for slowing down, looking inward, and practicing wisdom." I noted the enormous progress that had occurred in the last decade—meditation was receiving scholarly attention in the universities, neuroscience was successfully mapping the impact that meditation has on brain function,[5] and the popular press had moved meditation to the cover of major national magazines.[6]

The next morning, one of our fellows, Marilyn Nelson, an African American woman who has served as the poet laureate of Connecticut, described the poetry course she had created at West Point, where she was teaching at the time of her fellowship.[7] The core of her contemplative pedagogy, she said, was to ask her "students to explore several ways of listening for, and listening to, silence. I hope they will develop a contemplative attitude, and learn how to hear silence."

Many of her students continued their meditation practice after graduation while serving in Iraq. Nelson found a connection between meditation, inner peace, and peacemaking. One of her students, for example, set up a sister city program between her hometown in Kansas and the Kurdish village where she was deployed. In a visionary moment, Nelson suggested that "if people meditate together they can no longer be enemies. There's an image to conjure: armies meditating together. World leaders sitting for fifteen minutes of shared silence. Just think of the fruit that that could bear."

After Nelson's talk, I went out into the crisp air of early spring, feeling blessed by being part of this event. I reflected on the image of world leaders meditating together—and the unimaginable new vistas that had opened up from this fellowship program we had launched ten years ago. I started to walk slowly to Central Park. Christo's gates, hundreds of twelve-foot-high saffron constructions, had been erected, and that morning saffron banners had been unfurled from each gate in the fresh breeze. I went into the park from the northwest corner, down a long set of stone steps and along a narrow path pressed up against the west wall of the park, walking under a row of gates framing the vista. I had strolled these paths many times in the years when I lived in New York, but I saw them with fresh eyes through the gates.

I thought back to my first interview for the deanship at CUNY Law School. After a meeting with the chancellor at the East Side headquarters of the City University I had walked in the park, still overwhelmed by the strangeness, intensity, and vague menace of the city's streets. Washington had seemed so much more manageable and comfortable. Wondering what I had gotten myself into, I found Central Park to be a place of refuge, its granite outcroppings echoing the landscape of central Ontario, where I had met Susan.

After I became president of the Cummings Foundation and moved to Riverside Drive, the city began to seem more accessible and hospitable. My friend Paul Gorman and I used to walk these paths, deep in long, rambling talks about the life of the foundation that were infused by the natural beauty of the park and the distant views of the dense high-rise buildings on the surrounding streets, a unique blend of quiet open space with intense human activity. This formed the background—and a metaphor—for our conversations about a grants program that combined an activist commitment to social justice with a broader view cultivated through meditation practice. We talked about the subtle seductions of being a foundation president, where everyone wants something. "This is where the meditation comes in," said Paul. "It will give you some hope of holding onto your center, and walks in the park will help maintain that perspective."

As I walked through Christo's gates now, I reflected on how this ambitious work of art continuously reframed the landscape, making familiar paths and crossings look new and interesting. I thought of the critical turning points in my life, how each choice reframed my ambitions and opportunities—my decisions to leave corporate law practice, to start the Center for Law and Social Policy, to start the City University of New York Law School, to commit to daily meditation practice and yearly retreats, to become president of the Nathan Cummings Foundation, to leave the foundation and move to California.

I thought about the way that each gate that I had passed through had framed a choice, not only for the work that I would do but for the person that I would become. My decision to move to California to live without a job and without a title was my latest gate, and it felt as if it framed the practice of wisdom, both as an opportunity and a necessity.

As Susan and I settled into our California life—exploring remote corners of the state in our canoe, playing with grandchildren, participating in meditation retreats, flying back to New York for board meetings and theater—Susan's oncologist brought us up short with the news that the cancer was back, in a more aggressive and menacing form. He recommended a stem cell transplant, using her own cells.

After we had checked out information sources on the Web and sought a second opinion, we decided to proceed with this drastic treatment. Susan's stem cells would be drawn from her blood and frozen. Then she would receive massive chemotherapy, heavy enough to kill the cancer but also so strong that it would wipe out her immune system. Then her own stem cells would be transfused back into her, and they would begin to reconstitute a new immune system. For much of this period, she would be in the hospital in semi-isolation with few visitors.

Our decision to move to Berkeley had been prophetic. This oner-ous procedure was tolerable in part because we were so well sup-ported by our children—and our grandchildren who rode their bicycles below Susan's window and held up signs wishing her well. When I entered her room, I wore a yellow plastic coverall to pro-tect her from infection from the outside world. We decorated her walls with crepe paper flowers, the grandchildren's drawings, and a huge blowup of our official family photograph. For most of the time Susan was extremely weak; a trip to the bathroom, trailing her pole of dripping fluids, would be followed by a two-hour nap. She would fall asleep in the middle of *Tootsie* and *The Graduate*, our favorite movies to support us in Norman Cousins's laughter therapy.

In the long hours that I spent sitting in her hospital room I watched my anxious thoughts arise, but I was often able to let them go, rather than let them proliferate into nightmare scenarios of unbearable future suffering, hers and mine. I could deal with what was happen-ing at the time while she drifted in and out of sleep. Both of us were in the northwest quadrant of the medicine wheel in the cycle of our lives, connected to the interlocking cycles of the day and night, the seasons—a vision of birth and death, decline and renewal.

When her immune system had been obliterated and the course of chemical infusions had been completed, three technicians in plastic suits, like priestesses in special ritual garments, came into her room and began their magic—melting her frozen stem cells and slowly dripping them into her arm. Over the following days, her stem cells gradually brought a new immune system to life.

As she regained her strength over a period of months, we began a sporadic, continuing conversation about her disease and its treatment. We were awed by the power of the new technology and grateful for it. A few decades earlier, this treatment would not have been available. We were pleased to have the high-end insurance that made this costly procedure available to us and painfully conscious of the millions of uninsured people who would not be able to benefit from this technology.

We spoke of how valuable meditation practice had been to each of us. We also discussed the surprising gifts that her cancer had given us. I had uncovered my capacity to be a caregiver, not selfless, to be sure, but competent in a role that I would have thought was beyond me. Susan had developed her capacity to be cared for, to surrender to her situation, to be helpless, and to rely on me and on others.

During the course of her recovery she finished her book, *The Etiquette of Illness: What to Say When You Can't Find the Words*—truly the product of her practice of wisdom.[8] She had never written a book before and would not have done so if not for the experiences of her own cancer and her meditation practice. Our relationship to our elderly mothers and to other critically ill friends and relatives became deeper and more empathic. And our rich relationship with each other, after decades of marriage, was carried to a new level of intimacy and love, autonomy and interdependence. We honed our ability to relish each precious moment that we have together. Our harvesting these paradoxical rewards from the onset of her cancer was directly connected to the inner work that we had done—alone and together.

I thought of the person I was when I went to law school, and later, when I went off to our West Virginia cabin to deal with my shallowness crisis. I rarely used or heard the word *wisdom* at those times. I am wiser than I was then, and I am still practicing. My time in California is a time to consolidate this transformation, to bring it forward in the world, and to work at living more fully in compassion and wisdom.

EPILOGUE:
PRACTICING WISDOM

I N EARLY SPRING 2007, I went away for a few days' retreat at the Sky
Farm Hermitage on a hilltop north of Sonoma. Sister Michaela and
Brother Francis welcomed me and showed me around the four guest
cottages. I stayed in one that had been made from an old wooden
wine vat, about twelve feet across. They had cut out windows and a
door and turned it into a simple and satisfying monastic cell in which
to live for a few days. I cooked my own meals in the refectory and
picked up wisdom books from their little library—Thomas Merton,
Brother David Stendl-Rast, Simone Weil. Each morning I got up
before sunrise to do my Qi Gong practice among the live oak trees,
sometimes alone and sometimes joined by Sister Michaela.

The silence, beauty, and isolation were a wonderful background
for my reflections about making waves and riding the currents
through a lifetime. I thought of the institutions I had launched and
their ongoing success. None of them have developed in just the way
that I would have planned or predicted, but they have taken on
lives of their own, with excellent leadership that has realigned their
programs to meet the shifting opportunities and demands of a
changing world. They were all founded with a commitment to making waves, and they continue to do so.

I reflected on the practice of wisdom, the theme that has come to dominate my life. I imagined what a law firm thoroughly grounded in wisdom practice might look like. The lawyers would give more time to silence and introspection, and to assuring that their lives could be lived and enjoyed in balance, that career and ambition did not squeeze out family and personal growth. In their professional work, clear seeing would be valued—free from the screens of cynicism and materialism on one side, and ungrounded utopianism on the other. Core values of interconnection, humility, and kindness would be reflected in their choice of cases, the way they related to adversaries, and the positions they advocated. They would be as zealous and determined in serving their clients' interests as any other lawyer. They would work with their clients to explore the long-term consequences of the issues they took on. The lawyers would regularly check into the extent that they were honoring their commitment to cultivate wisdom and support each other in that commitment. They would monitor the success of their overall program to assure that the practice of wisdom was serving their public interest goals, and they would reassess their goals to see if they could be deepened to reflect the wisest understanding. The novelty of the project would call for a suitable modesty and caution in their hopes and expectations.

It is possible to imagine the practice of wisdom having a similar impact in many fields—such as philanthropy, medicine, and business.

The practice of wisdom doesn't give answers, much less assure that we will arrive at a state of being wise. But it can give resilience, balance, and depth, enabling us to confront adversity and suffering in our personal lives, as I have found in connection with Susan's cancer.

The practice of wisdom can also help with the management of difficult, contentious problems of public policy without falling back on clichés and stereotyping. Even one person who is committed to the practice of wisdom might shift the dynamic in a way that creates a space for the emergence of wisdom. In the political sphere, it is possible to imagine a time when voters will take a candidate's wisdom into account in choosing leadership.

The fellowships offered by the Center for Contemplative Mind in Society suggest one way to restore the practice of wisdom to its proper place in the education of young people—not as an abstract subject of intellectual analysis, but as the forging of the container that holds all the other subjects of study.

Each of us can bring the practice of wisdom into our careers, our politics, and the life choices we make, deepening and empowering our work for a more just, sustainable, and reflective world. It nourishes our equanimity and resilience to deal with overwhelming problems, our capacity for maintaining balance in our lives, and our ability to see clearly the conditions around us and understand them in a large perspective of constant change and interconnected relationships. It can help us deal with the problem of burnout—the exhaustion of idealistic ventures where there is a bottomless well of needs and our efforts always fall short. Practicing wisdom can create a new framework for addressing the unprecedented challenges facing the world, from nuclear proliferation to global climate disruption, with insight, clarity, and hope

Practicing wisdom keeps us alert to identifying wise people when they appear in our lives, and gives us the capacity to open to their wisdom and to learn from them. The practice of wisdom has transformative potential—for each person individually and for societies collectively at this critical moment in history. It can give us the courage to take the radical initiatives that are necessary to build a more just, compassionate, and sustainable world. It can help keep our lives in balance—making waves and riding the currents.

ACKNOWLEDGMENTS

Making Waves

ALTHOUGH THIS BOOK has focused on my role in launching new initiatives, in fact all of these ventures have been deeply collaborative. I want to acknowledge and thank the collaborators who started and carried on the *Selective Service Law Reporter*, the Center for Law and Social Policy, the Bazelon Center for Law and Mental Health, the Council for Public Interest Law, the Institute for Public Representation, the City University of New York Law School, the Nathan Cummings Foundation, the Center for the Advancement of Health, Demos: A Network for Ideas & Action, and the Center for Contemplative Mind in Society. We learned from, supported, and taught each other, providing mutual help in our work and in our lives. I have had the good fortune to work with a remarkable group of dedicated and competent people—including professional colleagues, staff, trustees, advisers, and students. I also want to acknowledge the successors who provided leadership after I left. Most of these organizations are still active and making waves. I am proud to be associated with them and to have supported future generations of leadership.

Since I can't mention each person by name, I will pick only two, both departed, to stand for the others, and in acknowledging their qualities and contributions, recognize and thank the whole group. Judy Sullivan, a former Maryknoll sister, served as my executive assistant at CLASP and then at CUNY Law School—which meant that she had to do everything at these new and understaffed institutions. Her commitment to justice, to the missions of these organizations, and her infectious joy in living infused and enriched both places. She died of cancer shortly after returning from serving as a Peace Corps volunteer in Bulgaria.

My successor at CUNY Law School, Haywood Burns, was a remarkable person and a friend since we met in college. He was a leading civil rights lawyer, a man of courage and determination, kindness and generosity. I was delighted when he succeeded to the deanship. We played basketball together, went dancing with our wives together, and practiced meditation together. He died in an automobile accident in 1996 in South Africa, the day after meeting his hero, Nelson Mandela. One of the blessings of my life has been working with Judy and Haywood—and others like them—in a shared effort to build a more just and compassionate world.

I want to say a special word about the Nathan Cummings Foundation. When I was hired to become its first president, I became an honorary member of a family that was full of talent and goodwill. I am grateful for having had the opportunity to help build this family foundation into a powerful force in the philanthropic community from its first year in operation. I am grateful to have participated in that network of family members, trustees, an experienced and creative staff, our partners in other foundations, and of course, the grantees whose work we were able to support. Again, I will acknowledge only one person by name. Adam Cummings, the youngest grandchild of Nathan Cummings, was only twenty when the foundation began. He faithfully attended board meetings, steeping himself in the areas in which the foundation was making grants. Increasingly, he assumed leadership responsibility, and during the past two years, became chair of the board. Throughout this period he did the inner work that informed and deepened his emerging skills as a leader, serving as a model for the next generation of family members who are now taking their places on the board.

Riding the Currents

Many friends and teachers have pointed me in the direction of cultivating wisdom. I had the good fortune of learning from teachers who were, in most cases, also friends. Before I had ever thought about wisdom, Winfield Scott began to teach me and my family, by his example, what a life of service, kindness, and generosity looks like. In retrospect, I recognize him as an important wisdom teacher. My debts to Ralph Siu and the Dalai Lama are apparent from the text.

Largely through my work at the foundation, I became involved in an extraordinary circle of wise teachers. Many of them had spent years in Asia, studying with masters in Buddhist and Hindu traditions. Others explored Jewish spiritual traditions. They were generous in their friendship and in their teaching. My meditation practice, which has been an important gift in my life, flows from my relationships with these wise and loving friends. Again, I will mention just one by name—Ram Dass was a pioneer in exploring frontiers of consciousness and cultivating wisdom. He suffered a serious stroke in 1997; the courage and good humor with which he has recreated a life of service have been an inspiration.

In the aggregate, I have gained an inestimable gift from these friends and teachers, and I am grateful for the strength of their commitment and their years of meditation for the purpose of gaining wisdom to share with others.

Some places of exceptional power have also affected my life and merit acknowledgment. The meditation centers where I have enjoyed meditative retreats are the Insight Meditation Society, in Barre, Massachusetts; the Vallacitos Mountain Refuge, in northern New Mexico; and the Spirit Rock Meditation Center and Green Gulch Farm Zen Center, both in Marin County. All have nourished my capacity for practicing wisdom.

The Book

I began this book while on a Rockefeller Foundation fellowship at the Bellagio Study and Conference Center in northern Italy, and I am grateful for their generous support and encouragement. Since then I have also worked at the Mesa Refuge in Point Reyes Station and at the Skyfarm Hermitage in Sonoma, both in California. The opportunity to focus fully on the manuscript during these residencies was important to moving it forward at critical points. I have also drawn on earlier writing I did while on the Georgetown Law Center faculty, during my Senior Fellowship at Yale Law School, and as a visiting scholar at NYU Law School.

I am especially grateful to Jane Anne Staw, my writing coach, who helped me to understand the craft of writing. Drawing on the wisdom in her 2004 book, *Unstuck*, she helped me press through periods when the work seemed stalled and unproductive. My agent James Levine has been a valued adviser and good friend.

Steve Piersanti, president of Berrett-Koehler, was a vigorous and attentive editor, and his probing questions helped me shape the book and draw out its deeper lessons. The Berrett-Koehler team has been notably supportive and skillful in bringing the book into the world. Sandra Beris copyedited the text with careful attention.

Several of my friends have read drafts of the text at various points, and I am grateful for their perceptive comments: Paul Gorman, Rick Ingrasci, Elizabeth Leiman Kraiem, Michael Rubin, Robert Scott, Cindy Spring, and Peggy Taylor. My daughter, Ruth Halpern, brought her gifts as a storyteller and her intimate familiarity with the subject to her reading of the text.

My thanks to my research assistants, Lark Curtin and Matthew Henjum, and to Susan Weiss and Sahib Amar Khalsa, who formatted and transcribed parts of the text.

My profound gratitude goes to my wife Susan, my life companion and partner. The blessing of our intertwined and evolving marriage has infused every aspect of my career and inner life. This book, which reflects our life together, is shaped by her perceptive review of numerous drafts.

To my beloved children and grandchildren, I pass on this work and this heritage, these challenges and opportunities.

NOTES

Prologue

1. See W. Welsch, "Wisdom: Philosophical Aspects," *International Encyclopedia of the Social & Behavioral Sciences*, 16504–16510. ("Wisdom is not a central topic of contemporary philosophy." P. 16505). There is, however, a growing academic interest in the subject among psychologists. Robert J. Sternberg, ed., *Wisdom: Its Nature, Origins, and Development* (New York: Cambridge University Press, 1990); Robert J. Sternberg and Jennifer Jordan, eds., *A Handbook of Wisdom: Psychological Perspectives* (New York: Cambridge University Press, 2005). See also Stephen S. Hall, "The Older-and-Wiser Hypothesis," *New York Times Magazine*, May 6, 2007.

Chapter 1: Awakening

1. James Ridgeway: "Who's Fit to Be Free?" *The New Republic*, February 4, 1967, 24–26; "The Rouse Case," *The New Republic*, June 1, 1967, 5.
2. Ken Kesey, *One Flew Over the Cuckoo's Nest* (New York: New American Library, 1962); R. D. Laing, *The Divided Self: An Existential Study in Sanity and Madness* (New York: Penguin, 1960); Thomas Stephen Szasz, *The Myth of Mental Illness: Foundations of a Theory of Personal Conduct* (New York: Hoeber-Harper, 1961).
3. In recognition of Judge Bazelon's path-breaking work, the Mental Health Project was renamed the Bazelon Center for Mental Health Law in 1993 (visit www.bazelon.org).
4. For an excellent overview of the contribution of Thurgood Marshall and the NAACP Legal Defense and Education Fund to the civil rights movement see Mark V. Tushnet, *Making Civil Rights Law: Thurgood Marshall and the Supreme Court 1936–1961* (New York: Oxford University Press, 1994).

5. Erving Goffman, *Asylums: Essays on the Social Situation of Mental Patients and Other Inmates* (Chicago: Aldine de Gruyter, 1961).

6. See *Rouse v. Cameron*, 373 F.2d 451 (D.C. Cir. 1966); *Rouse v. Cameron*, 387 F.2d 241 (D.C. Cir. 1967). For further discussion of the development of the right to treatment see Charles R. Halpern, "A Practicing Lawyer Views the Right to Treatment," in "The Right to Treatment Symposium," *Georgetown Law Journal* (special issue), March 1969, 782–817.

Chapter 2: Breaking Out

1. For decades, Dworkin has been a leader in American jurisprudence and Constitutional theory. See his most recent book, *Is Democracy Possible Here? Principles for a New Political Debate* (Princeton, N.J.: Princeton University Press, 2006).

2. Thurman W. Arnold. *The Folklore of Capitalism* (New Haven, Conn.: Yale University Press, 1937).

3. For further background on Abe Fortas, see Laura Kalman, *Abe Fortas: A Biography* (New Haven, Conn.: Yale University Press, 1990).

4. *U.S. v. Allis-Chalmers Mfg. Co.*, 1970 WL 539 (E.D. Wisc. 1970).

5. The musical *Hair* made its Broadway debut on October 17, 1967. See also the movie *Hair*, directed by Milos Forman (MGM, 1999).

6. Visit the Institute for Policy Studies at www.ips-dc.org.

7. See Paul Goodman, *Growing up Absurd* (New York: Vintage, 1962); Percival and Paul Goodman, *Communitas: Means of Livelihood and Ways of Life* (New York: Vintage, 1960); Ivan Illich, *Deschooling Society* (New York: Harper, 1974); Ivan Illich, *Medical Nemesis, the Expropriation of Health* (New York: Pantheon, 1979); Norman Mailer, *The Armies of the Night: History as a Novel, the Novel as History* (New York: Plume, 1995 [originally published 1968]).

8. Ram Dass's book, *The Only Dance There Is* (New York: Anchor, 1974), suggests that all life can be viewed as a dance. See also Ram Dass, *Be Here Now* (San Cristobal, N.M.: Lama Foundation, 1971).

9. See John H. Fenton, "Dr. Spock Guilty with 3 Other Men in Antidraft Plot; Convicted of Conspiracy to Urge Evasion of Service—Raskin Wins Acquittal," *New York Times*, June 15, 1968. See also *U.S. v. Spock*, 416 F.2d 165 (1st Cir. 1969), overturning the district court's guilty verdict for Raskin's codefendants.

10. Charles A. Reich, *The Greening of America* (New York: Random House, 1970).

Chapter 3: Social Entrepreneur

1. Rachel Carson, *Silent Spring* (New York: Mariner Books, 2002 [originally published 1964]).

Chapter 4: Creativity in the Courtroom

1. Visit the Children's Defense Fund at www.childrensdefense.org; Common Cause at www.commoncause.org; the Natural Resources Defense Council at www.nrdc.org; the Puerto Rican Legal Defense and Education Fund at www.prldef.org; and the Environmental Defense Fund at www.environmentaldefense.org.

2. See *Morales v. Turman*, 364 F.Supp. 1039 (E.D. Pa. 1975); *Mills v. Board of Education of the District of Columbia*, 348 F.Supp. 866 (D.D.C. 1972).

3. John A. McPhee, *Encounters with the Archdruid* (New York: Noonday Press, 1971).

4. *Wilderness Society et al. v. Hickel*, 325 F.Supp. 422 (D.D.C. 1970).

5. The National Environmental Policy Act of 1969 (NEPA), 42 U.S.C. § 4321 *et. seq.* (2000).

6. *Wilderness Society v. Morton*, 479 F.2d 842 (D.C. Cir. 1973).

7. See *Environmental Defense Fund, Inc. v. Hardin*, 428 F.2d 1093 (D.C. Cir. 1970); *Environmental Defense Fund, Inc. v. Ruckelshaus*, 439 F.2d 584 (D.C. Cir. 1971).

8. For more details on Campaign GM, see David Vogel, *Lobbying the Corporation: Citizen Challenges to Business Authority* (New York: Basic Books, 1978).

9. For more information on the Sullivan Principles, visit the Sullivan Foundation at www.thesullivanfoundation.org/foundation.

10. *Wyatt v. Stickney*, 344 F.Supp. 373, D.C. Ala. 1972; *Wyatt v. Aderholt*, 503 F.2d 1305 (5th Cir. 1974). The Court of Appeals affirmed the constitutional right to treatment for individuals civilly committed to state mental facilities.

11. See Charles R. Halpern and John M. Cunningham, "Reflections on the New Public Interest Law: Theory and Practice at the Center for Law and Social Policy," *Georgetown Law Journal*, May 1971, 1095–1126.

12. Colman McCarthy, "Laws, Lawyers, and the System," *Washington Post*, October 14, 1970.

13. For positive portrayals, see Simon Lazarus, *The Genteel Populists* (New York: Holt, Rinehart and Winston, 1974); Joseph C. Goulden, *The Superlawyers: The Small and Powerful World of the Great Washington Law Firms* (New York: Weybright and Talley, 1971). For a negative portrayal, see Rael Jean Isaac and Erich Isaac, *The Coercive Utopians: Social Deception by America's Power Players* (Chicago: Regnery Getaway, 1983).

Chapter 5: Community and Consciousness

1. Among his many books, see R.G.H. Siu, *The Tao of Science: An Essay on Western Knowledge and Eastern Wisdom* (Cambridge: Massachusetts Institute of Technology, 1957) and *Transcending the Power Game: The Way to Executive Serenity* (New York: Wiley, 1980).

2. Visit the National Women's Law Center at www.nwlc.org.

3. Visit the Center for Law and Social Policy at www.clasp.org.

4. *Wilderness Society v. Morton*, 495 F.2d 1026 (D.C. Cir. 1974), reversed by the Supreme Court in *Alyeska Pipeline Service Co. v. Wilderness Society*, 421 U.S. 240 (1975).
5. Visit the Institute for Public Representation at www.law.georgetown.edu/clinics/ipr/.
6. For an account of Agnew's tie-breaking Alaska pipeline vote, see Edward Cowan, "Senate 77-20, Votes for Alaska Pipeline; Court Test Barred, with 49-to-49 Tie Broken by Agnew," *New York Times*, July 17, 1973.

Chapter 6: Facing a Tough Reality

1. Gene I. Maeroff, "Dean Appointed, Moving City U's Law School Closer to Reality," *New York Times*, December 24, 1981. See also Aric Press, "A New Kind of Law School," *Newsweek*, September 26, 1983, 91.
2. See Charles R. Halpern, "A New Direction in Legal Education: The CUNY Law School at Queens College," *Nova Law Journal* 10 (Winter 1986), 549–574. Visit the CUNY Law School website at www.law.cuny.edu.
3. For background on Manes, see Richard J. Meislin, "Political Power and Influence Lost in a Swirling City Scandal; Manes's Life: Rapid Ascent, Dizzying Fall," *New York Times*, March 14, 1986.
4. *Scott v. Sandford*, 60 U.S. 393 (1856).
5. *Bowers v. Hardwick*, 478 U.S. 186 (1986). The decision in *Bowers*, upholding Georgia's sodomy law, was overruled in *Lawrence v. Texas*, 539 U.S. 558 (2003).

Chapter 7: Beginning Meditation

1. Visit the Omega Institute at www.eomega.org.
2. For a detailed presentation of the medicine wheel, see Hyemeyohsts Storm, *Seven Arrows* (New York: Ballantine Books, 1972).
3. Visit Thich Nhat Hanh's website at www.plumvillage.org.

Chapter 8: Convergence

1. Kathleen Teltsch, "Needy People Get New Ally in Foundation," *New York Times*, March 27, 1989.
2. For background on the Mapplethorpe trial, see Andy Grunberg, "Critic's Notebook; Cincinnati Trial's Unanswered Question," *New York Times*, October 18, 1990; Isabel Wilkerson, "Cincinnati Museum Quiet After Trial," *New York Times*, October 7, 1990.
3. For background on Mayor Rudy Giuliani's campaign against the Brooklyn Museum of Art, see Dan Barry and Carol Vogel, "Giuliani Vows to Cut Subsidy Over 'Sick' Art," *New York Times*, September 23, 1999.
4. Visit Demos at www.demos.org.
5. Visit the Surface Transportation Policy Project at www.transact.org.
6. Visit the Center at www.jewishhealingcenter.org.

7. For more information about Jewish spirituality, visit the Institute for Jewish Spirituality at www.ijs-online.org.
8. Rodger Kamenetz, *The Jew in the Lotus: A Poet's Rediscovery of Jewish Identity in Buddhist India* (San Francisco: HarperSan Francisco, 1994).
9. Daniel Goleman, *Emotional Intelligence: Why It Can Matter More Than IQ* (New York: Bantam Books, 2005 [originally published 1995]).
10. Ram Dass and Paul Gorman, *How Can I Help? Stories and Reflection on Service* (New York: Knopf 1985); Ram Dass and Mirabai Bush, *Compassion in Action: Setting Out on the Path of Service* (New York: Belltower/Random House, 1995).
11. Visit the Fetzer Institute at www.fetzer.org.
12. Bill Moyers, *Healing and the Mind* (New York: Doubleday, 1993).
13. See the Center for Contemplative Mind in Society at www.contemplative-mind.org.
14. Visit www.vallecitos.org.
15. Woody Allen, "The Shallowest Man," *Side Effects* (New York: Random House, 1975).

Chapter 9: The Northwest Passage

1. See Stephen S. Hall, "The Older-and-Wiser Hypothesis," *New York Times Magazine*, May 6, 2007.
2. See Norman Fischer, *Taking Our Places: The Buddhist Path to Truly Growing Up* (San Francisco: HarperSan Francisco, 2003). Also visit his website www.everydayzen.org.
3. To learn more about the ethical and social dimensions of biomedical research, visit the Center for Genetics and Society at www.geneticsandsociety.org.
4. See Christopher Hitchens, *God Is Not Great: How Religion Poisons Everything* (New York: Twelve Books, 2007); Sam Harris, *The End of Faith: Religion, Terror, and the Future of Reason* (New York: W.W. Norton, 2005); Richard Dawkins, *The God Delusion* (Boston: Houghton-Mifflin, 2006).
5. For information on scientific studies regarding the effects of meditation on the brain, visit the Mind and Life Institute at www.mindandlife.org and the Laboratory for Affective Neuroscience at the University of Wisconsin-Madison at www.psyph.pych.wisc.edu. See also Stephen S. Hall, "Is Buddhism Good for Your Health?" *New York Times*, September 14, 2003.
6. See, for example, *Time*, July 27, 2003.
7. See Marilyn Nelson's recent book of poetry, *The Cachoeira Tales and Other Poems* (Baton Rouge: Louisiana State University Press, 2005).
8. Susan P. Halpern, *The Etiquette of Illness: What to Say When You Can't Find the Words* (New York: Bloomsbury USA, 2004).

BIBLIOGRAPHY
AND RESOURCES

Public Interest Law

Aron, Nan. *Liberty and Justice for All: Public Interest Law in the 1980s and Beyond*. Boulder, Colo.: Westview Press, 1989.

Council for Public Interest Law. *Balancing the Scales of Justice: Financing Public Interest Law in America: A Report*. Washington, D.C.: Council for Public Interest Law, 1976.

Sarat, Austin, and Stuart Scheingold, eds. *Cause Lawyering: Political Commitments and Professional Responsibilities*. New York: Oxford University Press, 1998.

Weisbrod, Burton A., Joel F. Handler, and Neil K. Komesar. *Public Interest Law: An Economic Analysis*. Berkeley: University of California Press, 1978.

Philanthropy and Foundations

Dowie, Mark. *American Foundations: An Investigative History*. Boston: MIT Press, 2001.

Fleishman, Joel. *The Foundation: A Great American Secret? How Private Wealth Is Changing the World*. New York: Public Affairs, 2007.

Nielsen, Waldemar A. *The Big Foundations*. New York: Columbia University Press, 1972.

Nielsen, Waldemar A. *The Golden Donors: A New Anatomy of the Great Foundations*. New York: Truman Talley Books, 1985.

Wisdom

Fischer, Norman. *Taking Our Places: The Buddhist Path to Truly Growing Up*. San Francisco: HarperSan Francisco, 2003.

Goldstein, Joseph, and Jack Kornfield. *Seeking the Heart of Wisdom: The Path of Insight Meditation*. Boston: Shambala, 1987.

Remen, Rachel Naomi. *Kitchen Table Wisdom: Stories That Heal*. New York: RiverHead Books, 1996.

Sternberg, Robert J. *Wisdom: Its Nature, Origins, and Development*. New York: Cambridge University Press, 1990.

Sternberg, Robert J., and Jennifer Jordan, eds. *A Handbook of Wisdom: Psychological Perspectives*. New York: Cambridge University Press, 2005.

Tolle, Eckhart. *The Power of Now: A Guide to Spiritual Enlightenment*. Novato, Calif.: New World Library, 1999.

Walsh, Roger. *Essential Spirituality*. New York: Wiley, 1999.

Meditation

Cohen, Ken. *The Essential Qigong Training Course: 100 Days to Increased Energy, Physical Health, and Spiritual Well-Being*. Boulder, Colo.: Sounds True, 2005.

Goldstein, Joseph. *Insight Meditation: The Practice of Freedom*. Boston: Shambala 1993.

Hanh, Thich Nhat. *The Miracle of Mindfulness: A Manual on Meditation*. Boston: Beacon Press, 1975.

Kabat-Zinn, Jon. *Wherever You Go There You Are: Mindfulness Meditation in Everyday Life*. New York: Hyperion, 1994.

Kabat-Zinn, Jon. *Guided Mindfulness Meditation*. Boulder, Colo.: Sounds True, 2005 (audio).

Salzberg, Sharon and Joseph Goldstein. *Insight Meditation: An In-Depth Correspondence Course*. Boulder, Colo.: Sounds True, 1996 (audio).

INDEX

A

Adirondack Mountains, 186–191, 229, 234
aging, 241–242
Agnew, Spiro, 142
Alaska pipeline
  as abstraction, 136
  Alyeska case, 98, 103, 111
  Brower and, 92–95
  CLASP and, 92–101, 105, 141
  court of appeals and, 100–101, 137
  design of, 100–101, 141
  Exxon Valdez disaster and, 142, 201
  hearing on, 95–98
  Kramer and, 103
  Siu on, 107, 111
  U.S. Supreme Court and, 137–138
Allen, Woody, 112, 185, 193
  "The Shallowest Man," 237
Allis-Chalmers, 36–37, 40–41
Alpert, Richard. *See* Ram Dass
Alyeska case. *See* Alaska pipeline
American Bar Association, 149, 173, 193

American Council of Learned Societies, 227, 251
Amsterdam, Tony, 74
Angels in America (Kushner), 241
antiapartheid struggle, 102
Armies of the Night, The (Mailer), 44
Arnold, Thurman, 29–30, 38, 46, 47, 78
Arnold & Porter
  Folklore of Capitalism, The, 29
  founding of, 11–12
  hiring committee of, 37–38, 86
  norms of, 38–39, 83
  politically controversial clients of, 27–28, 55
  pro bono work of, 23, 41–42, 47, 49
  Raskin case and, 46, 47
  routine business of, 11–12, 25–26, 33–34, 41, 50, 54, 64
arts
  art censorship, 215–216
  Nathan Cummings Foundation and, 213, 215–216
Aspen Institute, 105
assertiveness workshops, 119–120
Asylums (Goffman), 17

authority
   challenging of, 76, 115–116
   CUNY Law School and,
      171–172, 177
   lawyer humor and, 177

B

Baez, Joan, 182
balanced life
   celebrating success and, 100
   CLASP and, 85
   CUNY Law School and, 178
   family life and, 34, 35–36, 85
   meditation and, 227
   practice of wisdom and, 6, 7,
      258, 259
Balancing the Scales of Justice, 137
Bazelon, David, 12–13, 14, 15, 19,
   20, 21
Bazelon Center for Mental Health
   Law, 267n.3. *See also* Mental
   Health Law Project
Berkeley Repertory Theater, 239
Bok, Derek, 64–65, 69
Boudin, Leonard, 45
Brooklyn Museum of Art, 216
Brower, David, 91–95, 97, 109, 111
Buddhism
   Joseph Goldstein on, 229–230
   Goleman on, 222
   Hood and, 178–182
   Jewish spirituality and, 220–221
   retreats, 202–207
   right livelihood and, 6
Burger, Warren, 73, 143–144
Burnett, Grove, 229
Burns, Haywood, 200
Bush, George H. W., 105, 201
Bush, George W., 105, 201, 246
Bush, Mirabai, 226
   Compassion in Action, 223

C

California, subculture of, 113–114,
   126
Campaign GM, 101
canoeing
   CLASP retreats and, 123
   exploring with, 253
   lessons in, 130–132
   meditation compared to, 182
   reading currents and, 131–132,
      147–148
   releasing tension with, 177, 183
   serenity in, 4–5, 124–125
Canoe in the Rapids (Homer), 182
Cardozo, Benjamin, 246
Caroline or Change (Kushner), 239
Carson, Rachel, 101
   Silent Spring, 58
Center for Contemplative Mind in
   Society, 226–227, 241, 251, 259
Center for Law and Social Policy.
   See CLASP (Center for Law
   and Social Policy)
change, constancy of. *See also*
   impermanence
   practice of wisdom and, 6
   rivers and, 130
Chayes, Abe, 69, 143–144
Children's Defense Fund, 90
Chinese baseball, 161–162
Choate Club, 67, 68
Christo's gates, 252, 253
Cincinnati Museum of Contem-
   porary Arts, 215
civil liberties, defense of, 57
civil rights
   CLASP students and, 87
   foundations' support for, 71
   mental illness and. *See* mental
      health and illness
   for racial minorities, 14

~~~~~~

Civil Rights Act of 1964, 47

civil rights movement, 30–32, 44, 53, 57, 83, 212, 218

clarity of vision
cultivation of, 136
meditation and, 227
paradoxes and, 68
practice of wisdom and, 6
vision quest and, 194

Clark, Ramsey, 72, 73, 108

CLASP (Center for Law and Social Policy)
assessment of, 105
board of trustees, 62–64, 72, 73–74, 77
clinical legal education, 64–65, 67–70, 74–77, 86, 87, 88–90, 113–115
consciousness, community and, 78, 120, 122–127
corporate responsibility issues and, 101–102
development of, 53–61, 253
dispersal of lawyers from, 136–137
environmental issues and, 72, 84, 91, 92–101, 105, 141, 218
feminists and, 87, 121
foundations and, 55, 58–59, 61, 62, 64, 70–72, 77, 104, 210
Arthur Goldberg and, 63–64, 72, 95
identity of, 82, 115
interconnection and, 111
mental health issues and, 83–84, 89, 91
naming of, 61–62
nonhierarchical approach of, 87, 103, 112, 115, 119–120
paradoxes of, 68
polarized thinking and, 107, 111, 120, 236

press and, 58, 104–105
retreats of, 122–125, 129
salaries and, 85
student program, 64–65, 67–70, 72, 74–77, 85–91, 113–115, 126–127, 145
successes of, 99–100, 107, 110, 245
weekly seminars of, 88–91
yoga classes and, 126–127, 234

clinical legal education (CLASP)
evaluation of, 75–76
experimental nature of, 89–90, 114–115
innovation of, 76, 86, 87
law schools' interest in, 64–65, 67–70, 74–77, 88–89, 113

Coffin, William Sloan, 45, 46

Cohen, Saul
challenge to autonomy of CUNY Law School, 162–165
commitments of, 158
official residence of, 155
relationship with, 160, 161, 176–177, 182
search for CUNY Law School dean and, 144–145
vision for CUNY Law School, 158, 163

community
CLASP and, 78, 120, 122–127
CUNY Law School and, 151, 171, 172, 174, 176
meditation and, 202, 224–225

compassion
Buddhism and, 205, 223
in legal analysis, 27
meditation and, 223, 227
practice of wisdom and, 7, 232, 256, 259
social justice and, 207

Compassionate Action Working Group. *See* Wisdom Party

consciousness, 112, 113, 227. *See also* meditation

consciousness-raising workshops, 119–120

CORE (Congress of Racial Equality), 31, 46, 57

corporate law practice
  legal education and, 24, 57–58, 76
  meaningful work in, 32–33
  norms of, 38–39
  pressures of, 244, 245–246
  pro bono matters and, 33, 41–43, 46–47
  public interest law contrasted with, 103
  routine business of, 11–12, 25–26, 33–34, 50

corporate responsibility issues, 55, 101–102

Cosmos Club, 92, 108–109, 160

Council for Public Interest Law, 137

counterculture, 113–115

Cowan, Geoffrey, 60, 81, 86, 137

Cowan, Rachel, 218–220

Crown-Zellerbach Corporation, 31, 46–47

culture wars, 215

Cummings, Herb, 211, 236

Cummings, Nathan, 209, 214. *See also* Nathan Cummings Foundation

Cummings family, 209, 210–214, 215, 218, 220, 233

CUNY Law School
  accreditation of, 173, 193
  challenges of leadership, 160–162, 173, 175–180, 191–192, 198–199, 211, 214, 245, 253
  community and, 151, 171, 172, 174, 176
  curriculum of, 164, 172, 174
  facilities for, 145, 158, 168, 179, 186, 213
  faculty of, 149–150, 163–164, 168, 171, 172, 175, 176, 177, 185, 191, 193, 201
  first graduation of, 173–174
  honorary degree recipients and, 173–174, 191
  innovations of, 150–152, 200
  location in Queens, 154–157
  public interest law and, 143–149, 151–152, 153, 156, 158, 163, 165–166, 167, 170, 171, 176, 245
  students of, 152, 159, 165, 166–171, 174, 175, 176, 177, 183, 185, 191, 193, 199–200

Cuomo, Mario, 157, 191

D

Dalai Lama, 1–3, 207, 220, 238

dancing, 44–45

DDT litigation, 101, 105

death and dying, 223, 236

Democratic Convention of 1968, 53

Demos, 216

draft law. *See Selective Service Law Reporter*

Dred Scott decision, 170

Dubos, René, 101

E

Earthjustice, 136–137

emotional intelligence, 119, 222

Emotional Intelligence (Goleman), 222

Encounters with the Archdruid (McPhee), 91

environmental advocacy and law
  Alaska pipeline and, 92–101,
    105, 141, 201
  CLASP and, 72, 84, 91, 92–101,
    105, 141, 218
  DDT and, 101, 105
  global warming and, 216–217
  meditation and, 227–232
  Nathan Cummings Foundation
    and, 213, 216–218, 219, 222,
    227–232, 234, 235
  as new field, 55, 59
Environmental Defense Fund, 90,
  101, 141
Etiquette of Illness, The (Susan
  Halpern), 255
ex-great-man syndrome, 72, 240
Exxon Valdez disaster, 142, 201

F
family life, 34, 35–36, 85
Fanghetto, Italy, 127–129, 190–191
Farmer, James, 31–32
fears, acknowledging of, 188–189
feminism, 44, 87, 121, 169, 219
Fetzer Institute, 225–226
First Amendment, 45, 215
Fischer, Norman, 242–243
Folklore of Capitalism, The
  (Arnold), 29
Ford Foundation, 56, 71, 212, 213
Fortas, Abe, 28, 29, 30, 78
foundations. *See also* philanthro-
  phy; Nathan Cummings
  Foundation
  Brooklyn Museum of Art and,
    216
  CLASP and, 55, 58–59, 61, 62,
    64, 70–72, 77, 104, 210
  corporate model for, 234
  entrepreneurial ability and, 24
  flattery and money, 213, 214,
    217, 224, 239–240

interconnections and, 216
Nielson on, 213
public interest law and, 137
social justice and, 55, 71, 77, 90,
  210–211
types of, 70–71
types of work styles and, 210
Frank, Barney, 65–66, 69–70
Free Southern Theater, 31
Freud, Anna, 14–15
Friedman, Gary, 248
Friends of the Earth, 95
Furness, Betty, 101

G
Gandhi, Mohandis, 207
Gay Men's Health Crisis, 171
Georgetown Law School, 138
Gestalt therapy, 176–177, 183
Giuliani, Rudy, 216
global warming, 216–217, 227
Goffman, Erving
  Asylums, 17
  Rouse case and, 18
Goldberg, Arthur, 63–64, 72, 95
Goldstein, Joseph, 223, 229–231,
  232
Goleman, Daniel, 222–223, 225
  Emotional Intelligence, 222
Goodman, Paul, 44
Gorman, Paul, 252–253
  How Can I Help?, 223
Greening of America, The (Reich),
  50
guided visualizations, 140–141

H
Hair (musical), 39–40, 268n.5
Halifax, Joan, 223, 228
Halpern, Bob (son), 186, 190, 191
Halpern, Hon. Philip (father)
  26–27, 84

Halpern, Susan (wife)
  Asian trip, 200–201
  California and, 253–254
  on career turning point, 49, 50,
    51
  on CUNY Law School, 160
  dancing and, 44–45
  Etiquette of Illness, The, 255
  European trip, 127–129
  family life and, 34, 35–36
  feminism and, 121–122
  meditation and, 182, 202–205,
    238, 255
  New York trip, 39–40
  Non-Hodgkin's Lymphoma and,
    236–238, 239, 254–256
  Ontario camp and, 5, 124
  social work career of, 148
  West Virginia cabin and,
    129–130
Hardwick, Michael, 173, 174
Harvard Law School, 64–65,
  67–70, 71
Harvard College, 65–66
Hawaii Law School, 178–179
Healing and the Mind (Moyers), 226
health system. See also mental
    health and illness
  human subjects and, 102, 247
  Nathan Cummings Foundation
    and, 213–214, 222–223,
    225–226, 234, 236–237
  stem cell research and, 246–249
Healy, Tim (President, Georgetown
  University), 146–148, 167, 175,
  176
Higginbotham, Hon. Leon,
  173–174
Holtzoff, Alexander, 19, 20, 21–22,
  23
Homer, Winslow, Canoe in the
  Rapids, 182
Hood, David, 178–180, 203

How Can I Help? (Ram Dass &
  Gorman), 223
humanistic psychology seminar
  (Devil's Thumb), 138–140

I
Illich, Ivan, 44
impermanence
  Buddhism and, 205, 230
  Chinese baseball and, 161–162
  practice of wisdom and, 6, 232
inner explorations. See also
    meditation
  medicine wheel, 194–196,
    198–199, 241, 254–255
  Nathan Cummings Foundation
    and, 222, 233–234
  practice of wisdom and, 5
  process of, 4
  skeptical voice, 193, 194, 196
  sweat lodge, 196–198, 199
  vision quest, 193–198
  visit to Dalai Lama and, 1–3
  Winter Quest, 186–192
inner knowing, 36
Insight Meditation Society, 223
insights
  sharing of, 5
  solitude and, 135
  taking wider view and, 109
  Winter Quest and, 187
Institute for Policy Studies, 43–45,
  71
Institute for Public Representation,
  138
Institute of Medicine, 247
interbeing, 228
interconnection
  Buddhism and, 205
  children and, 34–35
  CLASP and, 111
  environmental advocacy and,
    227–228, 230, 231

foundations and, 216
natural world and, 4–5, 191, 192, 193, 203, 228–230
practice of wisdom and, 6, 232
Interior Department, 93, 95, 97–98, 99, 100, 141–142

J
Jastrab, Joseph, 186–190, 193–198
Jew in the Lotus, The (Kamenetz), 220
Jewish Healing Center, 219
Jewish life program, Nathan Cummings Foundation, 213, 218–219, 221
Jewish meditation, 219, 233, 242
Jewish philanthropy, 218, 219, 221
Jewish Renewal communities, 219
Jewish spirituality, 213, 219–222
Johnson, Lyndon, 29, 30, 45, 46, 71, 83

K
Kamenetz, Rodger, *The Jew in the Lotus*, 220
Katz, Stan, 167
Kennedy, John F., 53, 92, 159
Kennedy, Robert, 14, 53, 159
Kesey, Ken, *One Flew Over the Cuckoo's Nest*, 10, 17
King, Martin Luther, Jr., 48, 53, 202, 207
Klein, Bob, 248–250
Kolleck, Teddy, 214
Kornfield, Jack, 223
Kramer, Victor, 27–28, 37, 103–104, 138
Kushner, Tony, 239–240
   Angels in America, 241
   Caroline or Change, 239

L
Laing, R. D., 10
lawyer humor, 38, 123, 177

Lawyers Constitutional Defense Committee, 30–32
leadership
   CLASP and, 76, 78, 84, 85, 115–116
   CUNY Law School and, 185
   development of, 84
   new generation of, 105
   Tavistock conference on, 116–119
Lederman, Janet, 138–140
legal analysis
   compassion in, 27
   legal education and, 56–57
   rationalism in, 26–27
legal education. *See also* clinical legal education; CUNY Law School; and other specific law schools
   corporate law practice and, 24, 57–58, 76
   elite edge of, 85–86
   Ford Foundation and, 71
   innovations in, 140–141
   legal analysis and, 56–57
   mental health and illness issues and, 14–15
   personal/professional integration and, 112
   public interest law and, 75, 143–144
   social justice and, 24, 56, 65
Legal Services program, 58
Lehman, Rob, 225–226
L'Enfant, Pierre, 50–51
Lerner, Michael, 219
Lesnick, Howard, 150–151
limousine liberals, 48–49
Long Island Expressway, 153–154, 191
Lowell, Robert, 44
Lyons, Oren, 173, 174

M

Mailer, Norman, 44
  The Armies of the Night, 44
Mandela, Nelson, 207
Manes, Donald, 155–157, 160, 164, 165
Mapplethorpe, Robert, 215
marriage
  balanced life and, 35–36
  feminist movement and, 121–122
  levels of, 255–256
Marshall, Thurgood, 14, 23, 54
Mathiessen, Peter, 228
Mayer, Buddy, 209, 212, 233
Mayer, Rob, 211, 222, 235–236
McPhee, John, *Encounters with the Archdruid*, 91
medicine wheel, 194–196, 198–199, 241, 254–255
meditation. *See also* inner exploration
  beginning meditation, 181–183, 231
  community and, 202, 224–225
  cultivation of wisdom and, 4, 6
  daily practice, 4, 189, 192, 199, 202, 203, 206, 227, 231, 253
  environmental advocacy and, 227–232
  general benefits of, 226–227
  Goleman on, 222
  in higher education, 251–252
  interbeing and, 228
  Jewish meditation, 219, 233, 242
  Jewish spirituality and, 220
  for lawyers, 227, 241, 242–245, 246
  Nathan Cummings Foundation and, 231, 232–233, 234
  Qi Gong, 243–244, 257
  retreats, 202–207, 228, 229–232, 241, 242–245, 246, 253

teachers, 204, 224
mental health and illness
  Bazelon's work on, 12–14
  legal advocacy and, 9–11, 15–16, 17, 22–24, 89, 91, 102–103, 247
  legal education and, 14–15
  rights of mentally ill, 23, 55
  right to treatment litigation and, 24
  treatment for, 10, 13, 15, 16, 17–18, 21, 22
Mental Health Law Project (Bazelon Center for Mental Health Law), 102, 179
mental hospitals, conditions of, 10, 13, 14, 16–18, 19, 102, 247
mental institutions, constitutional protections and, 22, 24
mental retardation
  right to public education and, 91
  right to treatment and, 24, 102
  scientific experiments and, 102, 247
Merton, Thomas, 257
mind-body approaches, 223, 225–226, 234
mindfulness, 202, 203
Mineral Leasing Act of 1926, 97, 98
Mississippi Freedom Summer, 30
Moore, James William, 56
Moorman, Jim, 59, 91–92, 94, 96–98, 99, 136–137
Moyers, Bill, 225–226
  Healing and the Mind, 226
Muir, John, 91
Murphy, Joe, 155, 159–160, 162, 164
music improvisation workshop, 183–185

N

NAACP, 57

NAACP Legal Defense and
   Education Fund, 23, 54, 58

Nader, Ralph, 54, 100, 141

Nathan Cummings Foundation. *See
   also* foundations; philosophy

   arts and, 209, 213, 215–216

   Dalai Lama meeting and, 2

   environmental advocacy and,
      209, 213, 216–218, 219, 222,
      227–232, 234, 235

   health system and, 209,
      213–214, 222–223, 225–226,
      234, 236–237

   inner exploration and, 222,
      233–234

   Jewish life and, 209, 213,
      218–219, 221.

   Jewish spirituality and, 213,
      219–222

   meditation and, 231, 232–233,
      234

   program areas of, 209, 211,
      213–214

   program development, 215–216,
      221, 252–253

   program evaluation and,
      235–236

   social justice and, 210–211, 212,
      221, 236, 253

National Environmental Policy
   Act, 84, 97, 98

National Institute of Law Enforcement and Criminal Justice, 108

National Religious Partnership for
   the Environment, 222

National Women's Law Center,
   120

National Women's Liberation
   Front, 121

Native American traditions,
   193–198, 199

Natural Resources Defense
   Council, 90, 141

natural world, connection to, 4–5,
   191, 192, 193, 203, 228–230

Nelson, Marilyn, 251–252

New Deal, 11, 28, 30, 77, 78

New Republic, The, 10, 23

New World Foundation, 71

New York Central Park, 252

New York City, 153–154, 252–253

New York Times, 149, 214, 222

New York University Law School,
   150, 154

Nhat Hanh, Thich, 202–207, 228,
   238

Nielson, Waldemar, 213

Nixon, Richard, 57–58, 71, 83, 84,
   85, 91, 95, 99, 123, 149

nonadversarial dispute resolution,
   248

nonjudgmental attention, 184

northwesters, 242

northwest passage, 241–242,
   254–255

O

oil companies, 92–101, 105, 107,
   110–111, 142, 244–245

oil spills, 93

old-boy network, 68

Old Farts Club, 177, 183

Omega Institute, 183–185,
   202–203

Omer-Man, Jonathan, 219

One Flew Over the Cuckoo's Nest
   (Kesey), 10, 17

P

peacemaking, 251–252

philanthropy. *See also* foundations;
   Nathan Cummings Foundation

   corporate sector distinguished
      from, 235

philanthropy (continued)
  corporate-type decision processes
    and, 234
  exchange relationship and, 212
  foundations and, 70, 212, 234
  Jewish philanthropy, 218, 219,
    221
Philip Morris, 33, 54
Phillips, Channing, 101
Porter, Paul, 25, 28, 29–30, 38, 48,
  77–78, 79
poverty law, 57, 137, 144, 171
practice of wisdom
  activist engagement integrated
    with, 5–6, 7, 206–207,
    248–250
  balanced life and, 6, 7, 258, 259
  children and, 35
  compassion and, 7, 232, 256, 259
  CUNY Law School and, 172
  essential nature of, 1
  law practice and, 246, 258
  northwest passage and, 241, 242
  as ongoing process, 236
  public interest law and, 258–259
  social transformation and, 214
  transformative potential of, 259
  visit to Dalai Lama and, 2–3
  yoga classes and, 127
present moment, 230
pro bono matters, 23, 33, 41–43,
  46–47, 49
Project on Corporate Responsibility, 101
public interest law. See also
  environmental advocacy and
  law; mental health and illness
  Asian trip and, 200–201
  backlash and, 142
  Carnegie Foundation programs,
    179
  CLASP and, 56, 75, 86, 88, 145

  corporate law practice contrasted
    with, 103
  creativity of, 90
  CUNY Law School and,
    143–149, 151–152, 153, 156,
    158, 163, 165–166, 167, 170,
    171, 176, 245
  establishment of, 141
  expansion of, 137
  framework of, 104
  health system and, 247–249
  legal education and, 75, 143–144
  practice of wisdom and, 258–259
public interest law firms
  awarding attorney's fees for,
    137–138
  balanced advocacy and, 73
  CLASP as, 58, 68, 99, 104
  coalition of, 137
  conservatives' network of, 142,
    149
  establishment of, 104
  membership organizations and,
    141

Q
Qi Gong, 243–244, 257

R
Rabbi Michael Lerner, 219
rachmunes, 13–14
Ram Dass, 223–224
  Compassion in Action, 223
  How Can I Help?, 223
Raskin, Marc, 43, 44, 45
Raskin case, 46
Reagan, Ronald, 16, 105, 142, 149,
  201
Redford, Robert, 216–217
Reich, Charles, 50
  The Greening of America, 50
Reinglas, Fred, 39–40

retirement, northwest passage,
    241–242
retreats
    CLASP and, 122–125, 129
    environmental advocacy and,
        228, 229–232
    for lawyers, 241, 242–245, 246
    Thich Nhat Hanh and, 202–207
Ridgeway, Jim, 10, 23
right livelihood, 6
Rockefeller Brothers Fund, 77
Roosevelt, Franklin D., 29, 78
Rouse, Charles, 11, 13, 15–19, 21,
    22
Rouse case
    court of appeals and, 22
    follow up on, 83–84, 89, 91
    hearing before Holtzoff, 19–22
    practices of mental hospitals,
        15–17, 18, 19–20, 22
    public policy challenges and, 25
    public service and, 49
    social justice and, 24
    treatment of patients and, 16–17,
        18, 21, 22, 247
Russian Jews, 219

S
sabbatical, 199–200
Sacks, Al, 68–69
St. Elizabeths Hospital, 15–18
Salzberg, Sharon, 223
Salzburg Seminar in American
    Studies, 105
San Francisco Zen Center, 242
Schachter, Zalman, 219
Schlesinger, Arthur, 66
Scott, Winfield, 127–128
Selective Service Law Reporter,
    42–43, 54, 71
Selective Service System, 41–43
"Shallowest Man, The" (Allen),
    237

shallowness crisis, 132–135, 256
shareholder activism, 102
Silent Spring (Carson), 58
Simplicity Manufacturing, 36–37
Siu, Ralph
    on Alaska pipeline, 107, 111
    appearance of, 107–108
    Chinese baseball and, 161–162
    connection with totality, 178,
        192
    conversations with, 183, 205
    CUNY Law School and,
        160–162, 177–178
    natural rhythms and, 110
    Thich Nhat Hanh compared to,
        206
    nonconfrontational style of, 108
    on outcome measures, 235
    preconceptions and, 120–121
    reflection on stages of life, 195
    on taking wider view, 109, 178
    as teacher, 111–112
    visualization of mind as still
        pond, 110, 111, 194
Sky Farm Hermitage, 257
Sobol, Dick, 83
social entrepreneurs
    abilities of, 24, 85
    identification of, 84
    values of, 84
social justice
    activist lawyers and, 53, 54–55
    CUNY Law School and, 149,
        166
    Demos and, 216
    legal education and, 24, 56, 65
    Nathan Cummings Foundation
        and, 210–211, 212, 221, 236,
        253
    rationalism and, 26–27
    wisdom and, 207, 224
    work for, 4, 24

social transformation, 207, 214

Society of American Law Teachers, 174

solitude, 132–133, 134, 135

Sorensen, Ruth Cummings, 211

South Africa, 102, 104, 179

Spirit Rock Meditation Center, 242–245, 246

spirituality. *See also* inner exploration; meditation

    Jewish spirituality, 213, 219–222

    Nathan Cummings Foundation and, 221–222, 236

    spiritual quest and, 54

Spock, Benjamin, 45

Stanford Law School, 74, 113–114, 126, 138

stem cell research, 246–250

Stendl-Rast, Brother David, 257

Stern, Phil, 47

Stern Family Fund, 71

success trap, 184

Sullivan, Leon, 102

Sullivan & Cromwell, 27

Sullivan Principles, 102

Surface Transportation Policy Project, 218

sweat lodge, 196–198, 199

Szasz, Thomas, 10

T

Tavistock Conference, 116–119

Terris, Bruce

    CLASP and, 59, 61, 63, 65, 67–68, 69

    environmental law firm of, 137

Tikkun (magazine), 219

Tobacco Institute, 33

transportation policy, 217–218, 235

U

UCLA Law School, 74, 85, 113

Udall, Stuart, 72

understanding, limits of, 6

United States Information Agency, 200–201

University of California, Berkeley, School of Law, 241, 246

University of Michigan Law School, 74, 75, 76

University of Pennsylvania Law School, 74, 150

U.S. Constitution, 22, 24

U.S. Supreme Court

    Alaska pipeline and, 137–138

    draft law and, 42

V

Vallecitos Mountain Refuge, 229–231, 243

values

    CUNY Law School and, 151

    environmental challenges and, 227

    of social entrepreneurs, 84

    work aligned with, 6, 78, 85

Vietnam War

    Thurman Arnold and, 46

    CLASP students and, 87

    Institute for Policy Studies and, 44, 45

    legal support for draft resistance, 41–43

    Nixon and, 71, 85

    perspective on, 123

    resistance to, 53

    Thich Nhat Hanh and, 202, 204

    Yale Law School and, 76

vision quest, 193–198

Voice of America, 137

W

War on Poverty, 83

Warren, Earl, 73

Washington Post, 44, 104–105

Watt, James, 149
Weathermen, 53–54, 85
Weil, Simone, 257
white male advantage, 172
Williams, Barbara, 92
Winter, Paul, 183–185
Winter Quest, 186–192
wisdom. *See also* practice of wisdom
    cultivation of, 2–3, 6, 35, 68,
        112, 136, 232
    expression of, 206
    lack of academic interest in,
        267n.1
    medicine wheel and, 198
    qualities of, 3, 206
    social justice and, 207, 224
    social transformation and, 207,
        214
Wisdom Party, 224–225, 226, 228

Women's Law Project, 120
women's liberation movement, 119,
    121–122
work, meaning in, 32–33, 85, 133
Wyatt case, 102, 247

y
Yale Law School
    Bazelon and, 12
    CLASP and, 74
    corporate law practice and, 24,
        57–58
    Goldstein and, 76
    legal education and, 56–58
    paradox of, 57–58
    sabbatical and, 200
yoga classes, 125–126

Z
Zwerling, Israel, 20–21

ABOUT THE AUTHOR

CHARLES HALPERN is an innovative social entrepreneur who has led the way in bringing inner work and the cultivation of wisdom into the world of social activism. As chair of the Board of the Center for Contemplative Mind in Society, he is helping to integrate contemplative practice into mainstream institutions, in order to develop greater clarity, compassion, and effectiveness to face the challenges of the twenty-first century.

With his extensive record of institutional creativity and achievement, supported by twenty years of meditation, Halpern is the ideal person to write about the intersecting arcs of effective work in the world and the cultivation of the inner wisdom to deepen and nourish it.

An honors graduate of Harvard College and Yale Law School, he left a prominent corporate law firm to establish the first public interest law firm, the Center for Law and Social Policy, in Washington, D.C., and to help launch the public interest law movement. After serving as a member of the faculty at Georgetown and Stanford Law Schools, he was chosen as the founding dean of the City University of New York School of Law, a school devoted to training advocates for the poor and disadvantaged. He has lectured in

Europe and Asia on public interest law, citizen participation in government processes, and new directions in legal education.

As the first president of the Nathan Cummings Foundation, he developed an innovative philanthropic program, supporting social justice advocacy and exploration of the contemplative perspective. He helped to launch many nonprofit organizations, assisting them to assemble resources and to develop effective programs.

During his years of creative leadership, Halpern has pursued a path of inner growth, which has energized and informed his work. His career has taken him from the inner circles of the legal establishment to the outer fringes of gritty New York politics, from vision quests in the New Mexican wilderness to the current debates about stem cell research.

Currently a visiting scholar at the University of California, Berkeley, School of Law, Halpern consults to educational institutions, nonprofit groups, and foundations on management and program development, with an emphasis on the integration of the contemplative perspective into the life of organizations. He leads meditation workshops and retreats.

He lives in Berkeley, California, with his wife of forty-seven years, Susan Halpern, author of *The Etiquette of Illness: What to Say When You Can't Find the Words*. They have three adult children and six grandchildren. They meditate regularly and explore the remote waterways of California by canoe.

Visit www.charliehalpern.com for photographs, drawings, cartoons, additional information on incidents and themes in the text, and developments since publication.

About Berrett-Koehler Publishers

Berrett-Koehler is an independent publisher dedicated to an ambitious mission: Creating a World that Works for All.

We believe that to truly create a better world, action is needed at all levels—individual, organizational, and societal. At the individual level, our publications help people align their lives with their values and with their aspirations for a better world. At the organizational level, our publications promote progressive leadership and management practices, socially responsible approaches to business, and humane and effective organizations. At the societal level, our publications advance social and economic justice, shared prosperity, sustainability, and new solutions to national and global issues.

A major theme of our publications is "Opening Up New Space." They challenge conventional thinking, introduce new ideas, and foster positive change. Their common quest is changing the underlying beliefs, mindsets, and structures that keep generating the same cycles of problems, no matter who our leaders are or what improvement programs we adopt.

We strive to practice what we preach—to operate our publishing company in line with the ideas in our books. At the core of our approach is stewardship, which we define as a deep sense of responsibility to administer the company for the benefit of all of our "stakeholder" groups: authors, customers, employees, investors, service providers, and the communities and environment around us.

We are grateful to the thousands of readers, authors, and other friends of the company who consider themselves to be part of the "BK Community." We hope that you, too, will join us in our mission.

A BK Currents Book

This book is part of our BK Currents series. BK Currents books advance social and economic justice by exploring the critical intersections between business and society. Offering a unique combination of thoughtful analysis and progressive alternatives, BK Currents books promote positive change at the national and global levels. To find out more, visit www.bkcurrents.com.

Be Connected

Visit Our Website

Go to www.bkconnection.com to read exclusive previews and excerpts of new books, find detailed information on all Berrett-Koehler titles and authors, browse subject-area libraries of books, and get special discounts.

Subscribe to Our Free E-Newsletter

Be the first to hear about new publications, special discount offers, exclusive articles, news about bestsellers, and more! Get on the list for our free e-newsletter by going to www.bkconnection.com.

Get Quantity Discounts

Berrett-Koehler books are available at quantity discounts for orders of ten or more copies. Please call us toll-free at (800) 929-2929 or email us at bkp.orders@aidcvt.com.

Host a Reading Group

For tips on how to form and carry on a book reading group in your workplace or community, see our website at www.bkconnection.com.

Join the BK Community

Thousands of readers of our books have become part of the "BK Community" by participating in events featuring our authors, reviewing draft manuscripts of forthcoming books, spreading the word about their favorite books, and supporting our publishing program in other ways. If you would like to join the BK Community, please contact us at bkcommunity@bkpub.com.